Ringing Church Bells

to ward off Thunderstorms

Ringing Church Bells
to ward off Thunderstorms
and other Curiosities
from the original
Notes and Queries

Edited by

Justin Lovill

The Bunbury Press

2009

First published in 2009
by the Bunbury Press
www.bunburypress.com

ISBN 978-0-9562046-0-8

A CIP catalogue record for this book is available from
the British Library

Typeset at the Bunbury Press
Printed by T. J. International Ltd, Padstow, Cornwall

To my parents

Contents

Introduction

> We would suggest that the reader for amusement
> scarcely could take up a miscellany that contains more
> anecdote and quaint accounts of odd things new to
> his mind, than a volume of *Notes and Queries*...
>
> *The Examiner*

The first number of *Notes and Queries* appeared on Saturday
3 November 1849, near the end of a year which also saw British
forces annexing the Punjab, a cholera epidemic claiming 14,000
lives in London, Dickens publishing the first instalment of
David Copperfield, Disraeli becoming Conservative leader in the
House of Commons, and the creation of the first bowler hat.
Subtitled 'A Medium of Inter-communication for Literary
Men, Artists, Antiquaries, Genealogists, Etc.', it was the brain-
child of William Thoms (1803-1885), himself an antiquary
and an editor. The idea was for the Notes section to serve as
a kind of public commonplace book, wherein readers could
share and set on record interesting or notable things they had
come across, while the Queries section was to be a message
board on which they could post requests for information on
vexing questions (or *vexatae quaestiones*, as they tended to say).

After a quiet start – only forty copies were sold on the first
day – success was rapid: by the end of December 1849 the first
four fortnightly issues had had to be reprinted, and over the
following years the format would be copied across the world,
from Somerset and Shropshire to Holland and France, from
the United States to India. Success would also be enduring:
Notes and Queries is still published today, as a specialist academic
journal concentrating on literature, while its title has been
adopted for, among other things, a long-running column in the
Guardian newspaper.

In its form and *modus operandi* the original *Notes and Queries* was remarkably forward-looking. It was the first periodical to be written more or less entirely by its readers, a fact which has prompted comparisons with the internet – in particular with 'virtual communities' such as newsgroups and with collaborative reference works such as Wikipedia. Moreover, it made the most of the then recent developments of the penny post and the national railway network. Its standard price was a modestly pitched threepence, but for a penny more you could have a stamped version sent to you direct from the publisher, and each issue, having been printed in London on a Friday, was despatched at once by train so that country booksellers would receive copies in that night's parcels and so be able to deliver to subscribers on the Saturday. *Notes and Queries* also circulated widely overseas – before long contributions were arriving from as far afield as Malta, Mauritius, Australia, and New York.

In its content, on the other hand, *N & Q* (as it quickly became known to its readers) was almost entirely backward-looking and parochial, being, in Thoms's words, 'a work devoted to obscure points of national history, doubtful questions of literature and bibliography, the discussion of etymologies, and the elucidation of old world customs and observances'. Very occasionally contemporary events do impinge: in 1852 the death of the Duke of Wellington leads to a note on the superstition that storms mark the passing of great men; in 1852 and 1853 the publication of *Bleak House* prompts correspondence on London street characters and spontaneous combustion; in 1854 and 1855 one knows the Crimean War is raging because there are debates about the effects of cannon-balls and the spelling of Sebastopol (should it be Sevastopol?); and, at the end of 1861, the death of Prince Albert is marked by a black-bordered notice: 'Death hath stricken a noble heart. The PRINCE CONSORT is no more...' Most of the time, however, we are firmly in the past as contributors root about among old books and memories, clutching after ghosts and relics. This predilection is well conveyed by the *noms de plume* which many of them adopted to preserve their anonymity: Ache, Antiquarius, Mr Blink, Bookworm, Clericus Rusticus, Dryasdust, Etymologious, Grime, The Hermit of Holyport, Nemo, Old Fogie, Peter the Saxonian, and Mr Scribe, to name but a few.

As this perhaps suggests, to modern tastes much of what they write about is rather dull. Few eyes and minds now would not grow weary as another eager genealogical quest starts up, or as wrangling continues down the years about how to pronounce the surnames Coke and Cowper, or as the umpteenth theory about the identity of the eighteenth-century letter writer 'Junius' is rehearsed. However – and it is a fairly big however – for anyone interested in the way those who went before us lived, who cares about literature or history, who is intrigued by old words and customs, there are, amid the dust, bright nuggets that catch the eye and keep you turning the pages in hope of more. How much did Byron's brain weigh? Why are Cheshire cats said to grin? Was the Duke of Clarence really drowned in a Malmsey butt? Why did people so fear to be buried on the north sides of churchyards? What was spur money, and why did choirboys get so excited about it? Indeed, it is hard to think of any other volumes where such a wide range of unexpected and out-of-the-way information can be found, and Grime, Ache, Bookworm and the rest turn out – with all their fustiness and pedantry – to be agreeably learned and engaging guides along the byways of times past.

The aim of the present book is simple: to extract the more interesting material that appeared in the first decade or so of *Notes and Queries* and present it in an approachable form for the curious general reader of today. To this end the following editorial steps have been taken.

❖ Material has been arranged in an alphabetical sequence from 'Actress: Who was the first in England?' to 'Words, Last, of the Great and Famous'. The hope is that this unthematic approach, in which Burial follows Bunkum and Monks follow Mince Pies, recreates something of the serendipity that characterised the original *N & Q*. It also yields a contents listing at the start of the book that doubles as a basic index.

❖ On each selected subject contributions that originally appeared scattered through the months and years have been gathered together and presented in the order of their publication in *N & Q*. The resulting sequences do not necessarily contain all the original contributions on the given subject: to avoid repetition and limit longueurs a great deal has been omitted.

❖ Many contributions appear exactly as in *N & Q*, but others have been shortened and otherwise adjusted – again, partly to avoid repetition, and partly to improve the sense of continuity between contributions. Such cuts and adjustments are not indicated in the text but the original *N & Q* page references are given in the Sources section at the back of the book for anyone who wishes to investigate further.

❖ *Q.* at the start of an entry indicates a Query, *N.* indicates a Note, and *R.*, *R2.*, et cetera, indicate responses. However, it should be noted that, because of the way subjects often lapsed only to recur years later, items marked *R.* et cetera may not originally have been conceived as responses to the contributions that precede them in this volume.

❖ Contributor names and such addresses as were provided appear as in *N & Q*. 'Editor' indicates contributions by William Thoms, who presided over the publication from its inception until 1872. Dates given after contributor names are those of publication in *N & Q*.

❖ The *N & Q* of this period contained many errors, not least because, in a pre-typewriter age, contributions were necessarily handwritten. Deciphering them cannot have been easy. Slips have been corrected silently wherever detected, but it is likely that some remain.

❖ Contributors tended to refer familiarly and in glancing form to authors and works now largely forgotten. As far as possible names, titles and publication dates have been identified and inserted, either in the text itself or in the Sources section.

❖ Quotations provided by contributors have sometimes been extended from the sources they cited if the additional material seems germane and reasonably interesting.

❖ Calendar years have been standardised to the modern reckoning, or New Style, and, except in quotations from old sources, to a day-month-year sequence (12 November 1815, and so on).

❖ Old spelling and punctuation have been treated pragmatically and inconsistently – that is, retained where it does not seem likely they will impede ready comprehension but otherwise modernised in part or in full.

❖ Square brackets indicate new insertions. Round brackets within *N & Q* material generally indicate insertions made in *N & Q*, but book titles and publication dates are given in round brackets whether they appeared in *N & Q* or have been inserted anew.

❖ While on many subjects the *N & Q* material requires no explanation or addition, in other cases it has seemed appropriate to provide supplementary notes to fill out the information available to the reader. Such new notes are indicated by ¶.

❖ Illustrations have been added from a range of largely nineteenth-century sources, often coming from books that would have been familiar to readers of the early *N & Q*.

ACTRESS: Who was the first in England?

Q. Is it a fact that the first woman to appear on the English stage was Mrs Coleman, who represented Ianthe in Sir William Davenant's *Siege of Rhodes* in 1656? ~ R. W. Hackwood, 14 Mar 1857

R. In April 1662 letters patent were granted by Charles II to Sir William Davenant authorising him to erect a theatre and establish a company of actors in London or Westminster, or the suburbs of the same. The letters patent recite that formerly the women's parts in plays had been represented by men in the habits of women, 'at which some have taken offence'. To remedy this abuse leave is given that all the women's parts to be acted in the company 'for the time to come may be performed by women'. Another company of actors under Thomas Killegrew was also authorised by the same letters patent and with the same privileges. I think, from the date of these letters, that the appearance of Mrs Coleman in 1656 must have been very nearly, if not quite, the commencement of the practice. ~ Pishey Thompson, Stoke Newington, 21 Mar 1857

R2. It is well known that at a much earlier time Queen Henrietta Maria, the wife of Charles I, and the young ladies of the court performed characters and danced in the plays and masques exhibited in the royal palaces. It is not, however, so generally known that in 1629 some French dramatic pieces were performed at the Blackfriars theatre, when, according to the custom on the Continent, the female parts were played by women – the first attempt to introduce female actors on our public stage. William Prynne animadverts on this breach of morality in a note to his *Histriomastix*: 'Some Frenchwomen, or monsters rather, on Michaelmas terme, 1629, attempted to act a French play, at the play-house in Blackfriers: an impudent, shamefull, unwomanish, graceless, if not more than whorish attempt.'

This upright but querulous old barrister was not the only reformer who felt the age scandalised by these doings, for a Thomas Brande thus stigmatised them in an address to William Laud, at that time Bishop of London: 'Furthermore, you should know that last daye (November 8) certaine vagrant French players, who had been expelled from their own country, and those women, did attempt, thereby giving just offence to all vertuous and well-disposed persons in this towne, to act a certain lascivious and unchaste comedye, in the French tongue, at the Black-fryers. Glad I am to saye they were hissed, hooted, and pippin-pelted from the stage; so that I do not thinke they will soone be ready to try the same againe.' Prynne, however, says 'there was great resort' to the play, which seems to have been acted more than once.

Mrs Coleman, wife to Mr Edward Coleman, is justly entitled to the distinction of having been the first *Englishwoman* who appeared upon our public stage. But she can only be regarded as an amateur; as, indeed, were all the actors in *The Siege of Rhodes* in 1656.

Among the professional ladies who obtained early celebrity on the boards, soon after the Restoration, we find the names of Katherine Corey, Anne Marshall, Rebecca Marshall, Eastland, Weaver, Uphill, Knep, Hughes, Rutter, Davenport, Saunderson, Davies, Long, Gibbs, Norris, Holden and Jennings. The first nine belonged to Killegrew's company, the remaining eight to

Davenant's. It appears from that invaluable record of passing events, Pepys's *Diary*, that Killegrew had female performers some months before Davenant. Pepys records witnessing *The Beggar's Bush* on 3 January 1661, and then for the first time he saw 'women come upon the stage'.

However, the very first appearance occurred slightly earlier, in Killegrew's production of *Othello* on 8 December 1660, for which Thomas Jordan wrote a prologue expressly 'to introduce the first woman that came to act on the stage'. It appears from this that the lady, who performed Desdemona, was an unmarried woman; and, as Anne Marshall was the principal unmarried actress in Killegrew's company at that time, she is perhaps entitled to this distinction. ~ Edward F. Rimbault, 13 June 1857

¶ The colourful account ascribed to 'Thomas Brande' was in a letter 'discovered' in the library at Lambeth Palace by the scholar and forger John Payne Collier, who published it in his *History of English Dramatic Poetry* (1831). Sadly, as no original letter or catalogue reference survives, it seems likely that it was one of his many fabrications.

An earlier non-speaking appearance than those mentioned was that of Anne of Denmark, wife of James I, who performed in court masques along with other members of the royal family. In June 1610, for example, she masqueraded as Tethys in *Tethys' Festival* while Prince Charles (later Charles I) represented Zephyrus and Princess Elizabeth (later Queen of Bohemia) represented the Thames. Twelve other rivers were embodied by ladies of the queen's bedchamber.

In his *Histriomastix: The Players Scourge* (1633) the Puritan pamphleteer William Prynne famously referred to 'women actors, notorious whores'. For this supposed aspersion upon Henrietta Maria and other critical passages he was sentenced by the Star Chamber to pay £5,000, have his book burnt by the public hangman, suffer 'perpetual imprisonment' in the Tower, and have both his ears cut off in the pillory. Undeterred, while in the Tower he wrote further pamphlets for which he was branded on both cheeks with the letters 'S L' (seditious libeller) and condemned 'to lose the small remainder of both his ears'.

The last court masque took place in 1640 and in September 1642, shortly after the outbreak of the Civil War, the public playhouses were closed by parliamentary ordinance. They did not reopen until 1660. In 1656, however, with radical Puritanism on the wane, Sir William Davenant managed to persuade the music-loving Cromwell that his planned entertainment *The Siege of Rhodes* was not a play but that new thing, an 'opera', and was thus permitted to stage it privately at Rutland House in Charterhouse Yard.

In July and August 1660, shortly after the Restoration, Charles II granted warrants to Davenant and Killegrew which allowed them to employ actresses. However, as the actor and playwright Colley Cibber recalled, the stage 'could not be so suddenly supplied', and it remained necessary for a while 'to put the handsomest young men into petticoats'. This caused some practical difficulties, as Cibber relates:

> The king coming a little before his usual time to a tragedy, found the actors not ready to begin... His majesty, not choosing to have as much patience as his good subjects, sent to them to know the meaning of it; upon which the master of the company came to the box, and, rightly judging that the best excuse for the default would be the true one, fairly told his majesty that the queen was not *shaved* yet.

The end of this transitional period was marked by the letters patent to Davenant and Killegrew of April 1662 which decreed that henceforth *all* women's parts should be performed by women.

The landmark performance of *Othello* in December 1660 and the performance of *The Beggar's Bush* seen by Pepys a few weeks later took place at the Theatre Royal, Vere Street, a converted real tennis court near present day Kingsway (Vere Street ran south-east from the end of Great Wild Street to Clare Market). The building was subsequently used as a drama school, a fencing college, a Nonconformist meeting house, a carpenter's shop, and a slaughterhouse, before being destroyed by fire in 1809.

As noted in *N & Q*, the case for Anne Marshall being the first professional English actress to appear on the public stage is strong if circumstantial; cases have also been advanced for Katherine Corey and Margaret Hughes.

ANGLESEY, MARQUESS OF: The curious after-life of his leg

Henry Paget, Earl of Uxbridge, commanded the British cavalry at the Battle of Waterloo and was made Marquess of Anglesey shortly after the victory. As the battle was coming to its end a grapeshot passed over the neck of the Duke of Wellington's horse and shattered Uxbridge's right knee. Looking down he is reported to have said, 'By God, sir, I've lost my leg!', to which Wellington replied, with a brief glance away from his telescope, 'By God, sir, so you have!' The leg then took on a life of its own.

Q. By whom was the epitaph on the leg of the Marquess of Anglesey written? I am unable to meet with it, and should therefore feel much obliged if the Editor would either insert it or refer me to a source where it may be found. The leg is, I think, buried in the garden of an inn near the field of Waterloo. ~ Oxoniensis, 27 Sep 1862

R. Among the curiosities of Waterloo, to the examination of which the most strenuous persuasion is used to invite the passing stranger, are the grave of the late Marquess of Anglesey's leg and the house in which it was cut off, where the boot belonging to it is preserved. The owner of the house, to whose share this relic has fallen, finds it a most lucrative source of revenue and will, in spite of the absurdity of the thing, probably bequeath it to his children as a valuable property. He has interred the leg most decorously within a coffin, under a weeping willow, and has honoured it with a monument and the following epitaph:

Here is interred the Leg
of the illustrious and valiant Earl Uxbridge,
Lieutenant-General of His Britannic Majesty,
Commander in Chief of the English, Belgian and Dutch Cavalry,
wounded on the 18th June 1815,
at the memorable Battle of Waterloo;
who, by his heroism, has contributed to the triumph of the cause
of human kind;
gloriously decided by the resounding victory
of the said day.

Some rollicking wag scribbled an infamous couplet beneath the inscription:

Here lies the Marquess of Anglesey's limb;
The Devil will have the remainder of him.

~ Editor, 27 Sep 1862

¶ After receiving his wound Lord Uxbridge was taken to 214 Chaussée de Bruxelles, a house in the village of Waterloo owned by M. Hyacinthe Joseph-Marie Paris. There the remains of his leg were amputated with a rather blunt-looking saw which is now in the National Army Museum.[1] Meanwhile Lady Uxbridge, who had travelled to Belgium with her husband, visited the battlefield in his barouche and, as she related in letters home, was delighted to find some 'grape' exactly the size of the piece that had caused his wound: 'It just fits the hole in his Cossacks which he wore that day – I need not tell you that I have saved them also, but the poor old farmer would keep the boot, and offered two guineas for it.'

Monsieur Paris then lost no time in burying the leg in his garden in a wooden coffin, ordering the elaborate tombstone from Brussels, and turning his house into part of the Waterloo tourist trail. Visitors – including the King of Prussia and the

[1] The museum also has a bloodstained glove that belonged to Thomas Wildman of the 7th Hussars, who assisted in the operation, and the complete skeleton of Marengo, Napoleon's Arab stallion captured at the end of the battle.

Prince of Orange – were shown the bloody chair on which Uxbridge had sat after the operation, and then to the 'grave' in the garden.

Back in London the Marquess of Anglesey, as he had become, was fitted with the first articulated artificial limb – the 'Anglesey leg' – which boasted hinges at the knee and ankle. He was offered an annual pension of £1,200 in compensation for his loss but declined it and continued undaunted in a long and distinguished career, becoming a field marshal, knight of the garter, and Lord Lieutenant of Ireland. In later life he returned to the house at Waterloo with two of his sons and, finding the table on which the operation had been carried out, was so chuffed that he ate his dinner at it.

Paris's descendants continued to earn from the leg until 1878, when one of the marquess's sons, on a later visit, discovered that the bones were not buried but on open display. There followed a protracted dispute that ended with the Paris family hiding the bones away until 1934, when the widow of the last Monsieur Paris found them in his study and burnt them.

ANIMALS: Were they put on trial in the Middle Ages?

Q. I met lately an interesting account of the process by which, during the Middle Ages, animals and insects (flies, rats, and others) were cited to appear in the courts and to show cause why they should not be destroyed as a nuisance – and, on their failure to appear, their extermination was decreed in due form of law. I shall feel greatly obliged to any of your correspondents who can refer me to further information. ~ J.E.T., 26 July 1856

R. I have recently encountered three anecdotes of medieval executions of animals – of the hanging of a bull for killing a girl; of a boar for killing a child; and of another boar for killing and eating a child. The first and third cases occurred in the Low Countries, and the second at Mâcon in Burgundy, all during the latter part of the fifteenth century. These *seem* to have been judicial acts, as the public executioner was employed under the superintendence of the authorities. What sanction can there have been for such an extraordinary procedure? ~ H. Pk., 2 Apr 1859

R2. According to the Roman law, if a man was hurt by a tame animal – as by a vicious horse or a dangerous bull – the owner afforded satisfaction by the surrender of the animal. The same rule extended to a man's slave and also to his son, both of whom were regarded as his chattels.

In the case of a man being killed by a domestic animal, the medieval codes applied the principle of the wergeld, or pecuniary satisfaction for a life. Sometimes the entire wergeld was due, sometimes half the wergeld, coupled with the surrender of the animal. The Burgundian law enacted that where one tame animal was hurt by another, the offending animal was to be surrendered.

Hieronymus Rorarius, a papal nuncio at the court of Hungary in the sixteenth century, wrote and published a treatise to prove that animals are rational and that they make a better use of their reason than man. He stated that it was customary in Africa to crucify lions, in order to deter them from entering towns, and he had himself seen two wolves hung from a gibbet in the forest between Cologne and Düren, as an example to other wolves.

The Roman custom of annually crucifying dogs, on account of their failure to give the alarm when the Capitol was scaled by the Gauls, must be considered as a commemorative, not a penal infliction.[1]

It may be observed that animals, though conscious of the idea of danger – without which they would not preserve their lives – are destitute of the idea of death, and the infliction of death upon one animal would not operate by way of example upon another animal. The same remark may indeed be extended to all punishments inflicted upon animals. A whipping administered to one dog is no warning to another dog. ~ L., 23 Apr 1859

[1] During the assault, in 390 BC, Rome's geese famously made good the failure of its dogs.

A sow on trial at Lavegny

R3. In France the examples are numerous, from the twelfth to the middle of the eighteenth century. M. Berriat-Saint-Prix has enumerated ninety-two cases: the first that of the trial of field mice and caterpillars at Laon in 1120, and the last that of a cow at Poitou in 1741. The accused animals consist of those previously named along with pigs, oxen, horses, Spanish flies, leeches, cocks, moles, snails, mites, grasshoppers, dogs, donkeys, goats, sheep, worms, and, towards the end of the sixteenth century, tortoises in Canada. At Lausanne, at the beginning of the thirteenth century, the bishop, William of Embleus, condemned the eels of the lake to be confined in one certain part of the water: the cause is not named. In 1587 there was a celebrated trial of the vine proprietors of St Julien versus the weevils, the vines having suffered by a visitation of the latter. ~ J. Doran, 12 Mar 1864

R4. Bartholomew Chassenée, President of the Parlement of Provence, defended some rats who were indicted at the beginning of the sixteenth century, and a treatise was published as late as 1668 by Gaspard Bailly, a lawyer at Chambery, on legal proceedings against animals, with forms of indictment and modes of pleading.

Such trials have taken place in England also. An account of one of these, of a dog, was published in a pamphlet, from which it appears that the trial took place near Chichester in 1771 and that the chief actors in it were four country gentlemen named Butler, Aldridge, Challen, and Bridger. Such proceedings appear strange to us, but they were, after all, but a grave  and formal mode of proceeding towards the same end which is attained in our days by a more summary process – the destruction of animals who have been the cause of death, or serious injury, to man. ~ F.C.H., 12 Mar 1864

¶ A comprehensive list of trials was assembled by E. P. Evans in his pioneering work, *The Criminal Prosecution and Capital Punishment of Animals* (1906). Discounting the burning of storks at Avignon in 666 as insufficiently supported by the historical record, the first case he lists is that of moles in the Valley of Aosta in 824. Later defendants included cockchafers at Avignon in 1320, sixteen cows and one goat at Rouvre in 1452, snails at Mâcon in 1487, grasshoppers in Lombardy in 1541, dolphins at Marseilles in 1596, a cow, two heifers, three sheep and two sows in Connecticut in 1662, turtle-doves in Canada at the end of the seventeenth century, a he-goat in Russia in the same period (banished to Siberia), termites in Brazil in 1713, a cock at Leeds in the nineteenth century, and last of all a dog at Délémont in Switzerland in 1906. In this final case a man called Marger was robbed and killed by another man called Scherrer who was aided in the attack by his son and their dog. The three culprits were tried. The two men were sentenced to life imprisonment, but the dog, seen as the ringleader, was condemned to death.

From early in their history such prosecutions had opponents who argued that animals had no understanding of right and wrong and so could not be held accountable for their actions.

But defenders of the practice found support in the Bible, pointing in particular to Exodus 2:28, where God tells Moses, 'If an ox gore a man or woman, that they die: then the ox shall be surely stoned, and his flesh shall not be eaten; but the owner of the ox shall be quit.' Moreover, as God had placed brute creation under the dominion of Man, animals which harmed humans were seen as violating the divinely sanctioned order. Trial and punishment, in this view, were not merely tools for the management of relations between rational human beings but part of a far grander scheme. Thus in 1580 the jurist Jean Bodin argued that the purpose of executions was not to punish criminals but to serve divine justice and 'obtain the blessing of God'.

However, the Bible could also be used for the defence. In the celebrated case of the weevils of St Julien, their advocate, Pierre Rimbaud, argued that his clients had not rendered themselves liable to excommunication because, as is recorded in Genesis, the lower animals were created before Man and God had instructed them to be fruitful and multiply – which He would not have done had He not intended that they should have suitable and sufficient means of support. After a prolonged legal process – delayed somewhat by the Duke of Savoy's troop movements – the weevils were offered a nearby piece of land outside the vineyards, but this was refused by their lawyers on the grounds that it was sterile and not productive of appropriate food. The upshot and final judgement are not known because the last page of the court records has been destroyed by rats or bugs of some kind – acting, it has been suggested, in sympathy with the weevils.

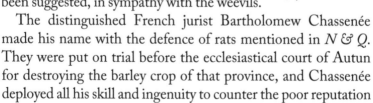

The distinguished French jurist Bartholomew Chassenée made his name with the defence of rats mentioned in *N & Q*. They were put on trial before the ecclesiastical court of Autun for destroying the barley crop of that province, and Chassenée deployed all his skill and ingenuity to counter the poor reputation of his clients. In the first place he argued that, as they were dispersed over a wide area and lived in numerous villages, a single summons was insufficient. This plea was admitted, a new trial date was set, and a new summons was read out from the pulpits of all the parishes inhabited by the rats. When once again they did not appear, Chassenée explained that the journey required of his clients was long and difficult and attended by great peril – not least from the ill-disposed cats of the area, who watched all their movements and lay in wait at every corner. Addressing the court at length on this point, he argued that if anyone was cited to appear at a place to which they could not come in safety, they might refuse the summons. This plea was accepted, and, as the plaintiffs were not prepared to be bound over for the good behaviour of their cats, the trial was adjourned without a new date being set.

In other cases courts did insist that some at least of the defendants appear to hear the charges against them. Thus in Lausanne in 1451 a number of leeches were brought into court to hear the instruction that they and their fellow leeches should leave the district within three days. Having failed to comply they and their fellows were exorcised – an action which provoked controversy but gained support not only from the learned doctors of Heidelberg but also, apparently, from events, for shortly after the excommunication all the leeches in the area died.

AUDREY, TAWDRY AND ETHELDREDA

Q. I copy the following paragraph from a scrap of printed paper lately placed in my hands:

> St Etheldreda, an English abbess who died in 679, is worth mentioning on account of a singular etymology connected with the name. Etheldreda was corrupted into Auldrey, and thence into Audrey; and it seems that at an annual fair in the Isle of Ely, called St Audrey's Fair, a sort of showy lace was sold which went by the name of St Audrey's lace. Another corruption was added to the series, and the word, say the

learned, was turned into Tawdry, and applied not only to lace but also to other articles of female attire more showy in appearance than intrinsically valuable. Another story tells us that St Audrey died of a swelling in the throat, which she considered a judgement for an inordinate love of fine necklaces in her youth.

Perhaps your insertion of the above may direct attention to a curious word, and be the means of determining the derivation.

St Etheldreda was third daughter of Anna, King of the East Angles, and she is said to have founded the abbey of Ely in the year 673. Ely Cathedral is dedicated jointly to St Peter and St Etheldreda, and arose out of the monastic foundation of the latter, whose legendary history is sculptured on the columns of some of the slender pillars which support the octagon tower and lantern, at the intersection of the nave and transepts. ~ Ned Alsned, 23 Mar 1861

R. Permit me to point out the following passage in Robert Southey's *Omniana*:

It was formerly the custom in England for women to wear a necklace of fine silk, called Taudry lace, from St Audrey. She, in her youth, had been used to wear carcanets of jewels; and, being afterwards tormented with violent pains in her neck, was wont to say that God in his mercy had thus punished her, and the fiery heat and redness of the swelling which she endured was to atone for her former pride and vanity. Probably she wore this lace to conceal the scrofulous appearance, and, from this, when it was afterwards worn as an ornament, which was common and not costly, the word tawdry may have been taken to designate any kind of coarse and vulgar finery.

~ W.H.W., 20 Apr 1861

¶ The saintly mode of life of Æthelthryth, traditionally known as Etheldreda, is recorded by the Venerable Bede, who says that she preserved her virginity through two marriages and, as a nun in her later years, wore only woollen garments, seldom washed in hot water, ate only once a day, and prayed assiduously. He also records that, sixteen years after her death, when her grave was opened so that her remains might be moved into the abbey she had founded, her body was found to be miraculously uncorrupted by decay.

In after years, at the fair held at Ely on 23 June – Etheldreda's feast day in the Roman calendar – ribbons which had touched her shrine were highly valued.

The expression 'Seynt Audries lace' is first recorded in 1530, and in *The Winter's Tale* (*c.*1610) Shakespeare has the shepherdess Mopsa reproach the Clown, 'Come, you promised me a tawdry-lace and a pair of sweet gloves.' The modern sense of deprecation first becomes apparent in Sir George Etherege's *The Man of Mode* (1676), as the rake Dorimant toys with Mrs Loveit: 'That ever I should love a woman that can dote on a senseless caper, a tawdry French ribbon, and a formal cravat...'

BASILISK: In Oxford in 1679

Q. From *A Guide to the Colleges and Antiquities of Oxford* (1702):

In the year 1679 an Italian surgeon, the Signor Govaro, came with letters of recommendation from Doctor Harvey and others. He had many wonderful things, and among them a basilisk, which he kept in a sealed glass case, and would have sold to the Museum for £100; but a dispute arose because he would not allow the case to be opened, as Doctor Radcliffe desired; so he took offence and went away. This was unlucky, for, whether it was a basilisk or not, the animal was a wonder and not known. It was said to have horns, an eagle's feet, and a dragon's tail; but, as no drawing was made, and those who saw it were in fear, we know not how this may be.

Is anything more known of this basilisk or its owner? Where is the most authentic history of basilisks? ~ J.A.A., 29 June 1861

R. The basilisk, or *regulus* of Pliny, must be ranked, with other myths of ancient zoology, as a portion of *unnatural* history. There was ground, however, for the fear amongst the naturalists at Oxford in 1679, for the opinion then prevailed that the basilisk could kill with a look. The 'sealed case' must have had some opening to admit of food. ~ T. J. Buckton, Lichfield, 20 July 1861

¶ Unfortunately no further information was forthcoming.

The mythical 'king of serpents' was said to be possessed of a lethal gaze and lethal breath and be hatched by a serpent from a cock's egg. Its name derives from the Greek *basiliskos*, little king, and is linked by Pliny and other writers to a coronet-like mark upon its head.

BELL, BOOK AND CANDLE: A medieval curse

Q. In Sir William Dugdale's *Baronage of England* it is stated that Humphrey de Bohun, Earl of Essex and Hereford, was present in 1253 'when that formal curse was denounced in Westminster Hall, against the violators of Magna Carta, *with bell, book, and candle*'. Can any of your readers refer me to a description of any such ceremony? ~ Vicar Choral, 9 May 1857

R. According to Holinshed, the Archbishop of Canterbury and thirteen bishops were present 'revested and apparelled in *pontificalibus*,[1] with tapers according to the manner', and 'the

---

[1] The vestments and insignia of bishops.

sentence of excommunication was pronounced against all transgressors of the liberties of the Church, and of the ancient liberties and customs of the realm'. At the end 'they threw away their extinct and smoking tapers, saying, "So let them be extinguished and sink into the pit of hell which run into the dangers of this sentence."' ~ Mackenzie Walcott, 30 May 1857

R2. Thomas Staveley, in his *History of Churches in England*, gives a full description of this ceremony, out of the Articles of the General Great Curse, found at Canterbury in 1562, as it is set down by Thomas Becon in *The Reliques of Rome*:

This was solemnly thundered out once in every quarter: the first Sunday of Advent, at coming of our Lord Jesus Christ; the first Sunday of Lent; the Sunday in the Feast of the Trinity; and the Sunday within the Utas (Octaves) of the Blessed Virgin our Lady St Mary. At which action the prelate stands in the pulpit, in his alb, the cross being lifted up before him, and the candles lighted on both sides of it, and begins thus, 'By Authority [of] God, Father, Son, and Holy Ghost...'

There follows a description of the persons cursed, and finally the curse itself:

'We denounce all those accursed that are so found guilty, and all those that maintain them in their sins, or give them thereto either help or counsel, for they be departed from God and all Holy Church: and that they have no part of the Passion of our Lord Jesus Christ, nor of no sacraments, nor no part of the prayers among Christian folk: But that they be accursed of God, and of the Church, from the sole of her foot to the crown of her head, sleeping and waking, sitting and standing, and in all her works; but if they have no grace of God to amend them here in this life, for to dwell in the pain of Hell for ever without end. *Fiat: Fiat.*[1] Do to the book: Quench the candles: Ring the bell: Amen, Amen.' And then the book is clapped together; the candles blown out; and the bells rung, with a most dreadful noise made by the congregation

---

[1] *Fiat.* Let it be done.

present, bewailing the accursed persons concerned in that black doom denounced against them.

~ J. B. Wilkinson, 20 June 1857

¶ The curious occasion recorded in Holinshed captures in miniature the tensions of the long reign of Henry III. He needed money with which to pursue an expansive foreign policy but was not trusted to abide by the constraints set on his role by Magna Carta, signed by his father King John in 1215. In 1253, as recorded by Holinshed, 'at length it was agreed that a tenth part of all the revenues belonging to the Church was granted to him for three years' space... and the king on the other part promised faithfully to observe and maintain the grant of the great charter'. The solemn service in Westminster Hall was designed 'for further assurance' of this undertaking. It did not work: relations between king and barons continued to deteriorate and ten years later civil war broke out.

The ceremony of bell, book and candle is thought to date from at least as early as the ninth century and was originally the ritual for the 'greater excommunication' of anathema: where ordinary excommunication involved exclusion from the worship and sacraments of the Church, anathema involved complete separation from the body of the faithful. The bishop pronounced excommunication surrounded by twelve priests carrying lighted candles. When the sentence had been pronounced the bell was rung as for the passing of a soul; the book, symbolising the Church and its authority, was closed in representation of the excommunicant's shutting out from the body of the faithful; and the candles were snuffed or dashed to the floor in token of the soul being extinguished and removed from the light of God.

Marlowe's Dr Faustus notably suffers this fate as friars appear on stage to deliver his comeuppance in Act 3, scene 2: 'Bell, book and candle, candle, book and bell, / Forward and backward, to curse Faustus to hell.'

In modern times the penalty of anathema has seldom been used and in 1983 it was abolished by the Catholic Church.

BENTHAM, JEREMY: A philosopher strangely preserved

Q. Where is Jeremy Bentham buried? I lately met a person who was quite positive that he was mummied, or in some way preserved, and was occasionally exhibited to a party of select friends. Can there be any foundation of truth in this extraordinary story? ~ D.L., 18 July 1857

R. It was part of Jeremy Bentham's will that his body should be devoted to the purpose of improving the science of anatomy, and in consequence it was laid on the table of the anatomical school in Webb Street, Borough. In compliance with Mr Bentham's wish, Dr Southwood Smith delivered a lecture on the occasion. After the usual anatomical demonstrations, a skeleton was made of the bones, which was stuffed out to fit Bentham's own clothes, and a wax likeness, made by a French artist, was fitted to the trunk. This figure was seated on the chair which he usually occupied, with one hand holding the walking-stick, called Dapple, which was his constant companion whenever he went abroad. The whole was enclosed in a mahogany case with folding glass doors, and may now be seen in University College, Gower Street. ~ Editor, 18 July 1857

¶ The pioneer of utilitarianism Jeremy Bentham, who famously argued that 'the greatest happiness of the greatest number' should be the guiding principle of conduct and laws, conceived what he called his 'auto-icon' some years before his death and accordingly left his body to his friend Dr Thomas Southwood Smith with detailed instructions for its preservation.

Southwood Smith delivered his lecture at the Webb Street School of Anatomy and Medicine on 8 June 1832, three days after Bentham's death, while thunder and lightning raged outside. Many years later he described the process whereby the auto-icon was subsequently created:

> I endeavoured to preserve the head untouched, merely drawing away the fluids by placing it under an air pump over sulphuric acid. By this means the head was rendered as hard as the skulls of New Zealanders, but all expression was gone,

of course. Seeing this would not do for exhibition, I had a model made in wax by a distinguished French artist, [who] succeeded in producing one of the most admirable likenesses ever seen. I then had the skeleton stuffed out to fit Bentham's own clothes, and this wax likeness fitted to the trunk.

The artist was Jacques Talrich, whose skill was much admired: Bentham's former friend Lord Brougham described the wax head as 'so perfect that it seems as if alive'.

In 1850, on giving up his consulting rooms in Finsbury Square, Southwood Smith found he no longer had a room large enough to hold the mahogany case and so donated it to University College, London.

In 1898 the auto-icon was examined by Professor Sir George Thane and T. W. P. Lawrence. They reported that the clothes were stuffed with hay and tow, that both hands were present inside the gloves, and that the wax head rested upon an iron spike. They found the real head 'wrapped in cloth saturated with some bituminous or tarry substance (a sort of tarpaulin) and then in paper, making a parcel, in the cavity of the trunk-skeleton, being fastened by strong wire running from the ribs to the vertebral column. On unpacking this the head itself was found to be mummified... In the sockets are glass eyes... The face is clean shaved – hair scanty, grey and long.'

Subsequently the real head was put on display on the floor between the auto-icon's legs and became an irresistible target: in October 1975 it was stolen by students from King's College, London, who demanded a ransom of £100 payable to the charity Shelter; £10 was paid and the head was returned. There are also stories of a second theft that led to the head being found in a left luggage locker at Aberdeen railway station, and an apocryphal tale that it was once used for football practice in the college's front quadrangle. Not surprisingly, the head is now locked away in a refrigerated safe in the college vault.

BILL OF FARE FOR A CHRISTENING, 1682

N. I send you a morsel, copied from a small manuscript volume of family memoranda belonging to a gentleman who has kindly permitted me to send it.

A BILL OF FARE AT THE CHRISTENING OF MR CONSTABLE'S CHILD, RECTOR OF COCKLEY CLEY IN NORFOLK, JAN. 2, 1682

1. A whole hog's head, souc'd [pickled], with carrotts in the mouth and pendants in the ears, with guilded oranges thick sett.
2. 2 ox.'s cheekes stewed, with 6 marrow bones.
3. A leg of veal larded, with 6 pullets.
4. A leg of mutton, with 6 rabbits.
5. A chine of bief, chine of venison, chine of mutton, chine of veal, chine of pork, supported by 4 men.
6. A venison pasty.
7. A great minced pye, with 12 small ones about it.
8. A gelt [gelded] fat turkey, with 6 capons.
9. A bustard, with 6 pluver.
10. A pheasant, with 6 woodcocks.
11. A great dish of tarts made all of sweetmeats.
12. A Westphalia hamm, with 6 tongues.
13. A jowle of sturgeon.
14. A great charger of all sorts of sweetmeats, with wine and all sorts of liquors answerable.

The child, a girle; godfather, Mr Green, a clergyman; godmothers, Miss Beddingfield of Sherson, and a sister-in-law of Mr Constable's.

The guests, Mr Green, Mr Bagg and his daughter, and the godmothers.

The parish[ione]rs entertained at another house with rost and boil'd bief, geese, and turkeys.

Soon after the child dy'd, and the funerall expences came to 6*d.*

~ Edw. Hawkins, 1 May 1852

BIRTH, MARRIAGE AND DEATH IN AN ESSEX PARISH

N. The following curious entries are to be found in the parish registers of Barking, Essex:

1558. Elizabeth and three of her children, buryed the xxvth of Novr.

1559. Julian, a stranger, buryed 28 Jany.

1568. Mother Durrant, bur. 20 Feby.

1574. Joane Ansell, servant with the basketmaker, bur. the 9th of februarye.

1575. A poore maid, who died in Illford Streat, bur. 15 Jany.

1578. Thomas Salinge, drowned at Ilford Bridge, bur. Feb. 16.

1587. Eve, daughter reputed of Christoper Valentine, bapt. 18 Aug.

1590. Mr Wild, one of her majesties chappell, bur. Aug. 4.

1592. Thomas Williams and Magdalen Milborne, *nec virgo nec vidua*,[1] marryed ultimo Januarii.

1592. Anne, an old woman who died in the cage, bur. Feb. 21.

1592. Thomas Wood, the reed reaper, bur. 7 Decr.

1593. John, a poore man, dyinge at the constables, bur. 27 Aprill.

1593. A poore man, who dyed in the feild beyond the brew-house, bur. Aug. 4.

1593. Peter Cecill, out of the cage, bur. 24 Novr.

1594. Dionice, servant wth Edward Fortescue, Esquier, was slaine, and buried April 1.

1595. Edward Snags, slaine at Nevilles house in Goodmay Street, bur. Feb. 13.

1595. John and Elizabeth, children of a travailler who was brought to bed at the Crowne at Illford, bapt. the 11th of Octr.

1596. Elizabeth, the wife of Mr John Tedcastle – bewailed of rich and poore – bur. Nov. 2.

1597. Two vagrant persons from Loxford, bur. 10 Feby.

1597. One other vagrant person, from Illford cage, bur. same day.

[1] Neither virgin nor widow.

1598. Margarett, daughter of a blind fidler, bapt. the 10th of Decr.

1601. Old Agnes, bur. 9 March.

1610. A driver unknown, diing sodenley at Ilford, bur. 27 June.

1654. Mr Chambells coachman, buried the 3 February.

1665. July 29. Nathaniel Pagit, and three of his children.

1665. Sept. 26. A glover, his wife, and his daughter.

1678. March 13. George Abell, out of Dagenham, killed by Loxford Bridge by the fall of a cart.

1684. April 22. Mr Edmund Halley of London, merchant murthered, and buryed in linen, £2 6s. pd. to this parish for ye use of the poor.

1717. Feb. 10. Thomas, son of John Archer, by his first wives own sister. (Baptised)

1720. March 13. Jasper, a black of Capt Brownes. (Buried)

1720. Aug. 22. A strange woman out of Parslowes cow-house. (Buried)

1737. Decr 29. Jane, an Indian black. (Buried)

1750. June 17. A stranger (suicide).

1796. Octr 6. William Goulstone, suffocated on a brick kiln.

~ Edward J. Sage, Stoke Newington, 11 Apr 1863

¶ Most parishes had a cage or similar secure place for the detention of those considered miscreants.

The entries for 1665 reflect the fact that Barking, along with surrounding areas, suffered heavily in the plague of that year.

The murdered merchant was the father of the astronomer Edmond Halley. A rich soap boiler and a yeoman warder of the Tower of London, he was found dead on the shore at Stroud, Kent. It was rumoured that he had been killed because he knew too much about the mysterious death of the Protestant plotter Arthur Capel, Earl of Essex, whose body had been discovered in the Tower on 13 July 1683, a day Halley was there. Like other wealthy people Halley was buried in linen, for which a penalty had to be paid – see WOOLLEN: Burial in.

BOILING TO DEATH: A punishment for cooks?

Q. In John Stow's *Chronicle of England,* edited by Edmund Howes, I find the two following notices:

> The 5th of April (1531) one Richard Rose, a cooke, was boiled at Smithfield, for poisoning of divers persons, to the number of sixteen or more, at ye bishop of Rochester's place, amongst the which Benet Curwine gentleman was one, and he intended to have poisoned the bishop himself, but he eate no potage that day, whereby he escaped. Marie[1] the poore people that eate of them, many of them died...

> The 17th March (1542) Margaret Dany, a maid, was boiled at Smithfield for poisoning of three households that she had dwelled in.

Query, was this punishment peculiar to cooks guilty of poisoning? And when did the latest instance occur? ~ L.H.K., 28 Dec 1850

R. The crime of poisoning was always considered most detestable because, of all types of murder, it can 'be the least prevented either by manhood or forethought' (Sir William Blackstone, *Commentaries on the Laws of England*). Nevertheless, prior to a statute of 1531 there was no peculiarity in the mode of punishment. The occurrence in that year to which the *Chronicle* refers appears to have excited considerable attention, probably on account of the supposition that the life of the bishop was aimed at; so much so, that the extraordinary step was taken of passing an Act of Parliament *retrospective* in its enactments against the culprit (who is variously described as *Rose, Roose,* otherwise *Cooke,* and *Rouse*), prescribing the mode of punishment as above and declaring the crime of poisoning to be treason for the future.

This horrible punishment did not long remain on the statute books, being repealed by statutes of 1547 and 1553, since when the punishment has been the same as in other cases of murder. ~ J. B. Colman, Eye, 10 Jan 1852

[1] An exclamation of surprise or indignation; originally the name of the Virgin Mary used as an oath.

R2. The Act of 1531 recites as follows:

One Richard Roose, late of Rochester in the county of Kent, cook, otherwise called Richard Coke, of his most wicked and damnable disposition did cast a certain venom or poison into a vessel replenished with yeast or barm standing in the kitchen of the Reverend Father in God John Bishop of Rochester at his place in Lambeth Marsh, with which yeast or barm and other things convenient porridge or gruel was forthwith made for his family there being, whereby not only the number of seventeen persons of his said family which did eat of that porridge were mortally infected and poisoned, and one of them, that is to say Benett Curwen gentleman, thereof is deceased, but also certain poor people were in like wise infected, and one poor woman of them, that is to say Alice Tryppytt widow, is also thereof now deceased. Our said Sovereign Lord the King of his blessed disposition inwardly abhorring all such abominable offences has ordained and enacted by authority of this present parliament that the said poisoning be adjudged and deemed as high treason [and] the said Richard Roose shall be therefore boiled to death without having any advantage of his clergy. And that from henceforth every wilful murder by poisoning shall be judged in the law to be high treason. And that every person attainted for any manner [of] poisoning shall not be admitted to the benefit of his or their clergy, but shall be immediately committed to execution of death by boiling...

~ Editor, 10 Jan 1852

R3. I have reason to believe that Mr Colman is wrong in his assertion that, prior to the statute of 1531, 'there was no peculiarity in the mode of punishment' for the crime in question. In the Chronicle of the Grey Friars of London, which I am engaged in editing for the Camden Society, I find the following in a statute of 1522: 'And this yere was a man soddene in a cautherne (cauldron) in Smithfelde, and lett up and downe divers times till he was dede, for because he wold a poisoned divers persons.'

Perhaps, therefore, the purpose of the Act referred to lay rather in depriving such culprits of their 'benefit of clergy' whereby they might have escaped the punishment already provided for their crime.[1]

Roose's own case is also recorded in the Chronicle of the Grey Friars: 'He was locked in a chaine and pulled up and downe with a gibbet at divers times till he was dede.'

A third instance occurs in 1542, when 'The 10th day of March was a maide boiled in Smithfelde for poisoning of divers persons.'[2] ~ John Gough Nichols, 31 Jan 1852

R4. On this subject it may be of interest to some of your readers that in the year 1392, when Florentius Wewelinghofen of Wewelkofen was Bishop of Utrecht, a certain Jacobus von Jülich, by means of forged credentials from the Pope, contrived to pass himself off for a time as suffragan to the same see. Upon the discovery of the cheat, however, Florentius summoned a synod of six bishops to Utrecht, who condemned the unfortunate pretender to be sodden to death in boiling water.

Perhaps one of your readers skilled in Roman ecclesiastical archaeology can inform the public whether this may not be the origin of the phrase *getting oneself into hot water...* ~ J. B. McC., British Museum, 21 Feb 1852

¶ The Roose case was so sensitive because John Fisher, Bishop of Rochester, was the principal supporter of Catherine of Aragon and an outspoken opponent of Henry VIII. In January 1531 a final attempt to persuade him to drop opposition to the king's planned divorce from Catherine failed, and in February he led bishoply resistance to the recognition of Henry as Supreme Head of the Church in England.

---

[1] Originally a privilege whereby clerics were entitled to be tried in ecclesiastical courts rather than the more severe secular ones, over time benefit of clergy had come to be allowed to anyone who could read a verse of Scripture, basic literacy being considered proof of clerical status. Henry VIII's action to restrict it was part of a long process of curtailment which culminated in its abolition in 1827.

[2] Notwithstanding the minor discrepancy between the dates in the Stow-Howes and Grey Friars chronicles, it seems very likely that the 'maide boiled' was Margaret Dany.

So when Roose put poison in the porridge some wondered whether Henry, or Anne Boleyn and her family, had been behind the deed. The king's public outrage, evidenced in his pushing for a harsh new law and exemplary punishment, may therefore have been an attempt to divert suspicion at a critical time. Certainly that seems to have been the view of Eustace Chapuys, the Spanish ambassador. 'The king', he reported on 1 March, 'was about two hours in the House of Lords and said a good deal to them about his love of justice, and his zeal for the good administration of the kingdom and the protection of his subjects. He also requested them to look into the case of the Bishop of Rochester's cook, which is a very strange one... The king has certainly shown some displeasure at this, but whatever demonstrations of sorrow he makes he will not be able to avert suspicion from falling, if not on himself, at least on the lady and her father.'

While there is nothing to indicate that Henry was himself behind the poisoning, Chapuys's pointing of the finger at the Boleyn faction is supported by modern historians. The porridge plot was not, after all, the only attempt to assassinate Fisher at this time – according to an early life of the bishop, while he was at Lambeth a short time later, 'sodenly a gunne was shott through the topp of his howse not far from his studye, where he accustomably used to sitt. Which made such a horrible noise over his heade and brused the tiles and rafters of the howse so sore, that both he and divers others of his servants were sodenly amased therat. Wherefore speedie search was made whence this shott shoulde come and what it ment. Which at last was found to come from the other side of the Thames out of the erle of Wiltshires howse, who was father to the ladie Ann.' Sir Thomas Boleyn, created Earl of Wiltshire two years earlier, had recently been allocated a set of rooms in Whitehall Palace.

Poison and optimistic potshots notwithstanding, Fisher continued to be a thorn in Henry's ample side for another four years. In 1535, however, he was convicted of treason for denying that Henry was Supreme Head of the Church in England and was beheaded on Tower Hill.

BOLEYN, SIR THOMAS: Going headless in Norfolk

Q. Sir Thomas Boleyn, the father of the unfortunate queen of Henry VIII, resided at Blickling, distant about fourteen miles from Norwich. The spectre of this gentleman is believed by the vulgar to be doomed annually, on a certain night in the year and for a period of one thousand years, to drive a coach drawn by four headless horses over a circuit of twelve bridges in that vicinity – these are Aylsham, Burgh, Oxnead, Buxton, Coltishall, the two Meyton bridges, Wroxham, and four others whose names I do not recollect. Sir Thomas carries his own head under his arm, and flames issue from his mouth. Few rustics are hardy enough to be found loitering on or near those bridges on that night. My informant averred that he was himself on one occasion hailed by this fiendish apparition and asked to open a gate, but he 'warn't sich a fool' as to turn his head, 'and well a didn't, for Sir Thomas passed me full gallop like', and he heard a voice which told him that he (Sir Thomas) had no power to hurt such as turned a deaf ear to his requests, but that had he stopped he would have carried him off.

This tradition I repeatedly heard in this neighbourhood from aged persons when I was a child, but I have never found more than this one person who has actually *seen* the phantom.

Perhaps one of your correspondents can give some clue to this extraordinary sentence? ~ E.S.T., 18 May 1850

¶ Later versions of the story have Sir Thomas's circuit increasing considerably, taking him as far east as Great Yarmouth and requiring him to cross forty bridges between midnight and cock-crow, pursued all the while by a howling pack of demon dogs. The flames shooting from his mouth and his penchant for carrying off those he catches have led folklore experts to link the story to the medieval tradition of the hell-wain, which carried off the souls of the damned.

As to the cause of the curse, some accounts say it is Henry VIII's revenge for Boleyn's part in bringing about his ill-fated marriage to Anne, others that it is rather a punishment for his supposed complicity in Anne's execution. In the latter stories the ride takes place on the night of 19 May, the anniversary of the execution. On the same night Anne herself also appears: according to Walter Rye, writing in Norfolk in the 1870s, 'nothing is more firmly believed than that Lady Anne Boleyn rides down the avenue of Blickling Park once a year with her bloody head on her lap, sitting in a hearse-like coach drawn by four black headless horses, and attended by coachmen and attendants who have, out of compliment to their mistress, also left their heads behind them.'

Sir Thomas causes concern in Norfolk

BOOK TITLES: Some curious

The following are among the more curious titles cited in the early years of *N & Q.*

♦ *A Sigh of Sorrow for the Sinners of Zion, breathed out of a Hole in the Wall of an earthly Vessel, known among Men by the Name of Samuel Fish.* Published by an imprisoned Quaker. No date.

♦ *Sternutatorium Hemicraniologicum, or, The Arte of Sneezing at Will and curing all sortes of Megrims and Disorders of the Head* by Thomas Whishe, Practitioner Extra to the Kinge's Grace. No date.

♦ *Remarks on the Profane and Absurd Use of the Monosyllable Damn* by the Rev. Matthew Towgood, 1746

♦ *A Philosophical Dialogue concerning Decency, to which is added a Critical and Historical Dissertation on Places of Retirement for necessary Occasions, together with an Account of the Vessels and Utensils in use amongst the Ancients* by the Rev. Samuel Rolleston, Archdeacon of Salisbury, 1751. Among other titles by the same author were *A Dissertation concerning the Antiquity of Malt Liquor* and *A Dissertation on Close-Stools.*

♦ *Some Observations on the Inconvenience of the Ten Commandments* by Mr Leycester, Barrister-at-Law of Lincoln's Inn, 1795

♦ *An Essay on the Probability of Sensation in Vegetables, with Additional Observations on Instinct, Sensation, Irritability, &c.* by James Perchard Tupper, 1811

BUNKUM

Q. From the *Illustrated News*, 26 June 1858:

> A diffuse and angry orator having made a somewhat irrational and very unnecessary speech in the House of Representatives in Washington, when nobody thought it worthwhile to contradict him, was afterwards asked by a friend who met him in Pennsylvania Avenue why he had made such a display. 'I was not speaking to the House,' he replied, 'I was speaking to Buncombe' – a county or district by the majority of whose votes he had been elected.

Where is Buncombe? And is this the origin of the phrase 'speaking Bunkum'? ~ William Fraser, Alton, Staffordshire, 31 July 1858

R. Buncombe is in North Carolina. Judge Halliburton of Nova Scotia thus explains this expressive word:

> All over America every place likes to hear of its members of Congress and see their speeches, and if they don't they send a piece to the paper enquirin' if their member died a natural death, or was skivvered with a bowie knife, for they hante seen his speeches lately, and his friends are anxious to know his fate... So every feller in bounden duty talks, and talks big too, and the smaller the State, the louder, bigger, and fiercer its members talk. Well, when a critter talks for talk sake, jist to have a speech in the paper to send home, and not for any other airthily purpose but electioneering, our folks call it *Bunkum*.

~ Editor, 31 July 1858

¶ The representative of Buncombe in question was Felix Walker, who held up Congress in this way *circa* 1820.

BURIAL 1: In an upright posture

Q. In the north transept of Stanton Harcourt Church, Oxon, is a circular slab of blue marble in the pavement into which is inlaid a shield of brass bearing the arms of the Harcourt family.

It is supposed to be the monument of Sir John Harcourt, who died in 1330. Tradition relates that the knight was buried beneath this stone in an erect posture, but assigns no reason for this peculiarity. Is the probability of this being the case supported by any similar burials elsewhere? Or does the legend merely owe its existence to the circular form of the stone? ~ Cheverells, 2 July 1853

R. Towards the close of the last century there lived in Kidderminster an eccentric person of the name of Orton, the landlord of the Bell Inn. During his lifetime he erected his tomb in the parish churchyard, with his *memento mori* inscription graven in large characters on the upper slab:

> Job Orton, a man from Leicestershire;
> And when he's dead, he must lie under here.

This inscription remains unaltered to this day, and may be seen on the right hand of the broad walk on the north side of the spacious churchyard. His coffin was constructed at the same time, and, until it should be required, was used as a wine bin. But, to carry his eccentricity even to the grave, he left strict orders that he should be buried in an erect posture, and tradition says that his request was complied with. His reason for such burial was that at the Last Day he might be able to rise from his grave before his wife, who was buried in the usual horizontal manner. ~ Cuthbert Bede, 16 July 1853

R2.   Pass, pass who will, yon chantry door,
> And through the chink in the fractured floor
> Look down, and see a grisly sight,
> A vault where the bodies are buried upright!
> There face by face, and hand by hand,
> The Claphams and Mauleverers stand...
> (Wordsworth, *The White Doe of Rylstone,*
> Canto 1, lines 245-250)

The note on this in Thomas Whitaker's *History of Craven* is as follows: 'At the east end of the north aisle of Bolton Priory

Church is a chantry belonging to Bethmesley Hall and a vault where, according to tradition, the Claphams were buried upright. I have looked into it through an aperture in the pavement.'
~ F.W.J., 3 Sep 1853

R3. In *The Ingoldsby Legends* we have the following regarding the beloved dog Tray and the possibility of a burial at Westminster:

> No! — Tray's humble tomb would look but shabby
> 'Mid the sculptured shrines of that gorgeous Abbey.
> Besides, in the place
> They say there's not space
> To bury what wet-nurses call a *Babby*.
> Even 'rare Ben Jonson', that famous wight,
> I am told, is interr'd there bolt upright,
> In just such a posture, beneath his bust,
> As Tray used to sit in to beg for a crust.

Is there any authority for this statement? ~ Erica, 5 Nov 1853

R4. Ben Jonson was buried thus at Westminster, probably on account of the large fee demanded for a full-size grave. It was long supposed by many that the story was invented to account for the smallness of his gravestone, but on the grave being opened a few years ago the dramatist's remains were discovered in the attitude indicated by tradition. ~ Henry Gough, Emberton, Bucks, 5 Nov 1853

R5. The German rogue Eulenspiegel (or Howleglass, as it is sometimes rendered) is another example of upright burial, as the following passage, translated by Thomas Roscoe, shows:

Howleglass was buried in the year 1350, and his latter end was almost as odd and eccentric as his life. For, as they were lowering him into the grave, one of the ropes supporting the feet gave way and left the coffin in an upright position, so that Howleglass was still upon his legs. Those who were present then said: 'Come, let us leave him as he is, for, as he was like nobody else when he was alive, he is resolved to be as queer now he is dead.' Accordingly they left Howleglass bolt upright, placing a stone over his head on which was cut the figure of an owl with a looking-glass under his claws, the device of his name.

His tomb was remaining thirty years ago under a large lime tree at Möllen, near Lubeck, and may still be there now. ~ J.R.M., A.M., 28 Jan 1854

R6. How strange it is that all of us should have forgotten Charlemagne. When his tomb at Aix-la-Chapelle was opened by the Emperor Frederick Barbarossa in 1165, 'he found the body of Charlemagne not reclining in his coffin... but seated in his throne as one alive, clothed in the imperial robes, bearing the sceptre in his hand, and on his knees a copy of the gospels' (Murray's *Handbook* to Belgium). The throne on which the body was seated, and the sarcophagus in which the feet of the dead king were placed, are still preserved in the cathedral, where I saw them last year, together with some portion of the robes and some curious ancient embroidery that are not usually exhibited to strangers. ~ W. Sparrow Simpson, 29 Apr 1854

¶ The poet and playwright Ben Jonson is the only person buried upright in Westminster Abbey. It is said that, in conversation with the dean about possible burial in Poets' Corner, he remarked that he was too poor for that: 'No, sir, six feet long by two feet wide is too much for me. Two feet by two feet will do for all I want.' Taking him at his word, the dean arranged for his interment not among the poets but in the northern aisle of the nave. In 1849 this resting-place was disturbed by a burial nearby and the clerk of works saw Jonson's leg bones fixed upright in the sand. He also saw Jonson's skull, still with some red hair attached, which rolled down from above the bones into the pit of the grave.

Perhaps the most celebrated vertical burial is that of Major Peter Labilliere. Eccentric and devout, he lodged at Dorking in his later years and before he died made two unusual requests. The first was that his landlady's youngest son and daughter should dance upon his coffin; the daughter, thinking this improper, was only prepared to sit on the coffin, but the son danced happily away. His second request was that he should be buried upside down at a favourite spot on nearby Box Hill; this was done on 11 June 1800, sprigs of box and of yew first being cast into the deep, round grave. This curious direction is attributed by some to the major's pious wish to emulate his namesake St Peter, who was crucified upside down, while others hold that it was so that on Judgement Day, 'when all things will be turned topsy-turvy', he should be the first one upright.

BURIAL 2: In unconsecrated ground

Q. Is there in existence any law rendering burial in consecrated ground compulsory? Most people have a strong desire to receive such interment, but a few might prefer to have their mortal remains deposited in some loved spot, far away from other graves, in a scene where many happy hours had been passed. It would be a very unusual thing, but, supposing such a desire to exist, could its execution be prevented? It is recorded that Manasseh, King of Judah, 'was buried in the garden of his own house, in the garden of Uzza' (2 Kings, 21:18). ~ Sampson Anramenii, 3 Apr 1852

R. Though not a lawyer, I venture to express the opinion that, if preferred, burial may take place in unconsecrated ground. The law exacts the registering of the death, and inhibits a clergyman from officiating except within the consecrated boundary. But, supposing a person to have the fancy to lie 'in some loved spot, far away from other graves', there seems to be no legal difficulty. In the shrubbery of Brush House, the residence of my friend and neighbour John Booth, Esq., MD, there is a mausoleum over the remains of his uncle, from whom he inherited the property. And was not Mrs van Butchell preserved many years after death in a glass case by her husband? ~ Alfred Gatty, 24 Apr 1852

R2. John Baskerville, the celebrated printer, directed that he should be buried under a windmill near his garden; this direction proceeded, alas, from disbelief in Revelation. A few years previously, in 1772, Mr Hull, a Bencher of the Inner Temple, was buried underneath Leith Hill Tower in Surrey, which he had erected on that beautiful and commanding spot shortly before his death.

Was not Mrs van Butchell, to whom Mr Gatty refers, to be seen some years ago in her glass case in the College of Surgeons? ~ J.H.M., 5 June 1852

R3. Two notable cases occurred some time ago in this neighbourhood, the one that of John Trigg, whose coffin is now to be seen placed on the beams of a barn at Stevenage, and the other that of Richard Tristram, who was buried in a field in the parish of Ippolitts. The gravestone marking the resting-place of Tristram was, till quite lately, an attraction in the neighbourhood, but a sacrilegious farmer, annoyed at the injury done to his hedges by the visitors to the tomb, has either removed the stone or sunk it below the level of the ground.

Local tradition assigns a singular cause to the burial of these two men in these spots. It is stated that they were shocked at the unceremonious way in which the sexton in a neighbouring churchyard treated some remains disinterred whilst digging a tomb, and therefore they left the most stringent injunctions that their burials might place them beyond the reach of similar usage. ~ L.W., Hitchin, 7 Aug 1852

¶ Mrs van Butchell was the wife of Martin van Butchell (1735–*c*.1812), who achieved eminence first as a dentist and then as a maker of medical trusses. He was also eminently eccentric, refusing to trim his beard lest his vigour should be diminished, riding in Hyde Park on a white pony painted with purple spots, and carrying for self-defence a large white bone which, it was said, had been used as a weapon of war in Tahiti.

His notoriety increased following the death of his first wife in 1775. Whether from a reluctance to lose her company or – as was rumoured – because a clause in the marriage settlement stipulated that his control of her fortune endured only while she remained above ground, he commissioned the eminent anatomist William Hunter to preserve her. It proved a milestone in the history of embalming. The impressive results were achieved by introducing powdered nitre and camphor into her abdominal cavity and injecting her vascular system with oil of turpentine and camphorated spirit of wine – leading one wag to refer to 'A wife that's dead, yet full of *spirits*.' Glass eyes were added and the body was then dressed in a fashionable lace gown and set upon a thin bed of plaster of Paris in a box topped by a removable glass lid. Thereafter van Butchell kept her in the parlour in his house in Mount Street, Berkeley Square, and observed regular visiting hours for friends and strangers alike.

This happy arrangement came to an end with the arrival of the second Mrs van Butchell. Her predecessor was promptly donated to the museum of the Royal College of Surgeons in Lincoln's Inn Fields, where she remained for some hundred and fifty years before being incinerated on the night of 10-11 May 1941 after a stray German bomb landed nearby.

The Famous Mr MARTIN VAN BUTCHELL

BURIAL 3: Alive

N. Newspaper paragraphs headed 'Buried alive!' appear at intervals sufficiently brief to keep the frightful possibility of such an occurrence vivid in the imagination. The ancients, as is well known, instituted their *conclamatio*[1] and other precautions to prevent this most horrible of fates. In *Romeo and Juliet*, Act 4 scene 3, the tender heroine soliloquises: 'How if, when I am laid into the tomb, / I wake... / ... There's a fearful point!', and the prevalence of such a fear may be gathered from the number of instances in which men have requested that, before the last offices are done for them, such wounds or mutilations should be inflicted upon their bodies as should effectually prevent the possibility of an awakening in the tomb. The late Francis Douce, the well known antiquary and lover of books, affords a notable example. The first clause of his will was as follows: 'I give to Sir Anthony Carlisle £200, requesting him either to sever my head or extract the heart from my body, so as to prevent any possibility of the return of vitality.'

In France, especially, premature interments seem in the past to have been startlingly numerous. Jean-Jacques Bruhier has collected and classified no fewer than 180 cases, many of which were doubtless attributable to hospital negligence.

For the behoof of those who may take an interest in this horrible subject, and wish to investigate it for themselves, I append the titles of a few volumes in my collection:

> *The Uncertainty of the Signs of Death, and the Danger of Precipitate Interments and Dissections Demonstrated*, 2nd edition, London, 1751

> *Observations on Apparent Death from Drowning, Hanging, Suffocation, by Noxious Vapours, Fainting Fits, Intoxication, Lightning, Exposure to Cold, &c.* by James Curry, MD, London, 1815

---

[1] Literally loud or combined shouting and the name given to the Roman practice of calling out a dead person's name three times before they were buried.

*The Danger of Premature Interment proved from many
remarkable Instances of Persons who have recovered
after being laid out for Dead* by Joseph Taylor, 1816.

~ William Bates, Birmingham, 9 Aug 1856

R. From Francis Bacon's *Historiae Vitae et Mortis* (1623):
There have been many instances of men left for dead, laid
out, and carried to burial – nay, of some actually buried – that
have yet come to life again. In the case of those buried, this
has been found by the bruising and wounding of their head
through the struggling of the body within the coffin. A most
memorable instance was that of Joannes Scotus, called the
Subtle, and a Schoolman, who, having been buried in the
absence of his servant (who knew his master's manner in such
fits), was by him digged up and found to have been buried
alive. The like happened in our days, in the person of a player
buried at Cambridge.

~ Mackenzie Walcott, 18 Apr 1857

R2. I have cut the following from the *Stamford Mercury* of
14 May 1858. If it be true it is worth a Note in your pages; if a
hoax, as I hope and believe, perhaps some correspondent will
prove it to be such.

BURIED ALIVE

A rich manufacturer named Oppelt died about fifteen years
since at Reichenberg, in Austria, and a vault was built in the
cemetery for the reception of the body by his widow and
children. The widow died about a month ago and was taken
to the same tomb; but, when it was opened for that purpose,
the coffin of her husband was found open and empty, and
the skeleton of the deceased discovered in a corner of the
vault in a sitting posture. A commission was appointed by the
authorities to examine into the affair, when they gave their
opinion that M. Oppelt was only in a trance when buried,
and that on coming to life he had forced open the coffin.

~ K.P.D.E., 5 June 1858

R3. In the *Gentleman's Magazine* for April 1801 there appears the following obituary notice:

Lately at Chester, aged 92, Christopher Lowe, many years bill-distributor for the Theatre Royal of Chester. This venerable patriarch was a native of Preston and, when in his sixteenth year, was afflicted with a fever of which he apparently died. He was laid out, shrouded, and coffined, and nearly three days after his supposed demise, while carrying on four men's shoulders to the grave, he suddenly knocked at the lid of the coffin and, to the ineffable amazement of the carriers and attendants, on opening it they found honest Christopher in a complete state of resuscitation. For many years after he used to amuse and astonish his neighbours and friends with 'the wonderful things he saw in his trance'.

~ T. N. Brushfield, Chester, 4 Dec 1858

R4. A belief in the bare possibility of living burial has been the cause of much misery to very many persons. I once conferred with a sensible medical man on this fearful subject. He stated that the moment of returning consciousness would be the last of existence, as suffocation must necessarily and speedily occur; but what a moment must *that* be! ~ Md., 23 Aug 1862

R5. N & Q has accumulated many valuable facts on this painful subject. It would be well to add the following to their number, with the Query, is it true?

At Asnières, France, an actor fell ill and apparently died. The day of the interment arrived, and when the persons who had to place the corpse in the coffin were about to perform that duty they were astonished to hear a deep sigh proceed from the body, followed by the words, *'Ah! Mon Dieu!'* M. Clair-Benié had awakened from a lethargy, and is now getting better.

(*Stamford Mercury*, 21 August 1863)

~ Grime, 19 Sep 1863

R6. To obviate this danger a custom obtains in the Campo Santo at Munich of leaving corpses with the lid of the coffin off, exposed on a marble slab for a day or two, with strings fastened to the hands and feet so that the least motion of the body causes a bell to ring. This bell being heard by a person set there purposely to watch night and day, any poor creature thus prematurely sent to their maker may be rescued. ~ P.A.L., 16 Nov 1867

¶ The death in Cologne of the medieval philosopher John or Joannes Duns Scotus (*c.*1265-1308) is as scantly documented as the rest of his life. The legend that he was buried alive flared into brief controversy in the early 1620s, at the time Francis Bacon was writing.

Bacon mentions wounds found on the heads of disinterred corpses, and other common 'signs' of premature burial were tearing to the hands and gnawing of the fingers, seen as proof that the victim had desperately clawed at the coffin lid to try to get out and then been forced to start eating their own hands. However, it is now known that rats, entering a coffin, tend to start their nibbling at the fingertips, damage the face, and generally inflict just such injuries as might be taken for evidence of a last desperate struggle in the grave.

Taphephobia – the fear of being buried alive – came into morbid fashion in the eighteenth and nineteenth centuries. It received an early boost from French physician Jean-Jacques Bruhier, who reviewed fifty-six cases of premature dissection or interment along with 125 narrow escapes in his *Dissertation sur l'incertitude des signes de la mort*, which went through several editions and translations in the 1740s. A hundred and fifty years later the fear was still high: in *Premature Burial and How It May Be Prevented* (1896), Colonel E. P. Vollum and William Tebb listed 161 cases of premature burial in Britain alone, along with 219 narrow escapes and ten premature dissections.

In the face of such alarming statistics it is not surprising that men such as Francis Douce took precautions. He was far from alone: William Blackett of Plymouth desired in his will of 1782 'that my body may be kept as long as it may not be offensive, and that one or more of my toes or fingers may be cut off, to secure a certainty of my being dead'; the Victorian novelist Edward Bulwer-Lytton left instruction that his heart should be punctured by his doctor before he was placed in his coffin; Harriet Martineau left her doctor ten guineas on the understanding that her head was to be amputated before she was interred; and as late as 3 August 1915 *The Times* would record that Miss Emily Harriet Ripley of Bayswater had left a doctor £20 on condition that, when she should be thought dead, he would see to it that her throat was slit from ear to ear to make sure.

The Germans tackled the problem on a larger scale and with characteristic thoroughness, building *Leichenhaüser* or 'waiting mortuaries' to give bodies time to revive. The first appeared in Weimar in 1791 and boasted a corpse chamber heated by steam to aid decomposition plus an attendant to look out for any sign of putrefaction. Over the following decades *Leichenhaüser* appeared all over Germany, with the bell-ringing arrangement noted in *N & Q* a standard feature. However, as Melanie King notes in her recent study, *The Dying Game*, 'One of the drawbacks of this alarm system was that decaying corpses had a habit of expanding and moving as putrefaction ran its course and so the bells were unwittingly set to jingling by the bloating cadavers.' Indeed, false alarms seem to have been the only kind: through the long history of *Leichenhaüser* there is not a single record of anyone coming back to life. In consequence, by the end of the nineteenth century many of the alarm systems had been removed and the mortuaries had begun to fall from favour, although some remained in use through to the 1940s.

Outside Germany waiting mortuaries were rare, but plenty of attention was given to the underlying question of how to be sure someone was dead. An early and simple test was the blowing of a bugle fanfare as loud as possible directly into the cadaver's ear. Another is suggested by the evidence of a mass grave for victims of the plague that ravaged Marseilles in 1720: when it was opened in 1994, inch-long bronze pins were discovered on two corpses in positions suggesting they had been driven under the nails of the large toes.

Slightly less excruciating tests would be developed by Jacob Winsløw (1669-1760), a Dane who had himself narrowly escaped premature interment as a child. He advocated irritating the nostrils with horseradish, tickling the nose with a feather, whipping the skin with nettles, pouring warm urine into the mouth, and tipping boiling Spanish wax over the head. A Swedish writer added the idea of placing a crawling insect inside the corpse's ear, and in 1854 a French doctor, Jules-Antoine Josat, invented a giant pair of tweezers which he called a *pince-mamelon*, or nipple-pincher. Apparently unimpressed by all such methods, another Frenchman, Dr Jean-Vincent Laborde, insisted that the only way to be sure was for the tongue of the deceased to be pulled rhythmically for three hours. When mortuary assistants complained that this was tedious work, Laborde invented an electric tongue-pulling machine to do the job for them.

If you did not want your tongue pulled for three hours you could always have a specially designed coffin. It is said that in 1792 Duke Ferdinand of Brunswick ordered one with a window, an air hole, and a lid secured not by nails but by lock and key. He then had a special pocket added to his shroud to hold not only the key for the lid but also one for the door of the vault in which the coffin was to be placed.

The subject also occupied the minds of a number of nineteenth-century writers. In 'The Premature Burial' Edgar Allan Poe cheerily imagined 'the stifling fumes of the damp earth – the clinging to the death garments – the rigid embrace of the narrow house – the blackness of the absolute Night'. Wilkie Collins visited a *Leichenhaüs* in Frankfurt and used the setting in his late novel *Jezebel's Daughter* (1880), in which a reviving body alerts the deadhouse attendant by ringing the bell, and Mark Twain, having visited Munich in the winter of 1878-9, described one of its waiting mortuaries in *Life on the Mississippi* (1883):

A watchman sits always alert and ready to spring to the aid of any of that pallid company who, waking out of death, shall make a movement – for any, even the slightest movement will twitch the wire and ring that fearful bell. I imagined myself a death-sentinel drowsing there alone, far in the dragging watches of some wailing, gusty night, and having in a twinkling all my body stricken to quivering jelly by the sudden clamour of that awful summons!

While its heyday is long past, taphephobia is itself not quite dead: modern undertakers report people asking for their mobile phones to be buried with them, turned off to ensure that sufficient charge will remain for the making of an unexpected call from the grave – signal permitting.

BURNING TO DEATH: When was it last a legal punishment in England?

Q. I think that some of your readers will be surprised to learn that, within the memory of witnesses still alive, a woman was burnt to death for the murder of her husband. A marine, her paramour and an accomplice in the murder, was condemned to be hanged. The post to which this woman was bound stood, till recently, in a field adjoining Winchester.

I know two persons still alive who were present. According to one of them, 'It was about sixty-five years ago. I sat in the crowd on my father's shoulder and saw them bring her and the marine to the field. They fixed her neck by a rope to the stake, and then set fire to the faggots and burnt her.' She was probably strangled by this rope.

Query, was this execution at Winchester in 1783 (or there-abouts) the last instance in England? ~ E.S.S.W., 1 June 1850

R. A woman was strangled and burnt for coining in front of the debtors' door, Newgate, on 10 March 1789. I believe this to be the last instance in which this old punishment was inflicted, at least in the metropolis. The burning part of the ceremony was abolished by a statute of 1790 and death by hanging made the penalty for women in cases of high or petty treason.[1]

E.S.S.W.'s informants are wrong in supposing that the criminals were burnt whilst living. The law, indeed, prescribed it, but the practice was more humane. They were first strangled – although it sometimes happened that, through the bungling of the executioner, a criminal was actually burnt alive, as occurred in the celebrated case of Catherine Hayes, executed for the murder of her husband in 1726. The circumstances of this case are so remarkable that I am induced to recapitulate the chief of them, in the belief that they will interest your readers.

John Hayes, who was possessed of some little property, lodged with his wife Catherine in Tyburn, now Oxford Road. Mrs Hayes prevailed upon two men, named Billings (who lodged in the house) and Wood (a friend of Hayes), to assist her in murdering her husband. To facilitate that object Hayes was induced to drink the enormous quantity of seven bottles (at that time full quarts) of Mountain wine, besides other intoxicating drinks. After finishing the seventh bottle he fell on the floor, but soon after arose and threw himself on a bed. There, whilst in a state of stupefaction, he was despatched by Billings and Wood striking him on the head with a hatchet. The murderers then held council as to the best mode of concealing their crime and it was determined that they should mutilate and dispose of the body. They cut off the head, Mrs Hayes holding a pail to

---

[1] Prior to this the punishment for women for these offences had differed from that for men largely out of delicacy, it being thought unseemly for their bodies to suffer the public exposure involved in suspension from a gibbet.

catch the blood, and she proposed that it should then be boiled until the flesh came from the skull. This advice was rejected on account of the time which the process would occupy, and Billings and Wood carried the head in the pail (it was at night) to the Horseferry at Westminster, and there cast it into the Thames. On the following day the murderers separated the limbs from the body, and, wrapping them together with the trunk in two blankets, carried them to Marylebone fields and placed them in a pond.

Hayes's head, not having been carried away by the tide as the murderers expected it would be, was found floating at the Horseferry in the morning. The attention of the authorities was drawn to the circumstance, and the magistrates, being of opinion that a murder had been committed, caused the head to be washed and the hair combed out, and then had it placed on a pole and exposed to public view in St Margaret's Churchyard, in the hope that it might lead to the discovery of the suspected crime.

Great crowds of persons of all ranks flocked to the churchyard to see the head, and amongst the rest a young man named Bennett. Perceiving the likeness to Hayes, whom he knew, he went immediately to Mrs Hayes on the subject – but she assured him that her husband was alive and well, which satisfied him. A journeyman tailor named Patrick also went to see the head, and on his return told his fellow workmen that it was Hayes. These workmen, who had also known Hayes, then went to look at the head and felt the same conviction. It happened that Billings worked at the same shop in which these men were employed in Monmouth Street, and when he came to work next morning they told him of the circumstance. Billings, however, lulled their suspicions by declaring that he had left Mr Hayes at home that morning.

After the head had been exhibited for four days in the churchyard the magistrates caused it to be placed in spirits in a glass vessel, and in that state it continued to be exposed to public view. Two friends of Hayes, named Ashley and Longmore, who had seen the head without imagining that it was his, some time after called on Mrs Hayes on separate occasions to enquire for her husband, whose absence began to be noticed. Ashley and Longmore were mutual friends, and, their suspicions being excited by the contradictory statements which Mrs Hayes had given to them, they went to look again at the head, and a minute examination satisfied them that it had belonged to Hayes. The apprehension of the murderers was the result. On the day they were brought up for examination, the trunk and limbs of the murdered man were found.

Wood and Billings confessed and pleaded guilty. Catherine Hayes put herself on her country and was tried and convicted. Wood died in prison. Billings was hanged in Marylebone fields, near the pond in which Hayes's body had been concealed. Catherine Hayes was executed at Tyburn, under circumstances of great horror, for, in consequence of the fire reaching the executioner's hands, he left his hold of the rope with which he ought to have strangled her before he had executed that part of his duty, and the result was that Catherine Hayes was burnt alive. The wretched woman was seen, in the midst of flames, pushing the blazing faggots from her whilst she yelled in agony. Fresh faggots were piled around her, but a considerable time elapsed before her torments ended. She suffered thus on 9 May 1726. ~ C. Ross, 22 June 1850

R2. Regarding the last instance of this punishment, the *Gentleman's Magazine* contains an account of the execution of nine malefactors at Newgate on 18 March 1789. Amongst them 'Christian Murphy, alias Bowman, for coining, was brought out after the rest were turned off, and fixed to a stake, and burnt, being first strangled by the stool being taken from under her.' However, from the very slight difference in date I am inclined to think that this is the same case alluded to by Mr Ross. ~ Old Bailey, 6 July 1850

R3. I was present at this execution. The number of those who suffered, and the burning of the female, attracted a very great crowd. After the other eight malefactors had been suspended the woman, in a white dress, was brought out of Newgate alone, and, after some time spent in devotion, was hung on the projecting arm of a low gibbet, fixed at a little distance from the scaffold. After the lapse of a sufficient time to extinguish life, faggots were piled around her, and over her head, so that her person was completely covered. Fire was then set to the pile, and the woman was consumed to ashes.

Thank God we now live in times when the law is less cruel, and more chary of human life. ~ Octogenarius, 21 Sep 1850

¶ The grisly story of Catherine Hayes inspired Thackeray's first novel, *Catherine*, serialised in 1839 and 1840, and her name reappeared in partnership with those of two other notorious murderers in *Vanity Fair*, in which Becky Sharp's formidable legal advisers are Burke, Thurtell and Hayes.

Catherine Hayes

BYRON'S BRAIN: How much did it weigh?

Q. Presuming that the respective weights of the brains of certain great men are known, I shall be glad to know the weight of Lord Byron's in illustration of the extraordinary weight the human brain will attain, particularly in persons of transcendent powers of mind with a healthy organisation. Also, what is the average weight of the human brain? ~ Konx Ompax, 13 July 1861

R. Thomas Moore, in his Life of Byron, gives a very minute account of the poet's personal appearance but does not say anything about his brain. He describes his head as 'remarkably small, so much so as to be rather out of proportion with his face'. This statement is confirmed by Colonel Napier, who says that, in a party of twelve or fourteen who were at dinner, not one could put on Byron's hat, 'so exceedingly small was his head'. He adds: 'My servant, Thomas Wells, who had the smallest head in the 90th regiment (so small that he could hardly get a cap to fit him), was the only person who could put on Lord Byron's hat, and him it fitted exactly.'

The following I cut the other day out of one of the London daily papers: 'It is said that a post-mortem examination of Lord Campbell took place. Amongst other things, the faculty speak of the enormous weight of the brain of the late Lord Chancellor. It weighed 53¼ ounces. Cuvier's was the largest ever known, being 59 ounces, but not healthy like Lord Campbell's. The average weight of brain is 46 ounces.' ~ L.F.L., Greenfield, near Manchester, 10 Aug 1861

¶ Eager to establish a biological basis for genius and exceptional talent on the one hand and for criminality on the other, nineteenth-century scientists developed a curious passion for weighing the brains of eminent men and notorious criminals. Byron's brain was one of the first to receive such attention. After the poet's death at Missolonghi on 19 April 1824 it was removed by the attending physician, Dr Bruno, and examined and weighed before being placed in an urn. 'The medullary substance was in more than ordinary proportion to the corticle,' Bruno noted in his report, 'and of the usual consistency. The cerebrum and the cerebellum, without the membrane, weighed 6 medical lbs.' The brain was then shipped back to England, along with the poet's coffin and two further urns containing his heart and viscera, and interred in the Byron family plot at Hucknall Torkard, Nottinghamshire.

The brain rotted quietly away, as brains tend to, but news of its apparently prodigious size was soon exciting anatomists, as Brian Burrell explains in his study, *Postcards from the Brain Museum*:

> Depending upon the system of weights employed and the interpretation of a 'medicinal pound', the brain might have weighed anywhere from 1,807 to 2,238 grams (the lower and more likely figure being a conversion from Venetian pounds; the higher, from English pounds, would make it the heaviest brain on record). In any case, it was a massive brain, at least 25 per cent bigger than the average, and the connection with his outsized reputation was soon made. Byron, the poster boy

for Romantic genius, became Exhibit A for the contention that great intellects are housed in large brains.

Byron may have been Exhibit A, but he was not to feature in the rankings of big brains produced over the following decades because professional anatomists considered Dr Bruno's information insufficiently reliable. No such reservations applied to the remains of the French naturalist Georges Cuvier, who had died in Paris in 1832. His autopsy was attended by ten leading physicians and his brain turned out to be enormous, weighing 1,830 grams.

As the mania took hold, even the absence of a brain did not dissuade the weighers. In 1865, when Dante's capacious skull was discovered at Ravenna, its cerebral cavity was carefully filled with rice grains which were then tipped out and weighed. Writing in the *Anthropological Review* in 1867, Professor Hermann Welcker concluded after various technical adjustments that in consequence '1,420 grams must be accepted as the probable weight of Dante's brain'. Disappointingly, however, this placed the brain of the greatest poet of the Middle Ages a long way down the table of twenty-seven that Welcker drew up. Indeed, it rated scarcely above the presumed mean weight of all male brains (1,390 grams).

Welcker's table included many now forgotten figures but also a handful of familiar names. In the following list W indicates brains actually weighed, C weights derived from skull circumference, and G weights arrived at after filling skulls with grains.

1st   Cuvier, naturalist, aged 63 – 1,830 grams (W)

6th   Robert the Bruce, King of Scotland, aged 54 – 1,610 grams (C)

7th   Schiller, author, aged 56 – 1,580 grams (C)

14th   Lord Campbell, Lord Chancellor, aged 80 – 1,520 grams (W)

21st= Schubert, composer, aged 69, & Dante, poet, aged 56 – 1,420 grams (both G)

In 1903 an updated list containing The Top 100 Brain Weights would be compiled by Edward Anthony Spitzka, an American anatomist who had inherited an extensive brain collection from his father (dutifully he added his father's brain to the collection). Three writers joined the rankings, with varying impressiveness: Turgenev took first place from Cuvier with an unprecedented 2,012 grams; Thackeray produced a creditable 1,658 grams; but Walt Whitman could manage only 1,282 grams.

Fortunately for Whitman the essential absurdity of the idea had by now become apparent, if not to Spitzka. Not only was it clear that brain weight depended on an array of factors – notably age at death, where the spinal cord had been severed, and whether cerebrospinal fluid and blood had been drained off before weighing – but in the 1880s various studies had demonstrated that criminals, too, had larger than average brains. Indeed Le Pelley, an assassin, produced a Byronic 1,809 grams, while the largest female brain recorded (1,565 grams) belonged to a woman who had killed her husband. Attempts were made to explain away this difficulty – criminals tended to die young, before brain shrinkage had set in, and death by hanging was thought to engorge the brain with blood, resulting in deceptively high brain weights – but this macabre scientific *cul de sac* was coming to be seen for what it was. If a final disproof were needed, Albert Einstein's brain would provide it: at 1,230 grams it was remarkably small.

CALUMNIATORS: A Polish punishment for

N. The enclosed extract deserves a corner in *N & Q*:

> The convicted calumniator of a senator in Poland was compelled, in full senate, to lie upon the ground under the stall of him whose honour he had attacked, and then declare aloud that in spreading abroad injurious reports against the honourable senator, he, the calumniator, had lied like a dog. He must then, three different times, imitate the barking of a dog.

> (M. le Chevalier de Polignac, *General History of Poland*)

~ R.R., 19 Apr 1856

CHARLESTON MAIDS: A petition of 1734

N. The following petition, signed by sixteen maids of Charleston, South Carolina, was presented to the governor of that province on 1 March 1734, 'the day of the feast':

To His Excellency Governor Johnson

THE HUMBLE PETITION OF ALL THE MAIDS
WHOSE NAMES ARE UNDERWRITTEN

Whereas we the humble petitioners are at present in a very melancholy disposition of mind, considering how all the bachelors are blindly captivated by widows, and our more youthful charms thereby neglected: the consequence of this our request is, that your excellency will for the future order that no widow shall presume to marry any young man till the maids are provided for; or else to pay each of them a fine for satisfaction, for invading our liberties; and likewise a fine to be laid on all such bachelors as shall be married to widows. The great disadvantage it is to us maids is that the widows, by their forward carriages, do snap up the young men, and have the vanity to think their merits beyond ours, which is a great imposition upon us who ought to have the preference.

This is humbly recommended to your excellency's consideration, and hope you will prevent any farther insults.

And we poor maids as in duty bound will ever pray.

P.S. I, being the oldest maid, and therefore most concerned, do think it proper to be the messenger to your excellency in behalf of my fellow subscribers.

~ Uneda, 18 June 1853

CHESHIRE CATS: Why are they said to grin?

Q. Will some of your correspondents explain the origin of the phrase 'grinning like a Cheshire cat'? The ingenious theory of someone, I forget who, that Cheshire is a county palatine,[1] and that the cats, when they think of it, are so tickled that they can't help grinning, is not *quite* satisfactory to... ~ K.I.P.B.T., 2 Nov 1850

R. Some years ago Cheshire cheeses were sold in this town moulded in the shape of a cat, bristles being inserted to represent the whiskers. This may possibly have originated the saying. ~ T.D., Bath, 16 Nov 1850

R2. I remember to have heard many years ago that it owes its origin to the unhappy attempts of a sign painter of that county to represent a lion rampant, which was the crest of an influential family, on the signboards of many of the inns. The resemblance of these lions to cats caused them to be generally called by the more ignoble name. A similar case is to be found in the village of Charlton, between Pewsey and Devizes, Wiltshire. A public house by the roadside is commonly known by the name of The Cat at Charlton. The sign of the house was originally a heraldic lion or tiger, or some such animal. ~ H., 24 Apr 1852

---

[1] From *palatinus*, of the palace; a county in which the earl or other lord is entitled to exercise royal privileges and sole jurisdiction.

¶ The expression is thought to date from the eighteenth century and was evidently in common use by 1808 when Charles Lamb wrote in a letter of palming off a pun 'upon Holcroft, who grinned like a Cheshire cat'. Lamb cited the county palatine theory but was clearly not impressed by it. The other two theories outlined in *N & Q* – of the decorated cheese and the signboard – remain those generally favoured. Lewis Carroll may well have had the former in mind in *Alice's Adventures in Wonderland* (1865): famously the grin is the last part of his Cheshire Cat to disappear, and the same would have been true of the cheeses if cut from the 'tail'.

Cheshire's fame for dairy produce also lies behind two other theories: first, that the county's plentiful production of milk and cream made its cats particularly happy; second, that the cats living in the docks at Chester could not stop grinning because the presence of a cheese warehouse ensured the disembarkation from docking ships of a very satisfactory supply of mice and rats.

CHURCH BELLS 1: For confession and pancakes

Q. Happening to be at Newbury on Shrove Tuesday I was struck with the tolling of the church bell as for a death, and, on enquiry, was informed that such was the custom of the place on this day. Does such a custom exist anywhere else, and what is the origin of it? ~ Newburiensis, 8 Apr 1854

R. From time immemorial what is called 'the pancake bell' has been rung on Shrove Tuesday in this place. All the apprentices whose indentures terminate before the return of the day assemble in the church belfry at eleven o'clock and in turn toll the tenor bell for an hour, at the sound of which all the housewives in the parish commence frying pancakes. ~ H.B., Hedon, 15 May 1858

R2. I well recollect as a schoolboy listening for the bell, which began at eleven o'clock, at which the master dismissed us an hour early with the words: 'There's the pancake bell; now, boys, go home and help your mammas to make pancakes.' It is a remnant of the Romish custom of ringing a bell to summon

the people to confession or shrift – hence *Shrove* Tuesday, being the day before the strict abstinence of Lent, which begins next day, Ash Wednesday. In my young Protestant mind the pancakes of the one day were associated with the hashed mutton of the next, and I believe many still make a like *hash* of the matter, unaware that the bell is a summons not to pancakes but to repentance.
~ T. J. Buckton, 12 Nov 1864

R3. John Taylor the 'water poet' has a curious account of the pancake custom in his *Jack a Lent* (1620):

Shrove Tuesday, at whose entrance in the morning all the whole kingdom is in quiet; but by that time the clocke strikes eleven, which (by the help of a knavish sexton) is commonly before nine, then there is a bell rung called the pancake bell – the sound whereof makes thousands of people distracted, and forgetful either of manners or humanitie; then there is a thing called wheaten floure, which the cookes do mingle with water, egges, spice, and other tragical magicall inchantments; and then they put it, by little and little, into a frying-pan of boiling suet, where it makes a confused dismall hissing (like the Lernaean snakes in the reeds of Acheron, Styx, or Phlegeton);[1] until at last, by the skill of the cooke, it is transformed into a forme of a flip-jack, called a pancake – which ominous incantation the ignorant people do devoure very greedily.

~ W. I. S. Horton, Rugeley, 12 Nov 1864

CHURCH BELLS 2: To ward off thunderstorms

Q. During the last two days a brisk gale has been blowing from the north-east, and while it continued two vessels were unfortunately lost at the mouth of the harbour with most of their crews. While the storm was at its height the Roman Catholic bishop ordered all the church bells to be rung for an hour, which was accordingly done, that the wind might cease and the sea be calmed. Of the result I need not remark.

[1] The snake-headed Hydra haunted the swamps of Lerna, near Argos. Phlegeton, like Acheron and Styx, was a river of the underworld.

This custom of ringing bells while storms are raging prevails not only in Malta, but also in Sicily and Sardinia, in Tuscany, and in France. It was only a short time ago that I read the following account in *Galignani's Messenger*:[1] 'A few days since, as two men residing in the commune of Bezant, Gers, were ringing the church bells, as is the custom in many parts of the country on the approach of a thunderstorm, the lightning struck the tower; and the electric fluid, penetrating into the belfry, killed them both.'

May I ask when this custom of ringing bells in storms originated; whether it is known in Protestant countries; and if the service of ringing them is not attended with danger? ~ W.W., Malta, 27 Nov 1852 & 28 July 1855

R. The custom is of very high antiquity in Christian times and its origin may, perhaps, be found in a still more ancient belief of heathen nations.

The Roman herdsmen in the time of Strabo were accustomed, as he tells us, to attach a bell to the necks of their flocks, and it was believed that noxious wild beasts were kept away by the sound.[2] So, too, it was believed that evil spirits would likewise flee from the sound of bronze instruments. Hence the custom of beating bronze vessels during an eclipse, which is referred to by Ovid, Livy, and Lucan. An old scholiast on Theocritus says it was the custom to beat bronze vessels and ring bells on a person's death, because the sound was believed to frighten away spectres and demons. In early ages, as is well known, evil spirits of the air were believed to be the cause of storms and tempests.

In the time of St Augustine it was believed that the demons of the air were driven away by the sound of church bells – so we find that the metal to which heathens had attached mysterious virtues had become a Christian preservative against the powers of evil.

The ordinance of blessing church bells has existed from a very early time, and one of its objects was declared to be that the

[1] A daily newspaper in English, published in Paris from 1814 until 1884.

[2] The Greek geographer made his first visit to Rome in 44 BC.

demons might be terrified by their sound. This, for example, is referred to in the fourteenth chapter of the Decrees of the Council of Cologne. William Durandus, in his *Rationale* (*c.*1286), says bells are rung in churches on the approach of a storm to the end that the devils, hearing the trumpets of the Eternal King (so were the bells deemed), might flee away in fear, and cease from raising the storm.

S.E.View of CALDECOT Church, RUTLAND
as damaged by a Thunder Storm. July 30.1797.

Many proofs might be cited to show that it was the custom in England before the Reformation to ring church bells in thunderstorms. Latimer, in one of his sermons, alludes to it, and my notes show that the custom prevailed at St Paul's, London, at Oxney Abbey, at Malmesbury, and in several parish churches. On the Continent the custom was common. In T. H. Dyer's *Life of Calvin* it is stated that in and before 1537, and until Calvin's preaching, the citizens of Geneva believed that the convent bells preserved all within their sound from storms and evil spirits. John Aubrey, in his *Miscellanies* (1696), mentions the custom at Paris at that time of ringing the great bell of

St Germains when a thunderstorm began. I believe the practice is continued in many parts of France at this day, but that it has ceased in what are called Protestant countries.

Whether or not the service of ringing bells in storms is attended with danger, I cannot illustrate by any examples. ~ W.S.G., Newcastle-upon-Tyne, 25 Dec 1852

R2. There can be no danger in the very act of ringing bells at such times, but there is always danger in being in any tower during a thunderstorm, if it be not protected by a lightning conductor. ~ H. T. Ellacombe, Clyst St George, 25 Dec 1852

¶ Decrying 'phantasies and delusions of the Devil', Hugh Latimer preached against the pre-Reformation use of church bells on the 21st Sunday after Trinity, 1552:

Ye know when there was a storm or a fearful weather, then we rang the holy bells, they were they that must make all things well, they must drive away the Devil. But I tell you, if the holy bells would serve against the Devil, or that he might be put away through their sound, no doubt we would soon banish him out of all England. For if all the bells in England should be rung together at a certain hour, I think there would be almost no place but some bells might be heard there...

In his *Miscellanies* John Aubrey also refers to practice in England: 'The like was wont to be done heretofore in Wiltshire. When it thundered and lightened, they did ring St Adelm's Bell at Malmesbury Abbey. The curious do say that the ringing of bells exceedingly disturbs spirits.' The practice was also adopted at St Mary's, Sandwich, its churchwardens' accounts for 1464 recording a charge for bread and drink for 'ringers in the great thundering'.

Other means of protection were also sought. In his *History of St Paul's Cathedral* Sir William Dugdale records that about the year 1315 a gilt pommel or ball and a new cross were placed upon the top of the cathedral's steeple, 'in which cross the relicks of divers saints were put by Gilbert de Segrave, then Bishop of London, with great and solemn procession, to the intent that God Almighty, by the glorious merits of His saints, would vouchsafe to preserve the said steeple from all danger of tempests'. According to a medieval chronicle the relics included 'a part of the wood of the Cross... wrought in the form of a cross', a 'stone from Mount Calvary', and a purse containing a piece of red silk 'in which were wrapped some bones of the Eleven Thousand Virgins'.[1]

The continuing reverence afforded to these defences is indicated by a contemporary account of a hallowing conducted by Thomas Savage, Bishop of London, on 17 May 1498. The steeple cross was set in the heart of the cathedral while bishop, canons and choir knelt all around and psalms and collects were recited. Then the bishop 'hallowed water and began *Asperges*, going about and casting holy water on every part of the cross with a stick bound full of hyssop during the whole psalm of *Miserere mei deus*. And that done the bishop sang the preface, hallowing and incensing the cross and other relics... And then was begun *O crux splendidior* and sung out and again repeated and in mean time the bishop censed it at every part, kneeling on his knees and put in the relics at four ends of the cross and closed them in with pins of timber and lead, and then opened the ball of the cross and put therein relics and it closed [and] again censed it about...'

St Paul's
A 14th-century view
from the west

Any protection did not last. On 4 June 1561 the steeple was struck by lightning, as recorded in a vivid account published six days later:

Between one and two of the clock at afternoon was seen a marvellous great fiery lightning, and immediately ensued a

[1] According to legend, as they returned from a pilgrimage to Rome the virgins had fallen prey to the Huns at Cologne and been slaughtered there along with their leader, the fourth-century British princess St Ursula.

most terrible hideous crack of thunder, such as seldom hath been heard. Divers persons being on the river of Thames, and others, being in the fields near adjoining to ye city, affirmed that they saw a long and a spear-pointed flame of fire (as it were) run through the top of the broch or shaft of Paul's steeple from the east westward. And some of the parish of St Martin's then being in the street did feel a marvellous strong air or whirlwind, with a smell like brimstone coming from Paul's Church, and withal heard the rush of ye stones which fell from their steeple into the church...

Between four and five of the clock a smoke was espied to break out under the bowl of the shaft. But suddenly after, as it were in a moment, the flame broke forth in a circle like a garland round about the broch and increased in such wise that within a quarter of an hour, or little more, the cross and the eagle on the top fell down upon the south cross-aisle. The steeple fell down on every side, and fired the other three parts, that is to say, the chancel or choir, the north aisle, and the body of the church, so that in one hour's space ye broch of the steeple was burnt down to ye battlements, and the most part of ye highest roof of the church was likewise consumed.

The cause of the disaster was debated with appropriate heat. On Sunday 8 June, with the ruins still smouldering behind him, the new and very Protestant Bishop of Durham, James Pilkington, preached a sermon at Paul's Cross in which he attributed the lightning to the wrath of God and warned of a greater plague to follow if amendment of life were not made in all estates. An anonymous Catholic countered in print that the fault lay rather in England's turning away from 'the old fathers and the old ways'. Pilkington responded with a comprehensive *Confutation* in 1563 in which he denounced the 'lying wonders' of the Catholic Church, including such 'witchcraftes' as 'ringinge the halowed belle in great tempestes or lightninges', and James Calfhill, a reforming prebendary of St Paul's, took up the theme two years later: 'We needed not to fear, if your opinion were true, the burning any more of Paul's. Make a cross on the steeple, and so it shall be safe. But within these few years it had a cross, and reliques in the bowl to boot. Yet they prevailed not: yea, the cross itself was fired first...'

The Catholic use of church bells against thunderstorms would also be scorned a few years later in a translation by Barnabe Googe of verses by Thomas Kirchmeyer, a celebrated Lutheran pastor:

> If that the thunder chance to roar,
> And stormy tempest shake,
> A wonder is it for to see
> The wretches how they quake,
> How that no faith at all they have,
> Nor trust in any thing,
> The clerk doth all the bells
> Forthwith in steeple ring:
> With wond'rous sound and deeper far
> Than he was wont before,
> Till in the lofty heavens dark
> The thunder bray no more.
> For in these christened bells they think
> Doth lie such power and might,
> As able is the tempest great
> And storm to vanquish quite.

CLARENCE, DUKE OF: Was he really drowned in a Malmsey butt?

Q. The curious and well known story of the Duke of Clarence, brother to Edward IV, having been drowned in a butt of Malmsey wine has been received with considerable scepticism by some of our historians, and certainly it would be difficult to conceive a fact *a priori* more improbable. Clarence had rebelled against his brother and been forgiven, but his discontented spirit made him again obnoxious to Edward and he was impeached for treason. The case was tried before the House of Lords, and Clarence was condemned to death. Some time elapsed before the law was allowed to take its course, and Edward caused the deed to be done in secret, not wishing that his brother should suffer the ignominy of a public execution. The method of his punishment was not made known, but if we may believe the chroniclers the general impression of the time was that he was suffocated in a cask of wine.

The only contemporary or near contemporary authorities for this extraordinary tale are Robert Fabyan and Philippe de Comines. However, their testimony would have been held amply sufficient to establish anything a degree more credible. Comines, it is true, was a foreigner, but Fabyan was an Englishman and a Londoner, and he had no doubt about the case whatever: 'The Duke of Clarence,' he says, 'thanne being prisoner in ye Tower, was secretely put to deth and drowned in a barell of Malvesye within the said Tower.' Nor is there any contradictory testimony.

Are we then to believe that this extraordinary mode of punishment was actually had recourse to?

A solution of this riddle has occurred to me. Does not Fabyan's account suggest that they killed the duke first and immersed him afterwards? May the butt not have been used to conceal the body after the deed, and then to commit it to the deep? The idea was not unnatural. A wine cask, taken out to sea as part of a ship's cargo, would create no suspicion. It might be tossed overboard and nobody one whit the wiser. ~ James Gairdner, 20 Sep 1856

Isabel, Duchess of Clarence (1451-1477)

R. I recollect that five years ago Sir Oswald Mosley,[1] in relating several incidents connected with the captivity of Lady Jane Grey, remarked that she had a weekly allowance of wine (I think Malmsey) for *a bath.* It was mentioned at the time as giving a rational explanation of Clarence's mysterious death. ~ H. Moody, Birmingham, 11 Oct 1856

[1] The great-great-grandfather of his namesake the Fascist leader.

George, Duke of Clarence (1449-1478)

R2. The story related by Mr Moody, on Sir Oswald Mosley's authority, appears to have been true of *Mary Queen of Scots*.

Speaking of the Earl of Shrewsbury's expenses at Tutbury in 1569, Strype says: 'In this castle this noble earl had Mary Queen of Scots in custody; which, whatsoever public allowance he had, was extraordinary expensive to him. And among other things provided, the wine only amounted to a considerable charge; for, when she bathed, she bathed in wine.' ~ J. Sansom, 25 Oct 1856

R3. The curious account of the death of this prince is, as justly stated by Mr Gairdner, received with considerable scepticism. It seems to be a tradition adopted, like many others, without reflection or any attention to detail. Why Malmsey? Any other wine, or even water, would have served the purpose. The general inference would be that Malmsey wine was kept in open butts, and that the prince was thrown into one of them, but butts or pipes are not sufficiently large for the purpose intended, being seldom larger in England (not being a wine country) than four feet in length.

As to the interesting suggestion of Mr Gairdner, it must be observed that a butt of wine, even without a human body, if thrown into the sea, will not readily sink, and consequently, it being intended to keep secret the death of the prince, this mode of proceeding would have been altogether fruitless. ~ J.B., 10 Jan 1857

¶ The word Malmsey is an English corruption of the Italian *Malvasia*, denoting the ancient port of Monemvasia in the Peloponnese, and was used originally for the sweet white wines produced in that region. They were greatly prized in northern Europe in the Middle Ages and by the fifteenth century Venetian traders were shipping considerable quantities to England, so it would not be surprising if Malmsey butts were to be found in the Tower in 1478.

Fabyan's *Chronicle* was not published until 1516, and it is not known how long before that date he wrote his account of Clarence's death. However, a similar account is found in another English chronicle which has been dated to *circa* 1480: 'Also the xviiith day of ffebruary was George, Duke of Clarence and brother unto King Edward, put to the deth within the Tower as a prisoner. Drowned in Malvesay.' In the same vein Domenico Mancini, a well connected Italian visitor to England, reported in 1483 that 'The mode of execution preferred in this case was that he should die by being plunged in a jar of sweet wine,' while another early account, that of Jean de Roye, adds various details: that the barrel was set on end; that Clarence was killed by being thrust in head first; and that afterwards his body was pulled out and beheaded.

While acknowledging the unanimity of the early chronicles, modern historians have naturally been reluctant to accept that so unusual, indeed unprecedented, a form of execution should have been adopted. In an attempt to counter this, in 1925 Dr Heinz Goldschmidt demonstrated that a similar method of execution – drowning in vessels of water – had in fact been quite common in the Netherlands. He cited more than a dozen instances between 1535 and 1730, including a 1558 case in which a man was drowned in a wine vat filled with water. Noting that Edward IV visited the Netherlands at the end of 1470, Goldschmidt went on to suggest that the mode of punishment had long predated the recorded cases and that the English king had learnt the trick there.

The idea that the butt might have contained not wine but water was taken up in 1936 by John Webster Spargo:

> If the butt had still contained wine at the time of the execution, it would not have been available for occupancy by Clarence, for the head of the barrel would still have been intact. The barrel must have been an old Malmsey butt which had been refilled with water... A barrel of this size always has some commercial value. When left standing dry such a container quickly becomes valueless through shrinkage of the wood; and, too, it is a useful reservoir for water.

Another theory is that Clarence was simply poisoned and that Malmsey was used to administer the poison. There is certainly evidence to suggest that he shared the fashionable taste for the drink – an ordinance for his household dated 9 December 1469 allows £20 for buying 'Malvesey and other sweet wines' – and it is easy to see how whispered reports of a death by Malmsey could have developed into a tale of strange drowning.

It is harder to explain why any secret method should have been adopted if Clarence was killed on the king's orders: as noted in *N & Q*, he had already been publicly tried and sentenced, so there was no great need to keep the deed secret or the body unmarked. Perhaps the king was squeamish and the executioners were instructed to avoid bloodshed, or perhaps Clarence tried to escape and events took an unscheduled turn. On the other hand, perhaps secrecy and lack of evident injury *were* required because the instigator was not the king: Shakespeare famously attributes the murder to Richard, Duke of Gloucester, later Richard III, while modern historians have speculated that, with King Edward reluctant to act, the real instigators may have been the family of his wife and queen, Elizabeth Woodville, anxious to remove Clarence as a threat to the succession of her son, the future Edward V.

COFFEE-HOUSES: When were they first in England?

N. In 1652 one Mr Edwards, a Turkey merchant, brought home with him a Greek servant, whose name was Pasqua, who understood the roasting and making of coffee, till then unknown in England. This servant was the first who sold coffee, and he kept a house for that purpose in St Michael's Alley in the City of London.

The first mention of coffee in our statute books is in 1660, when a duty of 4*d.* was laid upon every gallon of coffee made and sold, to be paid by the maker, while a statute of 1663 directs that all coffee-houses should be licensed at the general quarter sessions of the peace for the county within which they are to be kept.

In 1675 King Charles II issued a proclamation to shut up the coffee-houses, but in a few days suspended it by a second proclamation. They were charged with being seminaries of sedition. ~ Editor, 10 Nov 1849

R. From John Evelyn's *Diary*, May 1637: 'There came in my time to the college one Nathaniel Conopios out of Greece. He was the first I ever saw drink coffee, which custom came not into England till thirty years after.' ~ J.B., 5 Jan 1850

R2. As a supplement to your Note on coffee, I send you the following extracts.

John Aubrey, in his account of Sir Henry Blount, says of this worthy knight, 'When coffee first came in he was a great upholder of it, and hath ever since been a constant frequenter of coffee-houses, especially Mr Farr at the Rainbowe, by Inner Temple Gate, and lately John's Coffee-house, at Fuller's Rents. The first coffee-house in London was in St Michael's Alley, in Cornehill, opposite to the church, which was sett up by one Bowman (coachman to Mr Hodges, a Turkey merchant, who putt him upon it) in or about the yeare 1652. 'Twas about four yeares before any other was sett up, and that was by Mr Farr. Jonathan Painter, opposite to St Michael's Church, was the first apprentice to the trade, viz. to Bowman.'

Of this James Farr, Edward Hatton, in his *New View of London* (1708), says: 'I find it recorded that one James Farr, a barber, who kept the coffee-house which is now the Rainbow, by the Inner Temple Gate (one of the first in England), was in the year 1657 prosecuted by the inquest of St Dunstan's in the West, for making and selling a sort of liquor called coffee, as a great nuisance and prejudice to the neighbourhood, etc., and who would then have thought London would ever have had near three thousand such nuisances, and that coffee would have been, as now, so much drank by the best of quality and physicians?'

James Howell, in a letter prefixed to the 3rd edition of Walter Rumsey's *Organon Salutis* (1664), observes that 'This coffee drink hath caused a great sobriety among all nations. Whereas formerly apprentices and clerks with others used to take their morning draughts in ale, beer, or wine, which, by the dizziness they cause in the brain, make many unfit for business, they use now to play the good-fellows in this wakeful and civil drink. Therefore that worthy gentleman, Sir James Muddiford, who introduced the practice hereof first to London, deserves much respect of the whole nation.'

From these extracts it appears that the use of this berry was introduced by other Turkey merchants besides Edwards and his servant Pasqua.

Anthony Wood records in his Diary, under the year 1654, that 'Coffey, which had been drank by some persons in Oxon

1650, was this yeare publickly sold at or neare the Angel within the east gate of Oxon, as also chocolate, by an outlander or a Jew.' And in another place he says: 'This yeare Jacob a Jew opened a coffey house at the Angel in the parish of St Peter, in the East Oxon; and there it was by some, who delighted in noveltie, drank. When he left Oxon he sold it in Old Southampton buildings in Holborne neare London, and was living 1671.' ~ Edward F. Rimbault, 16 Mar 1850

¶ Coffee-houses are recorded at Mecca in 1511, Cairo in 1532, and in Constantinople in 1554, where they were encountered by early Western travellers: visiting Constantinople in 1610, George Sandys noted that 'Although they are destitute of taverns, yet they have coffa houses, which something resemble them. There sit they chatting most of the day, and sippe of a drinke called coffa in little China dishes, as hot as they can suffer it: blacke as soote, and tasting not much unlike it.' By the 1620s and 1630s small quantities were probably being imported to England for private use – William Harvey, famed for his treatise on the circulation of the blood, may have been drinking it as early as 1627, and, as John Evelyn recorded, Nathaniel Conopios was drinking it at Balliol College, Oxford, ten years later.

The owner, location and date of the first coffee-house in England are disputed. The honour is usually given to Jacob in Oxford in 1650 – his shop was in the High Street, near the site of the present day Examination Schools. However, as Markman Ellis has pointed out in his recent history of the coffee-house, this claim is not corroborated by leases or licences or other documentary evidence: it rests solely on the authority of Anthony Wood and the suggestion in a footnote by his late nineteenth-century editor, Andrew Clark, that the second of Wood's Jacob references quoted above dates from '1650 probably'.

Greater certainty attaches to the London claim. In 1651 Daniel Edwards, a Levant merchant and prodigious coffee drinker, returned from Smyrna to England bringing with him his servant Pasqua Rosee, who began serving coffee in

Edwards's house in Walbrook in the City. However, the drink proved so popular among Edwards's friends that this began to interfere with business and so he helped Rosee to establish a shop in a shed in St Michael's Alley, just off Cornhill – possibly as early as 1652, and certainly by 1654.

Rosee proved an adept entrepreneur, promoting coffee drinking with a pioneering handbill:

THE VERTUE OF THE COFFEE DRINK

The grain or berry called coffee groweth upon little trees only in the deserts of Arabia. It is brought from thence, and drunk generally throughout all the Grand Seignour's dominions. It is a simple, innocent thing, composed into a drink by being dried in an oven, and ground to powder, and boiled up with spring water, and about half a pint of it to be drunk fasting an hour before, and not eating an hour after, and to be taken as hot as possibly can be endured. It is very good to help digestion. It much quickens the spirits, and makes the heart lightsome; it is good against sore eyes, and the better if you hold your head over it and take in the steam that way. It suppresseth fumes exceedingly, and therefore is good against the headache. It is excellent to cure the dropsy, gout, and scurvy; also against the spleen, hypochondriac winds, and the like. It will prevent drowsiness, and make one fit for business. Therefore you are not to drink of it after supper, unless you intend to be watchful, for it will hinder sleep for three or four hours.

Made and sold in St Michael's Alley in Cornhill, by
Pasqua Rosee, at the sign of his own head

City alehouse keepers tried to nip this rival attraction in the bud, petitioning the lord mayor to close Rosee's shop on the grounds that he was not a freeman of the City. This challenge was adroitly overcome, however: Alderman Hodges – who was Daniel Edwards's father-in-law – simply set up his coachman, Bowman, who was free of the City, as Rosee's business partner, a manoeuvre which explains Aubrey's assertion above that Bowman was responsible for the first coffee-house. Soon, however, Bowman and Rosee were running rival houses on the same street by St Michael's Churchyard, and another competitor emerged in the form of James Farr, whose Rainbow Coffee-house was in Fleet Street. Thereafter the number of such houses rose rapidly: by 1663 there were eighty-two and by the reign of Queen Anne there were over 500.

There were early gainsayers: a 1663 satire referred to coffee as 'a loathsome potion... syrop of soot, or essence of old shoes', while another of 1674 suggested that the new drink 'made men as unfruitful as the deserts whence that unhappy berry is said to be brought'. But such squibs and scares had little effect. A more faithful and positive picture of these places where men of all classes could do business and hear what was afoot in the world is painted in a broadside song of 1667, 'News from the Coffee-House', in which the houses' powers are rated above those of the contemporary astrologers, William Lilly and John Booker:

> There's nothing done in all the world,
> From monarch to the mouse,
> But every day or night 'tis hurled
> Into the coffee-house.
> What Lilly or Booker can
> By art not bring about,
> At coffee-house you'll find a man
> Can quickly find it out.
>
> They'll tell you there what lady-ware
> Of late is grown too light;
> What wise man shall from favour fall,
> What fool shall be a knight;
> They'll tell you when our failing trade
> Shall rise again and flourish,
> Or when Jack Adams[1] shall be made
> Churchwarden of the parish.

[1] A third contemporary astrologer. His name became a byword for simpleton.

COMBUSTION, SPONTANEOUS: Does it exist?

At the end of the tenth instalment of *Bleak House*, published in December 1852, Charles Dickens described the death of the alcoholic rag-and-bottle shop owner Krook, whose scant remains are discovered by Guppy and Weevle as they enter his darkened shop at midnight. Dickens's unequivocal closing statement – that Krook had died of 'Spontaneous Combustion, and none other of all the deaths that can be died' – sparked a public debate that was soon taken up in *N & Q*.

Q. Is there such a thing as spontaneous combustion? ~ H.A.B., 19 Mar 1853

R. A most interesting discussion of this question is to be found in Justus von Liebig's *Familiar Letters upon Chemistry*. That chemist proves conclusively:

1. That of the cases adduced none is well authenticated, while in most it is admitted that the victims were drunkards, and that generally a candle or lamp was in the room, and after the alleged combustion was found turned over.

2. That spontaneous combustion is absolutely impossible, the human frame containing 75 or 80 per cent of water; and since flesh, when saturated with alcohol, is not consumed upon the application of a light, the alcohol burning off first, the causes assigned to account for the spontaneous ignition are *a priori* extremely improbable.

~ A. W. Wills, University College, London, 30 Apr 1853

R2. Leaving the philosophy of this question for the *savants*, I beg to add the following. Dr Lindsley has compiled a table of nineteen instances from the *Dictionnaire de Médecine* – not, however, of spontaneous combustion exactly, but of something akin to it, namely the rapid ignition of the human body (which *per se* is not combustible) by contact with flame, as a consequence of the saturation of its tissues by alcohol. It is as set out below.

'Is it the cinder of a small charred and broken log of
wood sprinkled with white ashes, or is it coal?
O Horror, he is here...'

	Works in which they are reported	By whom	Date of occur-rence	Age of the indi-vidual	Extent of the com-bustion	Immed-iate cause when known	Habit of life	Situation of the remains, etc.
1	*Actes de Copen-hague*	Jacobeus	1692	-	The whole body, except the skull, and last joints of the fingers	-	Abuse of spirits for three years	Upon a chair
2	*Annual Register*	Bianchini of Verona	1731	62	Except the skull, a part of the face, and three fingers	Took fire through sitting near a lamp	Indulged in frequent fomen-tations of camphor-ated spirits	Upon the floor
3	*Ibid.*	Wilmer	-	50	Except thigh and one leg	A light upon a chair near the bed	Took a pint of rum daily	Upon the floor near the bed
4	*Ency. Method.*	-	-	50	Except a few bones	-	Habitually drunken	-
5	*Acta Medica*	-	-	-	Except the skull and fingers	-	She drank brandy as her only drink	-
6	*Mem. on Spon. Com.*	Lecat	1744	60	Except a part of the head and limbs	A pipe which she was smoking	A drunk-ard	Near the chimney
7	*Ibid.*	Ibid.	1745	-	Ibid.	A fire	Habitually drunken	Upon the hearth
8	*Ibid.*	Ibid.	1749	80	A charred skeleton only left	Fire of the hearth	Drank brandy only for many years	Sitting on a chair near the fire
9	*Jour. de Méd.*	-	1779	-	Except a few bones, a hand, and a foot	A foot-stove under her feet	A drunk-ard	-

	Works in which they are reported	By whom	Date of occur-rence	Age of the indi-vidual	Extent of the com-bustion	Immed-iate cause when known	Habit of life	Situation of the remains, etc.
10	*Ibid.*	-	1782	60	Ibid.	A fire of the hearth	Ibid.	Upon the hearth
11	*Revue Médicale*	Julia Fontenelle	1820	90	Except the skull and a portion of skin	A candle	Abuse of wine and Eau de Cologne	In bed
12	*Ibid.*	Ibid.	1820	66	Except the right leg	Ibid.	Ibid.	In the same bed. Both burnt together
13	-	Gen. William Kepland	-	Very old	Almost wholly consumed	A lighted pipe	-	Upon the floor
14	*Journal de Florence*	Joseph Battaylila	1786	-	Skin of right arm and right thigh only burnt	-	-	Upon the floor. He lived four days after
15	*Revue Médicale*	Robertson	1799	-	Combus-tion incomplete	-	Abuse of brandy	Upon a bench
16	*Ibid.*	M. Marchand	-	-	Hand and thigh only burnt	-	-	Cured
17	*Journal Hosp. Hamp.*	-	-	17	One finger of right hand only burnt	A candle	-	Cured
18	-	Alph. Devengee	1829	51	Muscles of thighs, superior extremities, and trunk burnt	A foot-stove	Abuse of spirits	Upon a chair
19	*Dic. de Médecine*	-	-	-	Combus-tion almost complete	A foot-stove	Ibid.	Upon the floor

In addition the following case is related, on the authority of Dr Schofield of Upper Canada, in the *Journal of the American Temperance Union* for March 1837.

A young man, aged twenty-five, had been a habitual drunkard for many years. One evening at about eleven o'clock he went to a blacksmith's shop: he was then full of liquor, though not thoroughly drunk. The blacksmith, who had just crossed the road, was suddenly alarmed by the breaking forth of a brilliant conflagration in his shop. He rushed across and threw open the door, and there stood the man erect, in the midst of a widely-extended, silver-coloured flame, bearing, as the blacksmith described it, exactly the appearance of the wick of a burning candle in the midst of its own flame. He seized the young man by the shoulder and jerked him to the door, and the flame was instantly extinguished. There was no fire in the shop, and no article likely to cause combustion within reach of the individual. In the course of a short time a general sloughing came on, and the victim's flesh was almost wholly removed in the dressing, leaving the bones and a few of the large blood-vessels standing. The blood nevertheless rallied round the heart, and life continued to the thirteenth day, when he died, a loathsome, ill-featured and disgusting object. His shrieks and cries were described as truly horrible.

Two other cases have occurred recently, one in 1851 in Paris, and one last year somewhere in the north. Both may be found by reference to the newspapers. ~ Shirley Hibberd, 7 May 1853

R3. I have somewhere read an account of a drunkard whose body was so saturated with alcohol that, being bled in a fever, and the lamp near him having been overthrown, the blood caught fire and burst into a blaze. The account added that he was so startled by this occurrence that on his recovery he reformed thoroughly and prolonged his life to a good old age. ~ W. Fraser, Tor-Mohun, 25 June 1853

¶ As the responses above suggest, the idea of spontaneous combustion was taken up by Victorian social reformers more interested in painting a dramatic picture of the perils of alcohol than in scientific rigour. A comparable alacrity was evident in novelists seeking after literary effect – preceding Dickens there had been Captain Frederick Marryat, who combusted a character in *Jacob Faithful* (1834); Nikolai Gogol, who had a bibulous blacksmith catch fire 'inside' in *Dead Souls* (1842); and Herman Melville, who had a drunken sailor consumed by 'greenish fire, like a forked tongue' in *Redburn* (1849).

Such novelistic licence naturally exasperated sober rationalists like George Henry Lewes, the future husband-in-all-but-law of George Eliot. On 11 December 1852, within days of Krook's death appearing in print, he attacked the incident in forthright terms in the *Leader*, a periodical which he edited: 'It is a fault in Art, and a fault in Literature, overstepping the limits of Fiction, and giving currency to a vulgar error.' He added that he doubted whether Dickens would be able to find a single organic chemist to support him, spontaneous combustion being 'absolutely *impossible* according to all known laws of combustion, and to the constitution of the human body'.

Dickens responded by inserting a list of authorities in the next instalment of *Bleak House*, which appeared early in January 1853. Here and later he gave greatest prominence to the most celebrated of all cases, that of the Countess Cornelia Bandi, who died at Cesena in April 1731 at the age of sixty-two. Her death had been investigated by Giuseppe Bianchini of Verona, a noted legal and biblical scholar whose grisly, frequently reprinted and translated account provided Dickens with all the details he needed for Krook's death:

> In the morning the maid, going to call her, saw her corpse in this deplorable condition. Four feet distant from the bed was a heap of ashes, two legs untouched, stockings on, between which lay the head, the brains, half of the back part of the skull, and the whole chin burnt to ashes, among which were found three fingers blackened. All the rest was ashes, which had this quality, that they left in the hand a greasy and stinking moisture. The air in the room had soot floating in it:

a small oil lamp on the floor was covered with ashes, but no oil in it. Of two candles on the table, the tallow was gone, but the cotton left; some moisture about the feet of the candle-sticks; the bed undamaged, the blankets and sheets only raised on one side, as when one gets out of bed; the whole furniture spread over with ash-coloured soot, which penetrated the drawers and fouled the linen. This soot even got into a neighbouring kitchen, hung on its walls and utensils, and a bit of bread covered with it was refused by several dogs. In the room above the said soot flew about, and from the windows trickled down a greasy, loathsome, yellowish liquor, with an unusual stink. The floor of the chamber was thick smeared with a glueish moisture, not easily got off, and the stink spread into other chambers...

This and the other cases listed by Dickens left Lewes entirely unimpressed. On 5 February he published an open letter to the novelist in which he said that, like other admirers, he was 'grieved to see that an error exploded from science, but one peculiarly adapted to the avid credulity of unscientific minds, has been seriously taken up by you, and sent all over the world with your imprimatur – an act which will tend to perpetuate the error in spite of the labours of a thousand philosophers.' He then offered his own list of authorities headed by the eminent German chemist von Liebig, who had dismissed the phenomenon after a careful analysis of fifty cases.

After a further public attack a week later, Dickens replied to Lewes privately and politely but without giving an inch of ground. He insisted that before writing the scene he had 'looked into a number of books with great care, expressly to learn what the truth was', and argued that the eyewitness testimony of recorded cases outweighed scientific theory. Lewes returned to the attack in the *Leader* on 26 March, but Dickens would not back down: when *Bleak House* appeared in volume form in September the novelist spiritedly repeated his list of cases and insisted that 'I shall not abandon the facts until there shall have been a considerable Spontaneous Combustion of the testimony.'

COVENTRY: Why are people said to be sent there?

Q. Whence the origin of the expression 'Putting one in Coventry'? A friend informs me he has always understood that it took its rise thus: if a soldier was found to be a coward he was sent to Coventry, as being a central town of England, and a place where he was least likely to be exposed to the terrors of an unfriendly army. Is it so? Or is it derived from the French word *couvent*, a convent, which seems to me more apposite, as signifying seclusion from the rest of mankind? ~ Wm. W., Islington, 2 Oct 1852

R. The best explanation of this expression is that given in the Warwickshire volume of John Britton's *Beauties of England and Wales* (1814):

> The inhabitants of Coventry were formerly most decidedly averse to any correspondence with the military quartered within their limits. A female known to speak to a man in a scarlet coat became directly the object of town scandal. So rigidly indeed did the natives abstain from communication with all who bore his majesty's military commission, that officers were here confined to the interchanges of the mess-room; and in the mess-room the term of 'sending a man to Coventry', if you wish to shut him from society, probably originated.

~ Editor, 2 Oct 1852

R2. William Hutton, in his *History of Birmingham* (1782), gives a different origin of this expression, which he says arose as follows. The day after Charles I left Birmingham, on his march from Shrewsbury in 1642, the Parliamentary party seized his carriages, containing the royal plate and furniture, which they conveyed for security to Warwick Castle. They apprehended all messengers and suspected persons, and frequently attacked and reduced small parties of the Royalists, whom they sent as prisoners to Coventry. Hence the expression respecting a refractory person, 'Send him to Coventry.' ~ Philip S. King, 18 Dec 1852

¶ The above explanations from Britton and Hutton remain those most widely favoured, and the practice of sending Royalist prisoners to the Parliamentary stronghold of Coventry during the Civil War is also recorded in Clarendon's *History of the Rebellion* (1702-4). However, the fact that the idiomatic use of 'sending to Coventry' does not seem to have appeared in print until 1765 perhaps suggests that Britton's explanation, which is not tied to the Civil War period, is the more likely.

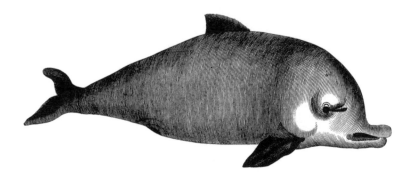

CROMWELL, OLIVER: Was his death portended by a storm and a whale?

Q. In his Diary Anthony Wood says, under 30 August 1658: 'Munday, a terrible raging wind hapned, which did much hurt. Dennis Bond, a great Oliverian and anti-monarchist, died on that day, and then the Devil "took Bond" for Oliver's appearance.' Meanwhile Lord Clarendon, assigning the Protector to eternal perdition and not liking to lose the portent, boldly says the remarkable hurricane occurred on 3 September, the day of Oliver's death.

James Heath, in his *Flagellum* (I have the 4th edition), says: 'It pleased God to usher in his end with a great whale some three months before, June 2, that came up as far as Greenwich, and there was killed; and more immediately by a terrible storm of wind: the prognosticks that the great Leviathan of men, that tempest and overthrow of government, was now going to his own place!'

Would some reader of better opportunities favour us with a record of these two matters of natural history? I have several works concerning Cromwell, but in no other do I find this story of a whale. ~ B.B., 15 Mar 1851

R. I take leave to inform B.B. that in a tract entitled *A Catalogue of natural Rarities, with great Industry, Cost and thirty Years' Travel in foreign Countries collected, by Robert Hubert, alias Forges, Gent., and sworn Servant to his Majesty. And Daily to be seen at the Place called the Musick House, at the Miter, near the West End of St Paul's Church* (1664) there is the following item: 'The vein of the tongue of that whale that was taken up at Greenwich, a little before Cromwell's death.' ~ W. Pinkerton, 12 Apr 1851

R2. B.B. may see, in the British Museum library, a tract of four leaves only, the title of which is as follows: *London's Wonder. Being a most true and positive relation of the taking and killing of a great Whale neer to Greenwich... upon the third day of June in the present year.* London, printed for Francis Grove, neere the Sarazen's head on Snowhill, 1658.

John Evelyn, who lived near Greenwich, notes in his *Diary* under the above-mentioned date as follows:

A large whale was taken betwixt my land butting on the Thames and Greenwich, which drew an infinite concourse to see it by water, horse, coach, and on foote, from London and all parts. It appear'd first below Greenwich at low water, for at high water it would have destroyed all ye boates; but lying now in shallow water incompass'd with boates, after a long conflict it was kill'd with a harping iron struck in ye head, out of which spouted blood and water by two tunnells, and after an horrid grone it ran quite on shore and died. Its length was 58 foote, height 16; black skin'd like coach leather, very small eyes, greate tail, onely two small finns, a picked snout, and a mouth so wide that divers men might have stood upright in it; no teeth, but suck'd the slime onely as thro' a grate of that bone which we call whale-bone; the throate yet so narrow as would not have admitted the least of fishes.

I turn now to the great storm that immediately preceded Cromwell's death:

> Tossed in a furious hurricane
> Did Oliver give up his reign.

So saith Samuel Butler, the witty author of *Hudibras* (3rd part, 1678), and to these lines his editor, Zachary Grey, adds the note: 'At Oliver's death was a most furious tempest, such as had not been known in the memory of man, or hardly ever recorded to have been in this nation. Though most of our historians mention the hurricane at his death, yet few take notice of the storm in the northern counties on that day the House of Peers ordered the digging up his carcass with other regicides.' ~ A. Grayan, 24 Apr 1852

¶ The Greenwich whale was also afforded significance by Dryden in his 'Heroic Stanzas', written to mark Cromwell's death:

> But first the ocean as a tribute sent
> That giant prince of all her watery herd...

On the storm night of Monday 30 August, while Cromwell lay on his deathbed in Whitehall, far away in Lincolnshire a 15-year-old boy was jumping first with the wind and then against it in order to measure what he called 'the vis of the storm'. He was Isaac Newton and next day he would tell his bemused schoolfellows that the storm was a foot stronger than any he had known before.

As noted in *N & Q*, Cromwell did not die until three days later, on the Friday afternoon, but the lapse of days was soon overlooked or forgotten and Clarendon, in his *History of the Rebellion* (1702-4), moved the storm to the Friday: 'This now was a day very memorable for the greatest storm of wind that had been ever known, for some hours before and after his death, which overthrew trees, houses, and made great wrecks at sea; and the tempest was so universal that the effects of it were terrible both in France and Flanders, where all people trembled at it...'

CURATES, PARSONS, RECTORS, VICARS

Q. It was remarked by the late Bishop Copleston that 'when once a word has slid from its first meaning, so as to cover other ideas besides that, it is very difficult to recall it.' In no case, perhaps, may this remark be better illustrated than in that of the terms *curate*, *parson*, *rector* and *vicar*. In popular phraseology we understand *parson* as meaning a clergyman, a person in holy orders, and *curate* as meaning the assistant of an incumbent. We also understand a *vicar* to be an incumbent, differing from a *rector* in nothing except the manner in which certain tithes are paid in. But let us turn to the original import of these names.

The word *parson*, from the Latin *persona*, as impersonating the parish at suits of law, originally denoted the rector, as distinct from the vicar or curate who was under him.

The word *curate*, from the Latin *curator*, properly denotes one who has the charge or care of. In the Prayer Book it is perpetually used to denote any minister who has the *cure of souls*, whether rector, vicar, or curate. I suppose it gradually came to be limited to the assistant or deputy in consequence of the fearful amount of non-residence on the part of incumbents in years past, the curate being generally the only person really having the cure or charge of the parish.

The term *vicar*, from the Latin *vicarius*, properly means a deputy and denoted an office much the same as the term *curate* does now. By degrees, as the rectorial tithes became impropriated, the officiating minister came to be regarded as an incumbent, under the name of *vicar*, or rector's deputy.[1]

Rector itself is a Latin word implying guide or ruler.

And now comes the question: can nothing be done towards recalling these names to something like their original and proper sense? ~ C. H. Davis, 1 Sep 1855

¶ C. H. Davis proceeded to detail six proposed changes of usage for inclusion in a reform bill expected in the next session of parliament – a quixotic endeavour, as he seems to have been aware.

CUSTARD: Why did the Puritans abominate it?

Q. Can any of your readers inform me why custard was held in such abomination by the Puritans? In the *Life* of Bishop Ken by W. L. Bowles we read that the clergy under Cromwell were subjected to a peculiar inquisition by 'Oliver's tryers' who questioned 'whether they had ever in their lives been present at a play, or whether they scandalously ate custard'. Bowles adds in a note: 'One clergyman was ejected from his living because he had "scandalously" eaten "custard", according to Warton. It is difficult to say what sin there was in eating custard, but some abomination was attached to it; and hence *Hudibras*: "And blaspheme custard through the nose." ' ~ W.N., 3 Apr 1852

R. The fact that custard was a condiment greatly beloved by the monks may have set the Puritans against it. There can be little doubt that their dish called 'almond-milk' or 'almond-cream' was the same as the custard of more recent times. In the *Continuations* of the history of the Abbey of Croyland we read

[1] Impropriation – the passing of church tithes or property to a lay individual or body – became increasingly common after the Dissolution of the Monasteries.

of Laurence Chateres, in the year 1413, giving £40 for the purchase of almond-milk on fish days. The regulations for the due and proper supply of this luxury were considered of such importance that they fill a whole page of the chronicle. Again, in the bill of fare of an abbey given by Thomas Fosbroke in his *British Monachism*, we find 'crem of alemaundys', which he explains as a compound of almonds with thick milk, water, salt, and sugar.

Of course I have suggested this explanation on the supposition that almonds form an essential part of custard. I certainly do not think that a proper custard can be made without them.
~ Henry T. Riley, 26 Aug 1854

A raid on the custard store

¶ In the first part of *Hudibras* (1663) Samuel Butler lists custard among a number of good things reviled by the Presbyterians:

> Rather than fail, they will defy
> That which they love most tenderly;
> Quarrel with minced-pies, and disparage
> Their best and dearest friend, plum-porridges;
> Fat pig and goose itself oppose,
> And blaspheme custard through the nose.

The detailed arrangements established at Croyland by the abbot, Thomas Overton, do indeed suggest that the monks took their almond-milk seriously. Six senior officers of the abbey – the master of the works, the almoner, the pittancer, the sacrist, the chamberlain, and the cellarer – each received ten marks in turn 'to supply three pounds of almonds, together with good bread and honey... on the fish days'.

DANTE AND MOUSETRAPS: A query for the curators of the Bodleian Library

Q. That very singular and caustic book *Il Vocabolario delle Opere di Santa Caterina* (Dictionary of the Works of St Catherine) by Girolamo Gigli was suppressed, and the author banished forty miles from Rome, by a decree of the Pope dated 21 August 1717. In its pages I find the following curious passage:

> The Florentines have, better than the inhabitants of the other Tuscan provinces, widely spread their idiom by means of commerce. And to this purpose I have read (but, from the treachery of my memory, for the moment I know not where) that, for the propagation of Florentine writings, the cheese merchants of Lucardo kept in their pay many writers to copy the best authors of the best age, and with these enveloped their buttery bantlings, in order that in the ports of the east and of the north, wherever such merchandise was marketable, the milk of the Florentine cows and that of the Florentine muses

might gain credit together. And this is so true that at Oxford, in the celebrated Bodleian Library, is still preserved a Dante, correctly copied from the first MS text, which had been used carefully to envelope a consignment of cheese at the time when the Bardi were merchants in England. It was known as the Lucardian Dante. The keepers of the great library kept always beside it two mousetraps on account of the persecution of this cheesy codex by the mice, so that at length it was called, in English, the Book of the Mousetrap.

Now Query, is there any tradition in the Bodleian respecting this Mousetrap Dante, and, if it is still there, does it still retain its cheesy flavour so as to require the protection of a trap? I know to my cost that hungry mice find unctuous hogskin binding very attractive, and, when hardly pressed for subsistence, will feed upon parchment or vellum, whether cheesy or not. ~ Periergus Bibliophilus, 5 Jan 1850

¶ The only response appeared on 23 March 1850 and referred to a purchase by the Bodleian of fifteen Dante manuscripts from a Venetian abbot. However, the purchase took place 'about the year 1822', over a hundred years after Gigli was writing, so the quest for the cheesy codex had come to nothing.

DAUGHTERS: Having nineteen

N. In the manuscript jottings of the engraver George Vertue we read: 'Died at Waldershare, in Kent, on Nov. 18, 1743, James Jobson, farmer, aged 112, who had seven wives, by whom he had thirty-eight children: nineteen sons and nineteen daughters.'

Farmer Jobson was more fortunate than good Dr Robert Hoadly Ashe, who had nineteen daughters but no son. Tom Dibdin has left us the following reminiscence of this clergyman:

I had the pleasure of sitting next to Dr Ashe at dinner, when he began a story with, 'As eleven of my daughters and I were crossing Piccadilly...' 'Eleven of your daughters, Doctor?' I rather rudely interrupted. 'Yes, sir,' rejoined the doctor, 'I have nineteen daughters all living; never had a son; and Mrs Ashe, myself, and nineteen female *Ashe plants* sit down one-and-twenty to dinner every day. Sir, I am smothered with petticoats.'

~ Editor, 3 Aug 1861

DEAD MEN'S HEADS: Unusual attachment to

1. MARGARET ROPER

Q. You have so many correspondents well versed in lore and legend that I am induced to beg through you for an explanation of the allusion in the following passage in Tennyson:

> Morn broaden'd on the borders of the dark,
> Ere I saw her, who clasp'd in her last trance
> Her murder'd father's head.

It occurs in 'A Dream of Fair Women', stanza 67. ~ W.M.C., Cambridge, 14 Dec 1850

R. The following extract from Sir James Mackintosh's *History of England* relates to Sir Thomas More's daughter and will serve to explain: 'The love of Margaret Roper continued to display itself in those outwardly unavailing tokens of tenderness to his remains. She procured his head to be taken down from London Bridge, kept it during her life as a sacred relic, and was buried with that object of fondness in her arms, nine years after she was separated from her father.' ~ X.Z., 4 Jan 1851

¶ Following More's execution on 6 July 1535 his body was buried in the church of St Peter in the Tower. As was the custom, his head was parboiled, fixed to a pole, and exhibited on London Bridge. One contemporary report refers to it turning black and being thrown into the river that November, but Thomas Stapleton, an early biographer of More, records that within a month Margaret Roper had persuaded the man who was responsible for the heads to sell it to her. According to Stapleton, she was then 'brought before the king's council and charged with keeping her father's head as a sacred relic... She answered that she had saved her father's head from being devoured by the fishes with the intention of burying it.' In fact she seems to have preserved it in spices in a leaden box until her death in 1544. She was buried in the More family tomb in Chelsea Old Church, her father's skull resting not in her arms but beside her.

Her husband William Roper died in 1578. His will stipulated that he should be buried next to her at Chelsea, but permission was refused and he was instead buried in the Roper family vault in St Dunstan's, Canterbury. As a result Margaret's body was moved from Chelsea to be reinterred beside him, and More's head went with her: it was seen when the Roper vault was opened in 1715, and again in 1835, as a letter in the *Gentleman's Magazine* of May 1837 explains:

> In the chancel of the church is a vault which, in newly paving of the chancel in the summer of 1835, was accidentally opened; and, wishing to ascertain whether Sir T. More's skull was really there, I went down into the vault, and found it still remaining in the place where it was seen many years ago, in a niche in the wall, in a leaden box, something of the shape of a beehive, open in the front and with an iron grating before it.

2. BESS AND CAREW RALEGH

N. The head of Sir Walter Ralegh, after his decapitation, was put into a red leather bag, over which his velvet nightgown was thrown, and the whole was then conveyed away in a mourning coach provided by Lady Ralegh. It is reported that she preserved this sad memorial in a case during her entire widowhood of twenty-nine years, prior to her son Carew obtaining it on her decease. He also kept it by him as his mother had done, and is said to have had it interred with him at Horsley, Surrey. In 1703 a head was dug up in that churchyard from the side of a grave where a Carew Ralegh was buried. There were no bones of a body, nor room for any, the rest of that side of the grave being firm chalk. An embalmed heart was also found under the floor of a room at Horsley which had once been a chapel. It has

been said that Carew carried about with him his father's heart.
~ Anon., 2 Jan 1858

¶ Sir Walter Ralegh was executed on 29 October 1618 in Old Palace Yard, Westminster, and buried headless in St Margaret's, Westminster.

Carew Ralegh died in London in 1666. On 1 January 1667 he was interred beside his father in St Margaret's and it is assumed that the head was buried there with him. However, the parish register at West Horsley records Carew Ralegh as having been buried *there* in September 1680, suggesting that his body may have been moved and reburied. If this did occur, the whereabouts of his father's head remains an open question...

DEATH WARNINGS IN ANCIENT FAMILIES

N. I marvel much that none of your contributors have touched upon the supernatural appearances, and other circumstances of a ghostly nature, that are said to precede a death in many time-honoured families of the united kingdoms. We have all heard of the mysterious 'White Ladye' that heralds the approach of death, or dire calamity, to the royal house of Hohenzollern. In like manner, the apparition of two gigantic owls upon the battlements of Wardour is said to give sad warning to the noble race of Arundel. The ancient Catholic family of Middleton have the same fatal announcement made to them by the spectral visitation of a Benedictine nun, while a Cheshire house of note, I believe that of Brereton, are prepared for the last sad hour by the appearance of large trunks of trees floating in a lake near their family mansion.

To two further families of venerable antiquity, both I believe of the county of Lancashire, the approaching death of a relative is made known, in one case by loud and continued knockings at the hall door at the solemn hour of midnight, and in the other by strains of wild and unearthly music floating in the air. ~ John o' the Ford, Malta, 21 Jan 1854

R. A drummer is stated to be heard in C— Castle, the residence of the Earl and Countess of A., going about the house playing his drum 'whenever there is a death impending in the family'. This warning is said to have been given shortly before the decease of the earl's first wife, and preceded the death of the next countess by about five or six months. Mrs Crowe, in her *Night Side of Nature*, observes hereupon: 'I have heard that a paper was found in her (the countess's) desk after her death, declaring her conviction that the drum was for her.'

Another legend is that a single swan is always seen on a particular lake close to the mansion of another family before a death, and Mrs Crowe speaks of many other curious warnings of death by the appearance of birds, as well as of a spectral black dog, which visited a particular family in Cornwall immediately before the death of any of its members. ~ Jas. J. Scott, Hampstead, 4 Feb 1854

¶ Catherine Crowe, author of *The Night Side of Nature* (1848), dates the drummer story to the period around Christmas 1844 and says she heard it from a friend connected to the case:

Miss D. was invited to spend a few days at C— Castle, with the Earl and Countess of A. She went, and whilst she was dressing for dinner, the first evening of her arrival, she heard a strain of music under her window, which finally resolved itself into a well-defined sound of a drum. During dinner she said, addressing Lord A., 'My lord, who is your drummer?', upon which his lordship turned pale, Lady A. looked distressed, and several of the company, who all heard the question, embarrassed. The lady, perceiving that she had made some unpleasant allusion, forbore further enquiry till she reached the drawing-room, when, having mentioned the circumstance again to a member of the family, she was answered, 'What! Have you never heard of the drummer-boy?' 'No,' replied Miss D., 'who in the world is he?' 'Why,' replied the other, 'he is a person who goes about the house playing his drum whenever there is a death impending in the family. The last time he was heard was shortly before the death of the last countess (the earl's former wife), and that is why Lord A. became so pale when you mentioned it...' Miss D. was naturally much concerned, and, indeed, not a little frightened at this explanation, and, her alarm being augmented by hearing the sounds on the following day, she took her departure from C— Castle.

This affair was very generally known in the north, and we awaited the event with interest. The melancholy death of the countess about five or six months afterwards, at Brighton, sadly verified the prognostic. I have heard that a paper was found in her desk after her death, declaring her conviction that the drum was for her...

The legend connected with the drummer is that either himself, or some officer whose emissary he was, had become an object of jealousy to a former Lord A., and that he was put to death by being thrust into his own drum and flung from the window of the tower in which Miss D.'s room was situated. It is said that he threatened to haunt them if they took his life; and he seems to have been as good as his word, having been heard several times in the memory of persons yet living.

Miss D. has been identified as a Miss Dalrymple. The castle is Cortachy Castle in Forfarshire, home of the Earl and Countess of Airlie. The story presumably relates to David, the 8th earl, who was born in 1785 and died in 1849. His first wife, Clementina, died in London in September 1835. He married again three years later and his second wife, Margaret, died on 17 June 1845. However, while Catherine Crowe's story seems to be supported by this last date of death, it is undermined by the fact that on the same day the countess gave birth to twin sons, suggesting that she died not as the result of a curse, but in childbirth.

DEATHBED SUPERSTITIONS

Q. When a curate in Exeter I met with the following superstition, which I do not remember to have seen noticed before. I had long visited a poor man, who was dying of a very painful disease, and was daily expecting his death. Upon calling one morning to see my poor friend, his wife informed me that she thought he would have died during the night, and consequently she and her friends *had unfastened every lock in the house*. On my enquiring the reason, I was told that any bolt or lock fastened caused uneasiness to, and hindered the departure of, the soul, and consequently, upon the approach of death, all the boxes, doors, etc., in the house were unlocked. Can any of your readers tell me whether this is in any way a general superstition amongst the lower orders, or is it confined to the West of England? ~ R.H., 16 Mar 1850

R. In the *Athenaeum* of 17 October 1846 it is stated that this remarkable superstition originates in 'the belief which formerly prevailed, that the soul flew out of the mouth of the dying in the likeness of a bird'. ~ Editor, 16 Mar 1850

R2. In my county, West Gloucestershire, they throw open the windows at the moment of death. ~ C.B., 30 Mar 1850

R3. Among the Jews at Gibraltar, where I have for many years been resident, there is another strange custom when a death occurs in a house. This consists in pouring away all the water contained in any vessel, the superstition being that the Angel of Death may have washed his sword therein. ~ Trebor, 18 May 1850

¶ The *Athenaeum* of 17 October 1846 detailed an additional step taken in Devonshire:

> The notion extends even to the supposition that a beam over the head of the dying man impedes the departure of the spirit. A clerical friend related to me that, in a village near Cullompton, he witnessed the death of a person, when the last moments seemed delayed by some unseen cause; and the relatives, in consequence, moved the bed – observing that over the place there was a beam concealed in the floor above. In consequence of such removal, as they said, the sick man 'went off like a lamb'.

113

DEVIL, THE: Did he appear on stage during *Dr Faustus?*

Q. In a curious Welsh work entitled *Gweledigaetheu y bardd cwsc* (Visions of the Sleeping Bard), first published in 1703, it is incidentally stated that the Devil appeared to play his own part in the interlude of *Dr Faustus* when acted at Shrewsbury. What is the foundation for this story, and where may I find further details about it? The Rev. D. Silvan Evans, in his excellent annotated edition of this Welsh classic, has no note upon the subject. ~ Aeron, 10 Apr 1858

R. There was long current a story that upon a certain occasion Satan actually made one of the party in Christopher Marlowe's *Dr Faustus*, with consequences very fearful to those who had assumed his shape. This strange tale is mentioned by William Prynne in his *Histriomastix* (1633), when writing against plays and lovelocks: 'The visible apparition of ye Devil appeared on ye stage, at the Belsavage Play-house in Queen Elizabeth's dayes, to the great amazement both of the actors and spectators, while they were prophanely playing the *History of Dr Faustus*, the truth of which I have heard from many now alive, who well remember it, there being some distracted with that fearful sight.' This story seems to have originated in an event recorded in *The Blacke Book* of Thomas Middleton, printed in 1604:

'Then, another door opening rere-ward, there came puffing out of the next room a villainous Leiftenant, without a band,[1] as if he had been new cut downe, like one at Wapping, with his cruell garters about his necke, which filthily resembled two of Derrick's necklaces.[2] He had a head of haire like one of the divells in *Doctor Faustus*, when the olde theater crackt and frighted the audience.'

The credulous John Aubrey, in his *Antiquities of Surrey*, probably alluding to this incident, wished his readers to believe that the Devil was a prompter to good works by making the actor Edward Alleyn quit the stage and piously devote his wealth to the founding of the College at Dulwich: 'The tradition runs thus: that Mr Alleyne, being a tragedian and one of the original actors in many of the celebrated Shakespear's plays, in one of which he played a demon, with six others, and was, in the midst of the play surpriz'd by an apparition of the Devil, which so work'd on his fancy that he made a vow, which he perform'd at this place.'

John Bowman, the actor, related to William Oldys a similar visitation during the reign of Charles II which occurred at the theatre in Dorset Gardens, where, in a dance of devils, one too many appeared: 'Some comical fellow among the comedians, having got into such a horrid dress as made him a much more infernal figure than the rest... so unexpectedly started up among them that they took him for the Devil indeed [and] were struck with a kind of panic, which soon infected the audience, and dispersed it in consternation. And after the like manner,' continues Oldys, 'may all the other apparitions of the Devil on the stage be probably accounted for.' ~ Editor, 10 Apr 1858

¶ Before the construction of permanent theatres in London the yards of coaching inns were often used for theatrical performances. At the Bell Savage on Ludgate Hill a portable stage

[1] Neckband or ruff.

[2] Gallows ropes. Thomas Derrick was a notorious Tyburn hangman of the time. His name became a byword for hangmen in general, and, as a result of his innovative use of a lifting device at the top of the gallows, later came to be used to denote cranes etc.

was erected in the cobbled courtyard and spectators could stand around it or watch from the galleries above. The Bell Savage also played host to other notable visitors beside the Devil: in 1595 William Banks exhibited his celebrated dancing horse Morocco there, five years before it climbed to the roof of St Paul's Cathedral; in 1616 Pocahontas was a guest; and in 1684 the first rhinoceros seen in England was put on show there.

The charged atmosphere at early performances of *Dr Faustus* is suggested by the fact that Edward Alleyn is said to have played the title role in a surplice with a cross stitched on the front as if to protect himself from damnation, while John Melton, in his *Astrologaster* (1620), paints a vivid picture of performances of the play at the Fortune Theatre: 'There indeede a man may behold shagge-hair'd devills runne roaring over the stage with squibs[1] in their mouthes, while drummers make thunder in the tiring-house,[2] and the twelvepenny hirelings make artificiall lightning in their Heavens.'

The Devil is also said to have appeared during a performance at Exeter, according to an old, undated manuscript note reprinted in the *Gentleman's Magazine* in September 1850:

Certaine players at Exeter, acting upon the stage the tragicall storie of Dr Faustus the Conjurer; as a certain number of devels kept everie one his circle there, and as Faustus was busie in his magicall invocations, on a sudden they were all dasht, every one harkning other in the eare, for they were all perswaded there was one devell too many amongst them; and so after a little pause desired the people to pardon them, they could go no further with this matter: the people also understanding the thing as it was, every man hastened to be first out of dores. The players (as I heard it) contrarye to their custome spending the night in reading and in prayer got them out of the towne the next morning.

---

[1] Small fireworks which burned with a hissing sound before creating a final explosion – unless, of course, they became damp.

[2] Attiring-house; dressing-room.

DOG-WHIPPING 1: In churches

Q. Can any reader throw light upon the following entry in the churchwardens' account book for the parish of Forest Hill, near Oxford? '1694. Pd. to Tho. Mills for whipping dogs out of church, 1*s.*' I am told by a friend that the office of dog-whipper existed about fifty years ago for the church of Heversham in Westmorland. ~ C.F.W., 15 Apr 1854

R. In 1659 Richard Dovey, of Farmcote in Shropshire, charged certain cottages with the payment of eight shillings to some poor man of the parish of Claverley who should undertake to awaken sleepers and whip dogs from the church during divine service. Ten shillings and sixpence per annum is now paid for the above service.

John Rudge, by his will dated in 1725, gave five shillings a quarter to a poor man to go about the parish church of Trysull in Staffordshire during sermons, to keep people awake and to keep dogs out of the church. This sum is still paid for that purpose.

At Chislet in Kent is a piece of land called Dog-whipper's Marsh, about two acres, out of which the tenants pay ten shillings a year to a person for keeping order in the church during divine service. Likewise there is an acre of land in the parish of Peterchurch, Herefordshire, appropriated to the use of a person for keeping dogs out of the church.

Many of your readers will call to mind the yelp of some poor cur who had strolled through the open door of a country church on some sultry day and been ejected by the sexton. I myself have often listened to the pit-a-pat in the quiet aisle, and I remember a disturbance once in church caused by the quarrel of two dogs. Such scenes, and the fact that dogs were considered unclean animals, most likely gave rise to the role of dog-whipper as a function of the sexton. It will also be remembered that some dogs cannot forbear a howl at the sound of certain musical instruments; and, besides the simple inconvenience to the congregation, this howl may have been considered a manifestation of antipathy to holy influences, much as the Devil was supposed to fear holy water.

Amongst other instances of the regular attendance at church of these 'unclean animals', I know one parish in Wales where a favourite dog always accompanied his master to church, and stood up in the corner of the pew, keeping watch over the congregation with the strictest decorum.
~ A Notary, 27 May 1854

R2. That persons bearing this office were attached to great houses in the sixteenth century is clear from the well known passage in *The Two Gentlemen of Verona*, Act 4, scene 4, where Lance says, referring to his incontinent dog Crab: 'I, having been acquainted with the smell before, knew it was Crab; and goes me to the fellow that whips the dogs. "Friend," quoth I, "you mean to whip the dogs?" "Ay, marry do I," quoth he...'
~ W.B.R., 27 May 1854

R3. In the bygone times in Scotland, when 'sacraments' and 'preachings' were held in the open air and country people gathered to them from considerable distances, many collies and other dogs which followed their masters were to be found attending. Sometimes they had to be driven off as, when psalm-singing began, they (through some sympathetical feeling) were apt to disturb the devotion by howling. The cattle browsing in the neighbouring fields, perhaps impelled only by curiosity, also drew around the worshippers, and the whole together presented a picture of primitive simplicity seldom now to be witnessed. ~ G.N., 2 Sep 1854

R4. The churchwardens of Great Staughton in Huntingdon-shire record the following disbursements:

> 1653. Itm. paide to Wm. Richards for whippinge the dogs out of the church, from Michaelm. till Christmas followinge... 1*s.*

> 1730. Pd. ye dogwhiper Hewitt... 2*s.* 6*d.*

> 1756. Pd. Robert Hewitt a quarter's pay, for looking after the people in the church, to keep them from sleeping... 2*s.* 6*d.*

> 1766. Aug. 22. Pd. for a dogwip for the church... 6*d.*

~ Joseph Rix, St Neots, 2 Sep 1854

R5. I find the following entry in the vestry book of Shrewsbury parish, in the diocese of Maryland: '1725. May 1. Agreed that Tho. Thornton shall keep and whip the dogs out of the church every Sunday till next Easter Monday, and also the cattle from about the church and churchyard, for 100lbs. tobacco.'

The value of the tobacco, which was a legalised and much-used currency in the southern colonies, had been fixed in 1715 at 10*s.* paper currency (equal to 7*s.* 6*d.* sterling of that period) per 100lbs., thus more or less consciously anticipating a decimal system of money. ~ I.H.A., 2 Sep 1854

R6. The office is not extinct. 'Dog-whipping, 2*s.* 6*d.*' still forms a regular item in the annual accounts of the sexton of the Collegiate Church of Middleham, Yorkshire, and is no less regularly paid, as I may stand witness. ~ T. H. Kersley, Canon and Sub-Dean, 15 Mar 1856

R7. The *Exeter Gazette* a few weeks since announced that 'Mr Jonathan Pickard, in the employ of the Rev. Chancellor Martin, has been appointed dog-whipper of Exeter Cathedral, in the room of Mr Charles Reynolds, deceased.' ~ Editor, 6 Sep 1856

¶ After the Reformation, when the chancel and altar became more accessible to the laity, the bringing of dogs to church was discouraged and communion rails were introduced in many churches, in part to protect the communion table from canine marauding.

Dog-whippers in Wales and bordering counties were commonly provided with tongs for restraining animals at a safe distance. These tongs were sometimes made of iron but usually of oak, and so bore the impressive teeth-marks of many generations of dogs.

In other places greater indulgence was shown: in the chancel arch of Northope Church in Lincolnshire there was, until about 1830, a small enclosed pew called the Hall Dog Pew in which the dogs from the nearby manor house would wait while their masters prayed.

Oak dog tongs,
Bangor Cathedral

DOG-WHIPPING 2: In Hull and York

Q. There was some time since the singular custom in Hull of whipping all the dogs that were found running about the streets on 10 October. Thirty years ago, when I was a boy, so common was the practice that every little urchin considered it his duty to prepare a whip for any unlucky dog that might be seen in the streets on that day. The custom is now obsolete, those 'putters down' of all boys' play in the streets – the new police – having effectually stopped this cruel pastime.

Perhaps some of your readers may be able to give a more correct origin of this singular custom than the one I now give from tradition. Previous to the suppression of the monasteries in Hull, it was the custom for the monks to provide liberally for the poor and for wayfarers who came to the fair held annually on 11 October. While they were busy in preparation on the day before the fair, a dog strolled into the larder, snatched up a joint of meat, and decamped with it. The cooks gave the alarm, and when the dog got into the street he was pursued by those waiting outside the gate to receive the monks' charity, who made him give up the stolen joint. Whenever, after this, a dog showed his face while the annual preparation was going on, he was instantly beaten off, a practice eventually taken up by the boys and, until the introduction of the new police, rigidly put in practice by them every 10th of October. ~ John Richardson, 13 Savile Street, Hull, 29 Oct 1853

R. This custom obtains, or used to, in York on St Luke's Day, 18 October, which is there known by the name of Whip-dog Day. The traditional account of its origin is that, in times of popery, a priest celebrating mass at the festival in a church in York unfortunately dropped the pyx after consecration, and it was snatched up suddenly and swallowed by a dog that lay under the table. The profanation of this high mystery occasioned the death of the dog, and a persecution began which has since continued to be severely waged on this day (St Luke's) against all of that species in the city. ~ R. W. Elliot, Clifton, 21 Jan 1854

DRAGONS: Were they really crocodiles?

Q. When passing through the city of Brünn, in Moravia, rather more than a year ago, my attention was drawn to the *Lindwurm* or dragon preserved there from a very remote period. This monster, according to tradition, was invulnerable except in a few well-guarded points, and, from his particular predilection for veal and young children, was the scourge and terror of the neighbourhood. The broken armour and well-picked bones of many doughty knights, scattered around the entrance to the cave he inhabited, testified to the impunity with which he had long carried on his depredations, in spite of numerous attempts to destroy him. Craftiness, however, at last prevailed where force had proved of no effect, for a knight stuffed the skin of a freshly killed calf with unslaked lime and laid it before the dragon's cave. The monster, smelling the skin, rushed out and instantly swallowed the fatal repast. Feeling afterwards, as may be readily expected, a most insatiable thirst, he hurried off to a neighbouring stream where he drank until the water, acting upon the lime, caused him to burst. The inhabitants, on learning the joyful news, carried the knight and the *Lindwurm* in triumph into the city, where they have ever since treasured up the memento of their former tyrant.

The animal or reptile thus preserved is undoubtedly of the crocodile or alligator species, although I regret it was not in my power to examine it more particularly, evening having set in when I saw it in the arched passage leading to the town hall, where it has been suspended. I fear also that any attempt to count the distinguishing bones would be fruitless, the scaly back having been covered with a too liberal supply of pitch with a view to protection from the weather.

Have any of your readers seen this *Lindwurm* under more favourable circumstances than myself, and can they throw any light on the genus to which it belongs?

Further, may it not be that the various legends respecting dragons and their like have their origin in the shape of crocodiles? ~ R.S. Jun., 28 Dec 1850

R. The subject on which R.S. Junior writes is of so much interest in many points of view that I hope that a few notices relating to it may not be considered unworthy of insertion.

In Murray's *Handbook* for Northern Italy mention is made, in the account of the church of St Maria delle Grazie near Mantua, of a stuffed lizard, crocodile, or other reptile, which is preserved suspended in the church. This is said to have been killed in the adjacent swamps in about the year 1406. It is stated to be six or seven feet long.

Eight or ten years ago I saw an animal of the same order, and about the same size, hanging from the roof of the cathedral of Abbeville, in Picardy. I then took it for a small crocodile, but I cannot say positively that it was one. I am not sure whether it still remains in the cathedral.

At the west door of the cathedral of Kraków are hanging some bones which are said to have belonged to the dragon which inhabited the cave at the foot of the rock (the Wawel) on which the cathedral and the royal castle stand; it was destroyed by Krak, the founder of the city. I regret that my want of osteological science prevented me from ascertaining to what animal these bones had belonged. I thought them the bones of some small species of whale.

I hope that some competent observer may inform us of what animals these and the *Lindwurm* at Brünn are the remains. It has struck me as possible that the real history of these crocodiles or alligators, if they are such, may be that they were brought home by crusaders as specimens of dragons, just as Henry the Lion, Duke of Brunswick, brought from the Holy Land the antelope's horn which had been palmed upon him as a specimen of a griffin's claw, and which may still be seen in the cathedral of that city. That such trophies should afterwards be fitted with appropriate legends is not surprising. ~ N., 18 Jan 1851

R2. The best authenticated dragon story is that of the one said to have been killed by Dieudonné de Gozon, a knight of Rhodes, and afterwards Grand Master of the Order of St John on that island, who died in 1353. The head of his dragon was carefully preserved as a trophy at Rhodes till the knights were driven out of the island in 1522. The Turks in turn preserved the head with equal care, so it was actually seen by Jean de Thévenot, the French traveller, as late as the middle of the seventeenth century; and from his description it appears to have been the head of a hippopotamus. I believe it really was that animal, which, before the invention of firearms, would have proved no contemptible antagonist to a knight on horseback confined with heavy armour and armed only with sword and lance. But how did it get to Rhodes? ~ William Pinkerton, 25 Feb 1865

R3. A late and learned antiquary and naturalist, Colonel Hamilton Smith, was of the opinion that many of the local traditions of encounters between knights and dragons may have had their origin in fact, and that in all cases the so-called dragon was a crocodile. In support of his opinion he showed a drawing made from a mural painting in a church on the island of Rhodes, representing a combat between a knight of St John and an unmistakable crocodile. Crocodiles are said to attain to a very great age, and Hamilton Smith believed it possible that some of the many imported into Europe by the Roman emperors may have escaped and survived to later times. ~ E. M'C., 25 Feb 1865

¶ The de Gozon story was first set down by Pfalzgraf Ottheinrich, a pilgrim who visited Rhodes on his way to the Holy Land in 1521. He was told of a young French knight who, having been forbidden to attack a dangerous dragon by the Grand Master, nonetheless returned to France to prepare for the ordeal, training his horse and dogs by setting them against a mechanical monster. The most unusual part of the story is this dummy dragon, described in detail by Giacomo Bosio in his history of the Knights of St John:

The dragon was made of canvas stuffed with tow, of the same size, form, and figure and of the same colours as the beast itself. It was of the size of an ordinary horse. It had the head of a serpent with ears the size and shape of a mule's, covered with a very hard and scaly skin, with a great and frightful mouth armed with very sharp teeth. Its eyes, deeply sunk in the head, glittered like fire and glared with horrible ferocity. It had four legs something like a crocodile's, with paws armed with very hard and sharp talons. From its back rose two wings, not so very large, which were the colour of a dolphin above and scarlet with some spots of yellow below. The body and legs were of the same colour as the wings, the belly red and yellow like the under side of the wings. It had a tail something like a lizard's. It ran with a speed greater than that of the swiftest horse, flapping its wings and making a tremendous noise.

Naturally de Gozon returned to Rhodes, slayed the dragon, and himself became Grand Master. The head of his supposed victim hung in a gateway on the island for several hundred years. It is thought that it disappeared *circa* 1839, a biologist having pointed out that it really belonged to a large crocodile.

GOZON KILLING the CROCODILE

EAR-PULLING TO ENCOURAGE REMEMBRANCE:
A Berkshire custom?

Q. R. B. Paul, author of *A History of Germany on the Plan of Mrs Markham's Histories* (1847), records that among the Ripuarian Franks the purchaser of land or houses, on paying the price before three, six or twelve witnesses according to the value of the property, administered a cuff to each of the same number of boys that had been present, and pulled their ears, by way of impressing the transaction on their memories. He then adds in a note that persons 'now or till lately alive in Berkshire' had informed him that they well remembered the ear-pullings inflicted on them by their fathers when they made a purchase of land. Is this custom now kept up in Berkshire or elsewhere? ~ P. J. F. Gantillon, 24 Nov 1855

R. The following extract from Benvenuto Cellini's Life, written *circa* 1560 and one of the most amusing autobiographies ever penned, seems to show that this curious custom is not peculiar to the purchase of lands, or to Germany or Berkshire, but was used elsewhere by parents on trivial occasions to sharpen their children's wits and memories:

> When I was about five years of age, my father was sitting alone in a little room, singing and playing on his fiddle. A good oak fire was burning and, the weather being exceedingly cold, he had drawn close to the fire. Then, looking into the flames, he saw a little animal resembling a lizard which was running about and enjoying itself in the hottest part of the fire. Instantly perceiving what it was, he called for my sister and me, and, after he had shown us the creature, he gave me a box on the ear. I fell a-crying, while he, soothing me with his caresses, said, 'My dear child, I don't give you that blow for any fault you have committed, but that you may remember that the little lizard which you see in the fire is a salamander – a creature which no one that I have ever heard of has ever beheld before.'

~ J.R.M., 22 Dec 1855

ELEPHANTS: Are they aroused by mulberry blood and human earwax?

Q. Dr Henry More, Fellow of Christ's College, Cambridge, wrote a work entitled *Enthusiasmus Triumphatus* (1656). In the preface he says, referring to his opponent Thomas Vaughan, author of *Anthrosophia Theomagica* (1650): 'These I spread before him like the bloud of mulberries before elephants in battel, to provoke his irascible.' Is there any foundation for the notion that elephants were thus exasperated? ~ Belphos, 15 Nov 1856

R. Your correspondent will find the relevant passage in the account of the war waged by Antiochus Epiphanes and Eupator against the Jews, given by the unknown author who wrote the 1st Book of Maccabees: 'To the end that they might provoke the elephants to fight, they showed them the blood of grapes and of mulberries.'

Dr More, by using the expression 'spread before' the elephants, evidently infers that the sight of the red juice or 'blood' of grapes and mulberries served to exasperate the animal. But the word in the Septuagint,[1] which is rendered 'showed' in the

---

[1] The most influential Greek version of the Old Testament. Unlike the Hebrew Bible it included the books known as the Apocrypha.

English version, is to be construed as physicians do when they talk of 'exhibiting medicines' to their patients. It means that the elephants were made furious by being forced to drink wine of grapes or mulberries. In this instance the 3rd Book of Maccabees is the best *scholium* on the 1st. It is not printed in our version of the Apocrypha, but will be found in the Septuagint. In describing the persecution of the Jews at Alexandria by Ptolemy Philopator in 210 BC the author relates (Chapter 5, verse 2) that the king, preparatory to causing them to be trampled to death by elephants in the hippodrome, ordered Hermo, the elephants' keeper, to dose the animals the day before with frankincense and undiluted wine, and the order was obeyed. The potion was repeated (verse 45) till the elephants were excited to madness by the wine – but instead of trampling the Jews they spent their fury on the armed troops and guards, of whom they destroyed numbers. ~ J. Emerson Tennent, 29 Nov 1856

A second improbable-sounding means of arousing elephants was mooted in the following year:

Q. In Lucknow human earwax is collected and is the chief ingredient in use for intoxicating elephants previous to their furious contests. Where can any scientific investigations into its nature be found? ~ J.P., 12 Sep 1857

R. The *Cyclopedia of Chemistry* (1854) says that earwax 'appears to consist of stearine, oleine, otine, yellow matter soluble in water, uncoagulated albumen, coagulated albumen, lactates of lime, and potash or soda'. What the 'yellow matter' may be is unknown, but certainly the ingredients seem totally inadequate for the purpose alleged. ~ Andrew Steinmetz, 26 Sep 1857

¶ J.P.'s query may have been suggested by remarks on earwax in Mrs Meer Hassan Ali's *Observations on the Mussulmans of India* (1832): 'The cleansing of ears is chiefly performed by men who, collecting this article, make great profits from the sale of it... It is the chief ingredient in use for intoxicating elephants previous to the furious contests so often described as the amusement of native courts.'

EPITAPHS: Some curious

✠ The following is, I think, terse and expressive on a talkative old maid:

> Here lies, return'd to clay,
> Miss Arabella Young,
> Who on the first of May
> Began to hold her tongue.

~ F.C.H., 23 Dec 1854

✠ The following is perhaps the briefest epitaph on record. It is said to have been written on Burbage the actor. This is it: 'EXIT BURBAGE.' Query, is there any authority for this? ~ Cuthbert Bede, 2 June 1855

✠ For brevity this epitaph beats that of 'O rare Ben Jonson!' Burbage was buried at St Leonard's, Shoreditch, but no inscription on his tomb has been recorded in the History of that parish. It first appeared in the additions to William Camden's *Remaines* published in 1674 by John Philipot, Somerset Herald, where it reads 'Exit Burbidge.' The epitaph on Dr Caius, founder of Gonville and Caius College, Cambridge, cannot be blamed for its prolixity: '*Fui Caius.*' ~ Editor, 2 June 1855

✠ An epitaph from Bideford, Devon:

> Here lies the body of Mary Sexton,
> Who pleas'd many a man, but never vex'd one:
> Not like the woman who lies under the next stone.

~ J.Y., 1 Dec 1855

✠ Within the church of Areley Kings, near Stourport, is the following:

> Here lieth the body of WILLIAM WALSH, gentleman,
> who died the third day of November, 1702, aged eighty-six,
> son of Michael Walsh of Great Shelsey, who left him a
> fine estate in Shelsey, Hartlebury, and Areley; who was
> ruinated in his estate by three Quakers, two lawyers,
> and a fanatic to help them.

~ Palque, 1 Dec 1855

✠ The following epitaph on a blacksmith is from a flat gravestone in the churchyard of Bradford, Yorkshire:

> My stithy and my hammer I reclined,
>
> My bellows too have lost their wind;
>
> My fire's extinguish'd, and my forge decay'd,
>
> And in my silent dust my vice is laid:
>
> My coal is spent, my stock of iron gone,
>
> My last nail driven, and my work is done.
>
> John Hill, died 1813.

~ N.L.T., 15 Nov 1856

✠ The late Sternhold Oakes was rather eccentric and offered a reward for the best epitaph for his grave. Several tried for the prize, but they flattered him too much he thought. At last he tried for himself, and the following was the result:

> Here lies the body of Sternhold Oakes,
>
> Who lived and died like other folks.

~ W.W., Malta, 14 Feb 1857

✠
> Beneath this stone old ABRAHAM lies:
>
> Nobody laughs, and nobody cries,
>
> Where he is gone, and how he fares,
>
> Nobody knows, and nobody cares.

The above is (or was some few years since) to be seen in Islington Churchyard on the monument of Abraham Newland, the well known principal cashier of the Bank of England, who died in November 1807 and was there buried. In his memoirs, published in 1808, I find these lines were his own composition.

~ John Tuckett, 25 Dec 1858

¶ In fact Ben Jonson's surname appears as 'Johnson' on the famous epitaph stone in Westminster Abbey, and Dr Caius was not quite as laconic as suggested. His epitaph is as follows:

Fui Caius.	(I was Caius.
Vivit post funera virtus.	Virtue lives beyond the grave.
Aetatis suae LXIII.	Aged 63.
Obiit 29 Julii	Died 29 July
Anno D. 1573.	1573.)

'The Puzzle'

An epitaph that might have appealed to *N & Q* readers. Published in 1756, it was dedicated to 'the penetrating geniuses of Oxford, Cambridge, Eton, and the learned Society of Antiquarians'. Latinate appearance notwithstanding, it records the last resting-place of Claud Coster, tripe-seller, of Impington, and his consort Jane.

EVENTS, GREAT, FROM SLENDER CAUSES

N. Dr Paris observes that 'the history of great events from small causes would form an interesting work', and I offer a few miscellaneous instances I have noted.

'How momentous', says Campbell, 'are the results of apparently trivial circumstances! When Mahomet was flying from his enemies he took refuge in a cave, which his pursuers would have entered if they had not seen a spider's web at the entrance. Not knowing that it was freshly woven, they passed by the cave – and thus a spider's web changed the history of the world.'

'What can be imagined more trivial,' remarks Hume in one of his essays, 'than the difference between one colour of livery and another in horse races? Yet this difference begat two most inveterate factions in the Greek[1] empire, the Prasini and Veneti, who never suspended their animosities till they ruined that unhappy government.'

If the nose of Cleopatra had been shorter, said Pascal, the condition of the world would have been different.

'The murder of Caesar in the Capitol was chiefly owing to his not rising from his seat when the Senate tendered him some particular honours,' says Richard Graves in *The Spiritual Quixote.* He adds that 'The negotiations with the Pope for dissolving Henry VIII's marriage (which brought on the Reformation) are said to have been interrupted by the Earl of Wiltshire's dog biting his holiness's toe, when he put it out to be kissed by that ambassador; and the Duchess of Marlborough's spilling a basin of water on Mrs Masham's gown, in Queen Anne's reign, brought in the Tory ministry, and gave a new turn to the affairs of Europe.'

Joseph Warton mentions, in his notes on Alexander Pope, that 'The coquetry of the daughter of Count Julian introduced the Saracens into Spain.' Further, he says that 'The expedition to the island of Ré was undertaken to gratify a foolish and

---

[1] i.e. Byzantine.

romantic passion of the Duke of Buckingham,' and that the Treaty of Utrecht 'was occasioned by a quarrel betwixt the Duchess of Marlborough and Queen Anne about a pair of gloves'.

Isaac D'Israeli, in his *Curiosities of Literature*, says that 'When Louis VII, to obey the injunctions of his bishops, cropped his hair and shaved his beard, Eleanor of Aquitaine, his consort, found him, with his unusual appearance, very ridiculous, and soon very contemptible. She revenged herself as she thought proper, and the poor shaved king obtained a divorce. She then married the Count of Anjou, afterwards our Henry II. She had for her marriage dower the rich provinces of Poitou and Guienne; and this was the origin of those wars which for three hundred years ravaged France, and cost the French three millions of men. All this probably had never occurred, had Louis not been so rash as to crop his head and shave his beard.'

We may add that Giotto, one of the early Florentine painters, might have continued a rude shepherd boy if a sheep drawn by him upon a stone had not accidentally attracted the notice of Cimabue; that Luther might have been a lawyer had he escaped the thunderstorm; and that if Mr Grenville had not carried, in 1765, his memorable resolution as to the expediency of charging certain stamp duties on the plantations in America, the western world might still have bowed to the British sceptre.

The story of Robert Bruce and the spider will bear a similar application, and doubtless many correspondents of *N & Q* can make interesting additions to the above examples. ~ N.L.J., 9 Sep 1854

R. There is a French book of this argument by M. Richer. Perhaps the subject is not a very wise one: a pair of gloves, or a wet gown, may give rise to a treaty, but there must be many greater causes behind the readiness to act. An accidental spark may blow up a fortress, but what should we say to the person who wrote a book on the spark, and forgot the gunpowder? ~ M., 7 Oct 1854

R2. According to Bishop Burnet the Habeas Corpus Act passed by a mere mistake, one peer being counted for ten, and that made a majority for the measure. ~ F.S., Churchdown, 19 July 1856

R3. When many Puritans emigrated or were about to emigrate to America in 1637, Cromwell, either despairing of his fortunes at home or indignant at the rule of government which prevailed, resolved to quit his native country in search of those civil and religious privileges of which he could freely partake in the New World. Eight ships were lying in the Thames ready to sail; in one of them, says Hume (quoting Cotton Mather and other authorities), were embarked Hazelrig, Hampden, Pym, and Cromwell. A proclamation was issued, and the vessels were detained by Order in Council. The king had indeed cause to rue this exercise of his authority. In the same year Hampden's memorable trial – the great case of Ship Money – occurred. What events rapidly followed! ~ J.H.M., 23 Aug 1856

R4. The following is from Arthur Stanley's *Historical Memorials of Canterbury*:

The Mission of Augustine is one of the most striking instances in all history of the vast results which may flow from a very small beginning – of the immense effects produced by a single thought in the heart of a single man, carried out conscientiously, deliberately, and fearlessly. Nothing in itself could seem more trivial than the meeting of Gregory with the three Yorkshire boys in the market-place at Rome: yet this roused a feeling in his mind which he never lost; and, through all the obstacles which were thrown first in his own way and then in that of Augustine, his highest desire concerning it was more than realised...

Let anyone sit on the hill of the little church of St Martin and look on the view which is there spread before his eyes. Immediately below are the towers of the great abbey of St Augustine, where Christian learning and civilisation first took root in the Anglo-Saxon race. From Canterbury, the first English Christian city – from Kent, the first English

Christian kingdom – has by degrees arisen the whole constitution of Church and State in England, which now binds
together the British Empire. And from the Christianity here
established has flowed, first, the Christianity of Germany,
then, after a long interval, of North America, and lastly we
may trust, in time, of all India and all Australasia. The view
from St Martin's Church is indeed one of the most inspiriting
that can be found in the world.

~ A.A.D, 20 Sep 1856

¶ Gibbon records the passions originally excited by the
Prasini (greens) and the Veneti (blues) in the circus at Rome,
and how the same affiliations reappeared in deadlier form in the
hippodrome of Constantinople during the reign of Justinian:
'The sportive distinction of two colours produced two strong
and irreconcilable factions, which shook the foundations of a
feeble government... Every law, either human or divine, was
trampled under foot, and, as long as the party was successful, its
deluded followers appeared careless of private distress or public
calamity.'

'Count' Julian, a rebel governor, controlled the vital stronghold of Ceuta in North Africa for the Christians as a vassal of
Roderic, the last Visigothic king of Hispania (modern day
Spain and Portugal). The story is that he sent his daughter
Cava to Roderic's court at Toledo to be educated and in show
of loyalty, but his trust was ill repaid when Roderic made her
pregnant. Outraged, Julian recalled his daughter and, in
Gibbon's words, 'offered his place, his person, and his sword, to
the successors of Mahomet'. With his help the Muslim armies
landed at Gibraltar in 711. By 718 they had conquered most of
the Iberian peninsula.

The expedition led by George Villiers, Duke of Buckingham,
to the Ile de Ré in 1627 was designed to boost the Huguenot
stronghold of La Rochelle and so weaken the position of
Cardinal Richelieu. Nearly 8,000 men set out in the summer;
only 3,000 returned to Portsmouth in November.

Luther is said to have been caught in a thunderstorm outside Erfurt on 2 July 1505. When lightning struck nearby he was thrown to the ground, crying out 'St Anne help me! I will become a monk.' Two weeks later, to the dismay of his father, he abandoned his legal studies and entered the city's Augustinian monastery. In Luther legend – as in the illustration above – the storm is often combined with the death at about the same time of his university friend Alexis.

Bishop Burnet's account of the passing of the Habeas Corpus Amendment Act of 1679 is as follows: 'It was carried by an odd artifice in the House of Lords. Lord Grey and Lord Norris were named to be the tellers. Lord Norris, being a man subject to vapours, was not at all times attentive to what he was doing, so, a very fat lord coming in, Lord Grey counted him for ten, as a jest at first – but, seeing Lord Norris had not observed it, he went on with this misreckoning... and by this means the bill passed.' In a note on this passage Speaker Onslow affirmed that the story was supported by the attendance and voting numbers set down in the minute book of the House of Lords for the day in question.

The idea that Cromwell came close to emigrating in 1637 is dismissed by modern historians, but it is thought that he did consider quitting England for the New World at other times. According to Clarendon, when the Grand Remonstrance was presented to Charles I in 1641, the future Protector whispered in the ear of Lord Falkland that, had it not gone forward, he had made up his mind to emigrate.

Pope Gregory's meeting with English boys in Rome was the supposed occasion of his famous remark, '*Non Angli sed Angeli*,' 'Not Angles but Angels.' It is said that, learning the boys were from the kingdom of Deira, which extended from the Humber to the Tees, he added a second pun, observing that they would surely be rescued *de ira*, from wrath.

FAMILIAR PHRASES: Some early origins of

N. I have recently remarked several phrases in vulgar use which are to be traced much further back than the present day, as may be seen from the following list:

• 'Fast and loose' will be found in Shakespeare, see *Love's Labour's Lost* (*c.*1595), Act 3, scene 1: 'As cunning as fast and loose.'

• 'Pumping' a man for information may be traced to Otway's *Venice Preserved* (1682), Act 2, scene 1, where Pierre says to Aquilina, 'Pump not me for politics...'

• Cowper has 'the worse for wear' in *John Gilpin* (1782).

• He has also to dash 'through thick and thin' in the same.

• 'Hobson's choice' is as old as the days of Milton, his younger days in fact.

• 'Veels within veels,' said Mr Samuel Weller in *The Pickwick Papers* (1837), and the verbal idea is in Ezekiel 1:16 ('their work was as it were a wheel in the middle of a wheel') and 10:10 ('as if a wheel had been in the midst of a wheel') .

Perhaps some of your readers will increase this random list.
~ W.T.M., Hong Kong, 19 Jan 1856

R. The following may be found in John Stanbridge's *Vulgaria Stanbrigi*, published by Wynkyn de Worde *circa* 1520, and strike me as curious and noteworthy:

- 'Thou hyttest the nayle on the heed.'
- 'He hath ordeyned a staffe for his owne heed.'
- 'Ryght on the nose...'
- 'A gyven hors may not be loked in the tethe.'
- 'He is an evyll coke that can not lycke his owne lyppes.'

~ Dunelmensis, 20 June 1857

R2. On reading Shacklock's *Hatchet of Heresies*, Antwerp, 1565, I have noted the following proverbial phrases:

- 'Do not these thynges differ as muche as chalcke and chese.'
- 'Playne as a pyke staff.'
- 'Labored with tothe and nayle.'
- 'Which no man can deny that Luther made with these choppynges and chaungynges.'

~ J.C.G., Ledbury, 22 May 1858

R3. I remember to have met in Pepys's *Diary* with the expression of someone's nose being put out of joint. ~ H.V.T., 26 May 1860

R4. Is not Chaucer the author of the phrase 'Murder will out'? In his *Nun's Priest's Tale* is the line: 'Mordre wol out, that see we day by day...' ~ W. H. Williams, 24 Nov 1866

¶ Some of the expressions cited date back a good deal further: 'thicce and thynne', for example, appears in the tenth-century *Exeter Riddle Book*, while Chaucer has 'thurgh thikke and thurgh thinne' in *The Reeve's Tale*.

The Pepys reference is to 31 May 1662: 'The queene is brought a few days since to Hampton Court; and all people say of her to be a very fine and handsome lady and very discreet, and that the king is pleased enough with her: which I fear will put Madam Castlemaine's nose out of joynt.'

'FIRST CATCH YOUR HARE...': Was this famous cookery instruction ever written?

Q. Mrs Glasse's *Cookery* is known to the present generation principally through this oft-repeated quotation. Did she ever write such a sentence? In her directions for cooking a hare she uses the word 'case', which is defined in some old dictionaries as to disembowel and skin. I have seen no edition containing the quotation as it is usually given. Until such is found, would it not be a graceful act on the part of facetious writers to let Mrs Glasse rest in peace? ~ G.D.Y., 6 Apr 1861

¶ The famously misquoted directions in Hannah Glasse's *The Art of Cookery Made Plain and Easy* (1747) are as follows: '*To roast a hare.* Take your hare when it is cas'd, and make a pudding...' A similar use of 'case' is found in Shakespeare: 'We'll make you some sport with the fox ere we case him' (*All's Well That Ends Well*, Act 3, scene 6).

There was a vogue for the 'facetious' form in the 1850s, when it was taken up by R. S. Surtees, Thackeray, and others – hence G.D.Y.'s letter – but the formula has been found as far back as the thirteenth-century treatise *De legibus et consuetudinibus Angliae* (On the Laws and Customs of England) by Henry of Bratton: '*Et vulgariter dicitur quod primo oportet cervum capere, et postea, cum captus fuerit, illum excoriare.*' 'And it is commonly said that first you must catch your deer, and afterwards, when it has been caught, skin it...'

FOOTBALL: Why was it outlawed?

Q. From an Act of Parliament of James I of Scotland, dated 1424: 'It is statute, and the king forbiddis, that na man play at the fute-ball under the paine of fiftie schillings, to be raised to the lord of the land als oft as he be tainted, or to the scheriffe of the land or his ministers if the lordes will not punish sik trespassours.'

Are any of your readers able to explain the reason for this curious enactment? ~ Quaesitor, Glasgow, 6 June 1863

R. The reason was that the game of football had infringed upon the more useful practice of archery. Even so early as 1349, in the reign of Edward III, that monarch was compelled to send a letter of complaint upon this subject to the sheriffs of London, declaring that the skill in shooting with arrows was almost totally laid aside for the purpose of useless and unlawful games, one of which was football. The danger, too, attending this pastime occasioned King James I of England, in the rules drawn up by himself for the recreations of his son Henry Prince of Wales, to give the following instructions:

> From this court I debarre all rough and violent exercises, as the *foote-ball*, meeter for laming than making able the users thereof; but the exercises that I would have you to use, although but moderately, not making a craft of them, are running, leaping, wrestling, fencing, dancing, and playing at the caitch, or tennise, archerie, palle-malle, and such like other fair and pleasant field-games.
>
> (*Basilikon Doron*, 1599)

~ Editor, 6 June 1863

¶ Edward III was neither the first nor the last king to try to suppress football. In 1314, during the reign of his father Edward II, a proclamation was issued by the Lord Mayor of London: 'For as much as there is great noise in the city caused by bustling over large balls... from which many evils might arise which God forbid: we command and forbid on behalf of the king, on pain of imprisonment, such game to be used in the city in future.' Richard II and Henry IV tried again in 1389 and 1401 respectively, but apparently to little avail.

One king, at least, does seem to have given the game his approval, for in 1526 Henry VIII ordered a pair of football boots from the Great Wardrobe. They were of leather, hand-stitched by the royal cordwainer Cornelius Johnson, and cost four shillings. But Henry was perhaps more serious about footwear than football: at the same time he ordered seventy-seven other pairs of boots, buskins, shoes and slippers.

More useful than football

FOX-HUNTING: Interrupted by the Civil War

Q. In his *Letters* Horace Walpole alludes to an anecdote of a country gentleman, during the Civil Wars, falling in with one of the armies on the day of some battle (Edgehill or Naseby?) as he was *quietly going out with his hounds.* Where did Walpole find this anecdote?
~ C., 8 Dec 1849

R. Our correspondent C.W.B. has kindly referred us to Dr Thomas's additions to Dugdale's *Warwickshire*, and we extract therefrom the following proof that Walpole had authority for his story:

> As King Charles I marched to Edgecote, near Banbury, on 22 October 1642, he saw [a man] hunting in the fields not far from Shuckburgh, with a very good pack of hounds, upon which it was reported that he fetched a deep sigh and asked who that gentleman was that hunted so merrily that morning, when he was going to fight for his crown and dignity. And being told that it was this Richard Shuckburgh, he was ordered to be called to him, and was by him very graciously received. Upon which he went immediately home, armed all his tenants, and the next day attended on him in the field, where he was knighted, and was present at the Battle of Edgehill.

~ Editor, 23 Mar 1850

FROGS: Swallowed, fried, et cetera

Q. I recollect seeing, more than forty years ago, one of my father's reapers, Mary Inglis by name, swallow several live frogs. It was done to cure herself of some stomach complaint. When asked what she swallowed them for she replied that there was 'naething better than a *paddy* for reddin' ane's puddins'. When she administered her remedy she held the reptile by the two hinder feet, and bolted it without any seeming repugnance! Mary is still alive, nearly fourscore years of age, in the village of Auchencrow. Can anyone say whether the swallowing of frogs was used as a remedy in former times? ~ Menyanthes, Chirnside, 22 Aug 1857

R. I remember that more than fifty years ago this practice was common with schoolboys, and I have seen it done often. It was alleged by those who did it that it was good to cleanse the stomach, which seems to have been the notion of Mary Inglis. But how far it was a practice seriously adopted as a remedy for any maladies, I cannot say. ~ F.C.H., 3 Oct 1857

R2. Swallowing live frogs appears to have been no uncommon medicine for weakness and consumption in the North Riding of Yorkshire. Several old people, dead years ago, have spoken of taking them when young, and have even added that they were delicious. ~ C.J.D.J., 3 Oct 1857

R3. This is practised in parts of Wiltshire, but not on human subjects. It is a remedy administered to cows when afflicted with a cessation of 'chewing the quid', or, as the more polite term it, 'chewing the cud'. ~ J.W., 20 Mar 1858

R4. Whilst strolling through one of the markets of Milan during the spring of 1855 my attention was attracted to a woman who appeared to be opening shellfish. Upon closer observation, however, I found she was preparing frogs for cooking. At her left hand was a sack almost full of these creatures. Taking them one by one on her knee, she denuded them of their skins in a very expert manner and then threw them into a dish, where they were crawling over each other and moving about in an awkward way, to the no small delight of a group of juveniles.

Mr Robert Fortune, in his last work, *A Residence among the Chinese* (1857), gives an account of a similar scene he witnessed in a street of Tse-kee, a city near Ning-po, and, from the following incident that occurred a few weeks ago, it appears that frogs are becoming an article of diet among the lower orders of this country also. In the neighbourhood of St Helens, Lancashire, a person observed some boys splashing about in a pond, and, going up to them, found they were catching frogs and cutting off their hind legs. He asked what they were going to do with them. The reply was, 'We putten um oth frying-pon, an' then 'ith oon – an' there graidley good.' Which means, in English, they fried and then ate them, and they were extremely good. ~ G., 1 May 1858

GAME FEATHERS IN BEDDING: Do they delay death?

N. I do not see that any of your numerous correspondents have mentioned the common belief among the poor in this county, Sussex, that a person cannot die if his bed is stuffed with game feathers. A friend of mine a little time back was talking to a labourer on the absurdity of such a belief, but he failed to convince the good man, who, as a *proof* of the correctness of his belief, brought forward the case of a poor man who had lately died after a lingering illness. 'Look at poor Muster S—, how hard he were a-dying. Poor soul, he could not die ony way, till neighbour Puttick found out how it wer. "Muster S—," says he, "ye be lying on geame feathers, mon, surely"; and so he wer. So we took'n out o'bed, and laid'n on the floore, and *he pretty soon died then!*' ~ Nedlam, 10 Apr 1852

R. In the adjoining county of Surrey the notion appears to be deeply rooted in the minds of the lower classes. A friend, residing in my parish of Betchworth, has given me several examples which have fallen under his notice during the past winter:

I was calling, a few weeks since, upon an old man whom I had left the previous day, apparently in a dying state. At the door I met an old neighbour, and enquired if he was still living. 'Yes, sir,' she said, 'we think he must change his bed.' 'Change his bed!' I replied. 'What do you mean?' 'Why, sir, we think he can't pass away while he lies in that bed. The neighbours think there must be game feathers in the bed.' 'Game feathers! What do you mean?' 'Why, sir, it is always thought a poor soul can't pass away if he is lying on game feathers.' 'Oh,' I said, 'there is nothing in that. That is not the reason of his lingering on.' 'No, sir,' she replied, 'I think so too, for I know the bed well. I was at the making of it, and the feathers were well picked over.'

Not long after I looked in upon another aged man, who had been confined to his bed upwards of four months, gently dropping into his grave without any other apparent complaint than old age. He was a fine, hearty old man, with a constitution which kept him lingering on beyond expectation. 'Well,' I said, 'how are you this morning?' 'Oh, sir, I have had a sad night. I hoped, when you left me, I should drop asleep and never wake more in this world.' 'Yes, poor fellow,' said his sister, who stood by his bedside, 'he does not seem able to die. We think we must move him to another bed.' 'Another bed! Why so?' 'Why, we think there must be wild feathers in his bed.' The old man evidently thought, with his sister, that his bed had something to do with the protraction of his life. He died, however, at length, without being moved. It is needless to remark that the superstition would no doubt have been confirmed, and the flickering lamp of life extinguished a few hours sooner, had they carried into effect their proposal to drag him from one bed to another, or to lay him upon the floor.

The woman who helped to lay out the corpse came to see me, and I took the occasion to ask if she knew the belief that a person could not die whilst lying upon game feathers. She assured me that she knew it to be the case, and that in two instances, when she had attended persons who could not die, they had taken them out of their beds and they had expired immediately. I found all expostulation in vain. No argument could shake so strong a conviction, and I have no doubt that this strange notion is extensively entertained by the peasantry in these southern counties.

I have since been informed that a similar belief exists in Cheshire, in regard to pigeons' feathers. ~ Albert Way, 1 May 1852

GLOVE-REMOVAL AND OTHER COURTESIES:
Did they originate in conflict?

Q. Why are gloves not worn before royalty? ~ F.E., 6 Apr 1850

R. Perhaps covered hands, as well as a covered head, may have been considered discourteous. ~ S. W. Singer, Mickleham, 10 Aug 1850

R2. Mr Singer's explanation is simple, and, I believe, correct. But why should uncovering either hands or head be a mark of respect? The solution seems to me of some curiosity, and may perhaps be to many of your readers of some novelty.

These and most other modern forms of salutation and civility are derived from chivalry, or at least from war, and they all betoken some deference, as from a conquered person to the conqueror – just as, in private life, we still continue to sign ourselves the 'very humble servants' of our correspondents.

The *uncovered* head was simply the head *unarmed*: the helmet being removed, the part was at mercy. So the hand *ungloved* was the hand *ungauntleted*, and to this day it is an incivility to shake hands with gloves on. Shaking hands itself was but a token of truce, in which the parties took hold each of the other's *weapon-hand*, to make sure against treachery. So also a gentleman's *bow* is but an offer of the neck to the stroke of the adversary, and the lady's *curtsey* is but the form of going *on her knees* for mercy.

This general principle is marked, as it ought naturally to be, still more strongly in the case of military salutes. Why is a *discharge* of guns a salute? Because it leaves the guns empty, and at the mercy of the opponent. And this is so true, that the saluting with blank cartridge is a modern invention. Formerly salutes were fired by discharging the cannon-balls, and there have been instances in which the compliment has been nearly fatal to the visitor whom it was meant to honour. When an officer salutes he points his drawn sword to the ground, and the salute of the troops is, even at this day, called 'presenting arms' – that is, presenting them to be taken. ~ C., 14 Feb 1852

¶ In similar vein it is said that the now convivial custom of chinking glasses or clinking tankards before drinking originally had a serious purpose: to spill liquid between vessels to reassure the drinkers that they were not about to be poisoned.

GOAT: Origin of the queen's regimental

Q. From the *English Churchman* of 18 January:

> The celebrated snow-white goat, presented by her majesty to the 23rd Royal Welch Fusiliers, died on the 20th of December. After weathering the campaign in Bulgaria, and marching proudly at the head of his regiment from Kalamita Bay to Sebastopol, he has at last fallen without wearing the Alma medal he had earned on the way. His stately demeanour and reverend beard made him a prominent feature in the appearance of the regiment as it moved along, and the gap left by his absence will force a recollection of the fine animal upon the memory of everyone familiar with the gallant 23rd. He had been hutted, and every care had been taken to protect him against the exposure and inclement weather, but all this attention was unavailing.

Her majesty's present suggests that it is a custom in regiments from mountainous districts to have such an animal attached to the corps, as a fond reminiscence and symbol of home and country. Perhaps some of your military readers can give more precise information. ~ J.M., 17 Feb 1855

R. The following particulars were communicated to the St Lucia *Palladium* in January 1846:

> The 23rd regiment, or Royal Welch Fusiliers, of which our governor is lieutenant-colonel, has, since its formation in 1689,

been the national corps of the principality of Wales. The battlefields of the Boyne, Blenheim, Ramillies – these famous plains have each trembled under their firm and sturdy tread, and the bones of many a brave Welshman lie mouldering there.

It has been the custom of this regiment from time imme-morial to be preceded in all its marches and accompanied in all its parades by a mighty goat, the emblem of old Cambria. It is on record that the goat of the regiment accompanied the Welch Fusiliers into action at Bunker's Hill, and James Fenimore Cooper, the American novelist, in one of his interesting national narratives, relates that such was the sanguinary nature of the contest that 'the Welsh Fusiliers had not a man left to saddle their goat'.

The last representative of this horned and bearded dynasty lately accompanied the regiment from Canada to Barbados. But poor Billy! Whether the climate disagreed with him, or he missed his native mountains, alas! he died, and great was the lamentation throughout the regiment.

This circumstance happened not long ago to be mentioned at the table of our gracious monarch, who directed that two milk-white goats of a magnificent Cashmere breed, peculiar in England to Windsor Park alone, and part of a flock sent to her majesty as a present from the Persian shah, be forth-with presented to the gallant 23rd to replace poor Billy's loss. We understand that this mark of her majesty's condescension has just been communicated to Colonel Torrens, and suitably acknowledged by his excellency. This gift sheds honour on her who gave, and on them who received. Good queen! Brave soldiers!

The governor spoken of is that able man and distinguished officer, Major-General Arthur Wellesley Torrens, one of the heroes of Inkerman. At the period in question he administered the government of this island. ~ Henry H. Breen, St Lucia, 5 May 1855

¶ The earliest reference to the Royal Welch's goat occurs in Major Robert Donkin's *Military Collections and Remarks* (1777) and suggests that the tradition was by then well established:

The royal regiment of Welch Fuzileers has a privilegeous honor of passing in review preceded by a goat with gilded horns, and adorned with ringlets of flowers... The corps values itself much on the ancientness of the custom. Every 1st March the officers give a splendid entertainment to all their Welch brethren, and, after the cloth is taken away, a bumper is filled round to his royal highness the Prince of Wales, the band playing 'The noble race of Shenkin', when a handsome drum-boy, elegantly dressed, mounted on the goat richly caparisoned for the occasion, is led thrice round the table in procession by the drum-major. It happened in 1775 at Boston that the animal gave such a spring from the floor that he dropped his rider upon the table, and then, bouncing over the heads of some of the officers, he ran to the barracks with all his trappings, to the no small joy of the garrison and populace.

Queen Victoria presented the regiment with its first royal goat in 1844, and the custom has been continued ever since. Each goat is called Billy, wears an elaborate silver headplate identifying it as a royal gift, has the rank of lance corporal, and is looked after by another corporal who bears the honorary title of goat-major. In June 2006, however, the goat was demoted for 'lack of decorum' during a parade to mark the queen's birthday held in front of foreign dignitaries at the Episkopi garrison in Cyprus. According to one soldier present, the goat 'was trying to head-butt the waist and nether regions of the drummers'. Subsequently an army spokesman hinted at a reprieve: 'His situation is currently being reviewed, and he could regain his rank.'

A month earlier the annual costs of ten army mascots had been revealed by the Ministry of Defence: £4,300 for two drum horses; £3,100 for two wolfhounds; £3,000 for two Shetland ponies; £700 for an Indian black buck; £700 for a ram; and £500 for two goats. It was pointed out by the minister responsible that the seemingly high wolfhound costs were a special case: 'These are wolfhounds which, as a result of generations of inbreeding, require a refined diet and a great deal of veterinary care.'

GOOSEBERRY, PLAYING

Q. I lately had an engagement to dine with my brother, who is a family man, and I was intending to drive over in the pony chaise. However, my brother's eldest daughter, who is about nineteen, happened to call in the course of the morning and overruled my proposal that we should ride together: she stated that she much preferred walking and requested that I would walk with her; so off we set together on foot. We had not gone a hundred paces when we were overtaken by a young gentleman of our acquaintance who remarked that he was going the same way as we were and, with our permission, would accompany us. I observed nothing particular on the road except that my niece and our casual companion seemed very much taken up with one another, and left me to my own meditations. But when we reached my brother's house, and the young gentleman had wished us good morning, my niece, to my great surprise, not only informed me that I was the kindest of uncles, but added that she could not express how much she felt obliged to me for 'doing gooseberry'. I begged to know what 'doing gooseberry' was; but she, with one of her sauciest smiles, merely replied, 'What you have been doing now.'

When the ladies had retired after dinner I mentioned this little occurrence in the hope of eliciting an explanation, but all the gentlemen present began laughing. Do enlighten my ignorance, for I assure you I never before met with or heard of the phrase 'doing gooseberry'. ~ An Old Bachelor, 20 Oct 1860

R. From the tenor of our correspondent's Query we infer that he and his brother reside in the *country*, and we would make this general observation – that though it may not be thought quite *the thing* if a young lady and her sweetheart are seen rambling through bypaths and shady lanes *alone*, yet if they take the same walk accompanied by the young lady's aunt, married sister, grand-mamma, or uncle, there is no violation of the 'strictest propriety'. The party thus sanctioning is said to 'do gooseberry'. We confess that, had he asked for the *origin* of the phrase, we should have

151

felt at a loss, though very possibly some other correspondent may yet come to our assistance. ~ Editor, 20 Oct 1860

R2. Is not this a short form for 'doing gooseberry picker'? The person who plays the part so obligingly performed by An Old Bachelor is sometimes called a 'gooseberry picker'. This seems more readily comprehensible than the shortened expression his niece employed, and suggests a possible origin for the saying, in some now forgotten story of a love-plot successfully carried out while the chaperon was innocently picking gooseberries. ~ T.E.S., 10 Nov 1860

HARE, MAD AS A MARCH

Q. In Mr Mayhew's very interesting work, *London Labour and the London Poor* (1851), a collector of hareskins, in giving an account of his calling, says: 'Hareskins is in – leastways I c'lects them – from September to the end of March, when hares, they says, goes mad.' Is anything known as to the origin of the well known saying 'as mad as a March hare'? ~ L.L.L., 20 Sep 1851

R. '*As mad as March Hare* is a very old saying. March is the rutting time of hares, and they are then very excitable.' I contributed this explanation to Thomas Wright's *Dictionary of Obsolete and Provincial English*, and perhaps you will permit me to add that I have had ocular demonstration of its correctness. After two or three warm days in early spring I have seen hares performing strange antics – running a few feet up the stems of trees which were slightly out of the perpendicular, falling down on their backs, leaping up into the air, and uttering strange cries which are called by old hunting authors 'beating' or 'tapping'. If any reader of *N & Q* still has his doubts, let him ask some intelligent gamekeeper, the best of field naturalists; or, still better, let him ascend a tree in a covert well stocked with these pernicious animals, on such a day as I have described, after five o'clock p.m., and keep quiet, and he will soon see and hear for himself. ~ E.G.R., 23 Jun 1860

HEDGEHOGS: The surprising voracity of

Q. In the few books on natural history to which I have access the voracity of the hedgehog is not noticed. I beg, therefore, to ask whether a tragical event which has recently taken place in my house is consistent with the habits of this animal, generally described as harmless.

Our kitchen being infested with cockroaches, I offered a shilling to any village boy who could procure me a hedgehog. A female, with a young one, was soon brought, and, besides having the run of the beetles at night, these animals had always bread and milk within their reach. One day, however, the servants heard a mysterious crunching sound in the back kitchen and found, on examination, that nothing was left of the young hedgehog but the skin and prickles – the mother had devoured her little pig! A friend has since informed me that a gamekeeper told him of a hedgehog eating a couple of rabbits which had been confined with it, and killing others beside. Our cruel beast runs about the house very nimbly at night, and takes high jumps if interrupted. The cockroaches have greatly diminished in number. ~ Alfred Gatty, 17 Nov 1855

R. Many years ago a hedgehog was placed in one hamper, a wood pigeon in another, and two starlings in a third. The lid of each hamper was tied down with string, and the hampers were placed in a garden-house, which was firmly secured in the evening. When I entered the garden-house the next morning I found the strings of all the hampers severed, the starlings and wood pigeon dead and eaten, feathers alone remaining in their hampers, and the hedgehog alive in the wood pigeon's hamper. As no other animal could have got into the garden-house, I came to the conclusion that the hedgehog had killed and eaten the birds. ~ C. S. Greaves, 15 Dec 1855

153

HERMITS, ORNAMENTAL

Q. Keeping a poet is a luxury enjoyed by many, from the queen down to Messrs Moses, Hyam and Co.,[1] but the refinement of keeping a hermit would appear to be a more *recherché* and less ordinary appendage of wealth and taste. I send you an advertisement for, and two actual instances of, *going a hermiting* from my scrapbook:

> A young man, who wishes to retire from the world and live as a hermit in some convenient spot in England, is willing to engage with any nobleman or gentleman who may be desirous of having one. Any letter directed to S. Lawrence (post paid) to be left at Mr Otton's, No. 6 Colman's Lane, Plymouth, mentioning what gratuity will be given, and all other particulars, will be duly attended to.
>
> (*Courier*, 11 January 1810)

Can anyone tell me whether this retiring young man was engaged in the above capacity? I do not think so, for soon afterwards an advertisement appeared in the papers which I have reasons for thinking was by the same hand: 'Wants a situation in a pious regular family, in a place where the Gospel is preached, a young man of serious mind, who can wait at table and milk a cow.'

It is clear at least that the following instance proved unsuccessful.

Mr Hamilton, once the proprietor of Painshill, near Cobham, Surrey, advertised for a person who was willing to become a hermit in that beautiful retreat of his. The conditions were that he was to continue in the hermitage seven years, where he should be provided with a Bible, optical glasses, a mat for his bed, a hassock for his pillow, an hour-glass for his timepiece, water for his beverage, food from the house, but never to exchange a syllable with the servant. He was to wear a camlet

---

[1] A reference to Elias Moses & Son Ltd and Hyam & Company, well known firms of tailors specialising in ready-made clothes. Moses & Son, in particular, were noted for their versified advertisements.

robe, never to cut his beard or nails, nor ever to stray beyond the limits of the grounds. If he lived there, under all these restrictions, till the end of the term, he was to receive 700 guineas. But on breach of any of them, or if he quitted the place any time previous to that term, the whole was to be forfeited. One person attempted it, but a three weeks' trial cured him.

A gentleman residing near Preston, Lancashire, was more successful in his singularity. He advertised a reward of £50 a year for life to any man who would undertake to live seven years underground without seeing anything human, and to let his toe and finger nails grow, with his hair and beard, during the whole time. Apartments were prepared underground, very commodious, with a cold bath, a chamber organ, as many books as the occupier pleased, and provisions served from the gentleman's own table. Whenever the recluse wanted any convenience he was to ring a bell, and it would be provided for him. Singular as this residence may appear, an occupier offered himself, and actually stayed in it, observing the required conditions for four years. ~ Florence, Dublin, 7 Feb 1852

R. Some fancy of this kind at Mr Weld's of Lulworth Castle, in Dorsetshire, exaggerated or highly coloured by John O'Keeffe, was supposed to afford the title and principal incident of the latter's extravagant but laughable comedy *The London Hermit, or, Rambles in Dorsetshire.* This play was first performed in 1793, with great success, and was revived in 1822.

I, too, have heard the story as told of Mr Hamilton and Painshill, but I a little doubt it because, when I visited it as a show place a great many years ago, I saw no hermitage. ~ C., 28 Feb 1852

R2. In *Blackwood's Edinburgh Magazine* for April 1830 it is stated by Christopher North[1] that the then editor of another magazine had been 'for fourteen years hermit to Lord Hill's father; and sat in a cave in that worthy baronet's grounds with an hour-glass in his hand, and a beard once belonging to an old

[1] Pen-name of the prolific journalist and critic John Wilson (1785-1854).

goat, from sunrise to sunset; with orders to accept no half-crowns from visitors, but to behave like Giordano Bruno.'

This is certainly strange training for a future editor. Perhaps some of your contributors can tell whether Sir John Hill really kept such an appendage at Hawkstone? ~ J. S. Warden, 13 Nov 1852

R3. Visiting the grounds at Hawkstone two-and-forty years ago, the hermitage was shown, with a stuffed figure dressed like the hermit of pictures seen by a dim light. Visitors were told that formerly it had been inhabited in the daytime by a poor man to whom the eccentric, but truly benevolent, Sir Richard Hill gave a maintenance on that easy condition, but that the popular voice against such 'slavery' induced the worthy baronet to withdraw the reality and substitute the figure. ~ Henry Walter, 18 Dec 1852

¶ In 1737 the Hon. Charles Hamilton (1704-1786) purchased 200 acres of desolate heathland sloping down to the River Mole, near Cobham, Surrey, and over the next thirty years he turned it into the influential landscape garden of Painshill. Along with exotic trees and shrubs he introduced a thirty acre lake, two vineyards, and a range of follies – including a hermitage – to furnish entertaining surprises for visitors walking through the grounds. In 1773 debts forced him to sell Painshill and later it fell into neglect. In 1980 a large portion of the original site was bought by the local authority and the grounds have since been restored by the Painshill Park Trust.

Thomas Weld (1750-1810) of Lulworth Castle succeeded to the family estates in 1775. A devout Catholic, he gave sanctuary to Trappist monks exiled from Revolutionary France, helping them to establish a monastery in the grounds. He also helped exiled Jesuits, giving them the house and grounds in Lancashire that would become Stonyhurst College. The playwright John O'Keeffe spent the summer of 1791 in the Lulworth area and visited the castle.

The *N & Q* references to Hawkstone Park, near Shrewsbury, mention a rather confusing range of Hills. Work on the picturesque grounds was begun in the 1740s by Sir Rowland, first baronet, and after his death in 1783 was continued by his son Sir Richard (1733-1808). Sir Richard was succeeded by his younger brother John, whose son Rowland (1772-1842) was one of Wellington's generals and became Lord Hill in 1814.

A *Guide* to the Hawkstone grounds by Thomas Rodenhurst, published in 1784, lists their many attractions including over ten miles of walks, rocks which are compared to the ruins of Palmyra, a wax effigy of an ancestor in a many-chambered grotto, a walled and turreted vineyard, a menagerie, a Gothic greenhouse, an Elysian Hill, a Stately Lion, an Awful Precipice, and the hermitage, complete with hermit. Forty years later, according to *The Shropshire Gazetteer* (1824), little had changed except that the hermit appears to have been stuffed and ingeniously mechanised:

> You reach a little cottage in which there is the figure of a hermit, in a sitting posture, and with a table before him, on which are a skull, an hour-glass, a book, and a pair of spectacles. The figure rises at the approach of strangers, and appears to repeat some lines which are fixed up in the inside of the habitation, under the motto *Memento Mori*.

It is said that in its heyday – from the late eighteenth to the early nineteenth century – Hawkstone attracted 10,000 visitors a year. In the twentieth century the estate changed hands and the park was neglected, but since 1993 much of the original scheme has been restored, the hermitage included, and the grounds are again open to the public.

Such restorations of eighteenth-century gardens have led on in recent years to a minor revival in ornamental hermits. In June 2002 Painshill's recreated hermitage was inhabited by artist David Blandy, who dressed as a Buddhist monk and listened to 1970s soul music to pass the time. More recently it has hosted an annual hermit 'event': 'HUNT THE HERMIT,' says the advertising for a weekend in September 2008. 'Search for our hermit around the park – if you find him he may not speak but he will reward you!'

The idea was also adopted for an 'art installation' at the wilderness end of the Shugborough estate in Staffordshire.

Even the old practice of advertising for a hermit was revived, the following notice appearing in the *Guardian*, the *Stage*, the *London Review of Books*, and the *Staffordshire Newsletter* in August 2002: 'RESIDENT HERMIT required for Great Haywood Cliffs, County of Staffordshire, to perform the role of resident hermit 20-22 September 2002. Wilderness and stipend provided.'

This appeal was syndicated by Reuters and the organiser received 250 applications, some from as far afield as America, India and Australia. The winner was Ansuman Biswas, chosen for his 'sincerity and commitment to solitude'. He may have been disappointed: during his weekend stint he had over 400 visitors.

HOUR-GLASSES IN PULPITS

Q. What early evidence exists of preaching by the hour-glass? If the Fathers of the Church timed their sermons by any instrument of the kind we should expect their writings to contain internal evidence of the fact, just as frequent allusion is made by Demosthenes and other ancient orators to the *clepsydra* or water-clock, by which the time allotted to each speaker was measured. Besides, the close proximity of such an instrument would be a constant source of metaphorical allusion on the subjects of Time and Eternity.

At all events there appears to be indisputable evidence of the use of the hour-glass in the pulpit in this country. In the churchwardens' accounts of the parish of St Helen, Abingdon, we find the following for 1591: 'Paide for an houre-glasse for the pulpit, 4*d*.' Among the accounts of Christ Church, St Catherine's, Aldgate, under the year 1564, this entry occurs: 'Paid for an hour-glass that hangeth by the pulpitt when the preacher doth make a sermon that he may know how the hour passeth away.' And in Thomas Fosbroke's *British Monachism* (1802) we find the following passage: 'A stand for an hour-glass still remains in many pulpits. A rector of Bibury, Gloucestershire, used to preach two hours, regularly turning the glass. After the text the esquire of the parish withdrew, smoaked his pipe, and returned for the blessing.' ~ A.W.S., Temple, 18 June 1853

R. In *The Last Battell of the Soule in Death* (1629) Zachary Boyd says: 'Now after his battell ended hee hath surrendered the spirit... His houre-glasse is now runne out, and his soul is come to its wished home, where it is free from the fetters of flesh.'

This divine was minister of the barony parish of Glasgow, the church for which was then in the crypt of the cathedral, and I have no doubt that an hour-glass was there used from which he draws his simile. However, to judge from their contents, Mr Boyd's sermons must each have occupied at the ordinary rate of speaking at least an hour and a half.

Though sermons are now generally restricted to no more than an hour's delivery, the practice of extended preaching in the olden times in the West of Scotland long prevailed. Within my own recollection I have heard sermons of nearly two hours' duration, and among some early Dissenters the services on sacramental occasions lasted continuously from ten o'clock on Sabbath forenoon to three or four o'clock the following morning.

There is a traditional anecdote of an old Presbyterian clergyman, unusually full of matter, who, having preached out his hour-glass, was accustomed to pause, say to the precentor 'Another glass and then,' turn the hour-glass over, and recommence his sermon. ~ G.N., Glasgow, 23 July 1853

R2. There is an example in the church of St Alban, Wood Street, Cheapside. The church was rebuilt by Sir Christopher Wren and finished in 1685, showing that the hour-glass was in use to at least that date. ~ J. D. Allcroft, 23 July 1853

R3. The following is from *A few Hints on the Practical Study of Ecclesiastical Antiquities, for the use of the Cambridge Camden Society* (1839):

> HOUR-GLASS STAND. A relick of Puritanick times. They are not very uncommon; they generally stand on the right-hand of the pulpit and are made of iron. A curious revolving one occurs at Stoke D'Abernon, Surrey, and in St John Baptist, Bristol, where the hour-glass itself remains. Though a Puritanick innovation, it long kept its place. John Gay writes:

'He said that Heaven would take her soul no doubt, / And spoke the hour-glass in her praise quite out', and it is depicted by the side of a pulpit in one of Hogarth's paintings.

~ W. P. Storer, Olney, Bucks, 27 Aug 1853

R4. There is an hour-glass stand at Tawstock Church, Devon, but it has been displaced: I saw it lying among fragments of old armour, banners, etc., in a room above the vestry. It represents a man's arm, cut out of sheet iron and gilded, the hand holding the stand. It turned on a hinge at the shoulder and lay flat on the panels of the pulpit when not in use. When extended it would project about a yard. ~ Balliolensis, 17 Sep 1853

R5. The hour-glass was used equally by Catholics and Protestants. In an account of the fall of the house in Blackfriars, where a party of Romanists was assembled to hear one of their preachers in 1623, the preacher is described as 'having on a surplice, girt about his middle with a linen girdle, and a tippet of scarlet on both his shoulders. He was attended by a man that brought after him his book and hour-glass.' (Samuel Clark, *The Fatal Vespers*, 1657) ~ Edward F. Rimbault, 18 Mar 1854

¶ At Earl Stonham in Suffolk four pulpit hour-glasses survive: two last for an hour, one lasts for half an hour, and one – which must have been a welcome sight to many eyes – lasts a quarter of an hour. Elsewhere surviving glasses are few but over a hundred stands can still be seen, including the one lighted on by Balliolensis at Tawstock, which has been restored to its place in the church. On arriving at Tawstock in the 1980s the present incumbent, the Rev. John Carvosso, also found an hour-glass, the sands of which had absorbed moisture over the centuries and so would not run. He placed it in his airing-cupboard for several years but, while improved, it still lasts for almost three hours.

The carrying of an hour-glass behind Father Drury at the 'Fatal Vespers' of 26 October 1623 was apter than he knew. In a third-floor garret in the French ambassador's house a large congregation had gathered to hear the celebrated preacher, but when he had been speaking for half an hour the floor gave way under their combined weight and Drury, along with ninety-four others, was killed – an accident interpreted by Protestants as a divine judgement upon Jesuits. It seems unlikely that the hour-glass survived.

Hugh Peters,
a notable seventeenth-century glass turner

HUMAN SKIN: Used in bookbinding et cetera

Q. I have somewhere heard or read of two or three human skins having been prepared and tanned like leather, and of a pair of shoes or boots having been made of such leather. Can any of your readers give me any information respecting them? ~ R. W. Hackwood, 26 July 1856

R. The Royal Infirmary at Bristol boasts of a valuable anatomical museum, formed by the late Mr Richard Smith, who was senior surgeon of that institution from 1796 until his decease in 1843. He was one of the leading men of his day, well known for his high professional character and attainments, and a frequent contributor on historical subjects to the *Gentleman's Magazine.* Amongst his peculiarities Mr Smith had almost a morbid curiosity in criminal cases – a trait of character that may be veiled as *a love of forensic medicine.* This is well seen in his museum – a small but sombre apartment containing a valuable collection of pathological and anatomical preparations.

Amidst other material therein none is more interesting than that relating to John Horwood. He was a youth of eighteen, the first criminal hanged at Bristol New Drop, 13 April 1821, for the murder, under aggravated circumstances, of his sweetheart, Eliza Balsum, at Hanham, by hurling a stone at her. In a case against the wall of the museum hangs the skeleton of this malefactor. Near it lies a book compiled by Mr Smith, evidently *con amore*, in which are enshrined the most minute details of the murder: cuttings from newspapers; the actual indictment; briefs of the counsel; correspondence; broadsheets; not excepting prints of the judge, the chaplain, a pencil sketch of the corpse, a chart of phrenological development, etc., altogether forming a collection that exhausts the repulsive subject and displays in a marked manner the *penchant* of the compiler.

This collection of Horwoodiana is half-bound in folio, and on the back is a label (about 6 inches by 3 inches) of the human cuticle tanned. It is somewhat of the texture of light-coloured Russia leather, with tooled border lines in gold, with a skull and crossbones stamped as ornament in each corner, and the following inscription in old English character, also gilt:

Cutis Vera

Johannis Horwood [1]

A memorandum within the book sets forth that 'the bones were macerated and the skin tanned at the infirmary'. ~ F.S., Churchdown, 27 Sep 1856

R2. While at Leyden in 1818 I remember seeing in a museum, amongst Boerhaave's surgical collection,[2] a pair of lady's shoes, with high heels, made of human leather from the skin of a man who had been executed. The nipple was placed as an ornament in front of the instep. ~ Henry Stephens, 27 Sep 1856

R3. In 1829 the now notorious William Burke was executed in Edinburgh for the murder of several individuals whose bodies he afterwards disposed of to a surgeon for dissection. A portion of his skin was tanned. It was very thick, of a dark blue colour, and much like Morocco leather. I remember well that the publisher of Burke's Trial at the time had a good piece of it, which he cut up and gave to various of his friends. ~ T.G.S., Edinburgh, 27 Sep 1856

R4. Rather more than thirty years ago (I forget the exact year) Kezia Westcomb was executed for murder at Exeter. According to the law of those days her body was sent to the dissecting room.[3] A portion of her skin was tanned into leather and used for the binding of a copy of *Paradise Lost*. The volume is now in the possession of the gentleman for whom it was bound, who is well known in Exeter. ~ Crowdown, 14 Apr 1866

R5. The late Mr Muskett, the bookseller of Norwich, had a portion of tanned skin of one Johnson, executed at Norwich for

---

[1] 'The true skin of John Horwood.'

[2] Hermann Boerhaave (1668-1738), Dutch botanist and physician.

[3] Between 1752 and 1832 the law provided that the bodies of those executed for murder should either be hung in chains or delivered to surgeons for dissection.

murder some fifty years ago, with which he had bound a copy of Johnson's *Dictionary*, now in the possession of one of Mr Muskett's brothers. ~ G.A.C., 19 May 1866

R6. I recollect being told in my younger days that a soldier named Steptoe had been executed at Reading, between sixty and seventy years since, for murder. The body was dissected, the skin tanned, and *gloves* made of it as a relic, several persons having taken a deep interest in the fate of the malefactor. It is said he was a great penitent as well as a great sinner and that he sang some hymn of his own composing, to the 'Dead March' in Handel's *Saul*, as he stood under the gallows beam. ~ L.W., 19 May 1866

R7. It is affirmed that, among the cruelties of the French Revolution, the skins of the victims were tanned and made into boots. ~ W. Winters, Waltham Abbey, 26 Mar 1870

R8. The famous Bohemian chief in the wars of the Hussites, J. Troknov, was better known by the name of Ziska, from his being blind in one eye. He died of the plague in 1424. It is said that his adherents then stretched his skin on a drum, the sound of which, they pretended, had the virtue to frighten their enemies out of their wits and put them to flight. ~ P.A.L., 7 Dec 1872

R9. The following is from an article by Mr Abraham Hayward, QC, in the *Edinburgh Review*, October 1866:

Not content with emptying the tombs, the heroes and heroines of the Reign of Terror danced among them, and once a woman stood at the cemetery entrance distributing copies of *The Rights of Man*, bound in human skin supplied to the binder by the executioner. M. Villenave possessed one of these copies. What would not an English collector give for one? What would not the drum made out of Ziska's skin fetch at Christie's, should it accidentally turn up?

~ Sparks H. Williams, Kensington Crescent, 3 May 1873

HUMBLE PIE

Q. In a bill of fare in *The Accomplisht Lady's Delight, in Preserving, Physick, Beautifying, and Cookery* (1683) I find reference to 'an umble pye'. Query, does the phrase 'to eat humble pie' owe its origin to this dish? ~ J. T. Hammack, 24 Nov 1849

R. I venture to submit that the *humble pie* of that period was indeed the pie named. It was made out of the 'umbles' or entrails of the deer, a dish of the second table, inferior of course to the venison pasty which smoked upon the dais, and therefore not inexpressive of that humiliation which the term 'eating humble pie' now painfully describes. The 'umbles' of the deer are constantly the perquisites of the gamekeeper. ~ A.G., Ecclesfield, 8 Dec 1849

¶ Umble (or entrail) pie may have been humble but it was good enough for Pepys. In his *Diary*, 8 July 1663, he records that 'Mrs Turner came in and did bring us an umble pie hot out of her oven, extraordinary good...'

HYDROPHOBIA: Were sufferers smothered between feather-beds?

Q. I can recollect, when I was a boy, to have been much surprised and horrified with accounts that old people gave me, that it was the practice in decided cases of *rabies canina* to suffocate the unfortunate patient between feather-beds. Perhaps some of your readers may be able to state where mention is made of such treatment, or what could give rise to such an opinion in the public mind ? ~ Indagator, 3 Jan 1852

R. To prevent possible misconceptions I may state that the established practice of the medical profession in hydrophobia is the same as their duty prescribes in all other diseases, viz. to endeavour to find a cure, to lengthen life, and to diminish suffering. In popular talk, with which doctors have nothing to do, two ways of dealing with hydrophobic patients are mentioned. One is to smother them between two feather-beds, the other is to give them their quietus with a dose of laudanum. I never knew or heard of either being done, and sincerely hope they are fables. At all events no respectable medical man would allow them to be attempted, even with the sufferer's consent. Such an act would be MURDER, and all concerned in it, even by suggestion, would be liable to a criminal prosecution. If such things have really ever been done in this country, or in earnest suggested, I hope the instances will be communicated to your pages, authenticated with name, time, and place. But it is hardly to be credited that we are so little removed from barbarism. ~ William E. C. Nourse, 28 Bryanston Street, 28 Aug 1852

R2. In the *London Medical Journal* for 1787 it is stated that Henry Rider of Richmond was seized with hydrophobia on Friday 23 February 1787, having been bitten by a dog *eighteen months* before – that is, in August 1785. From the beginning of the attack on the Friday he was convinced of the nature of the disease, and that a fatal result was inevitable. On the Sunday (the 25th), at midday, he imagined he was to be smothered betwixt two feather-beds, and the medical gentleman in attendance adds: 'Every time I came to see him he apprehended it was to give the fatal order. No persuasion could remove this unhappy idea from his mind, and he evidently suppressed his complaints in order to conceal, as he supposed, from me the necessity of my proceeding to the last extremity.' Death put an end to the poor man's suffering on Monday the 26th, at 4 a.m.

The narrative is curious and is highly creditable to the skill and humanity of the professional attendant. ~ Λ, 28 Aug 1852

R3. When I first went to school at Eton, in 1794, I well remember a story, which all the boys believed, that the ostler at the Christopher Inn, when in the last stage of hydrophobia, was smothered under a feather-bed by his attendants, in order to put a termination to his sufferings. ~ Braybrooke, 28 Aug 1852

R4. Mrs Duff, wife of Lord Fife, then Colonel Duff, died of undoubted hydrophobia about the year 1806. It was induced by a bite *on the nose* from a favourite Newfoundland dog. The report was widely spread that she 'had to be smothered', which was of course groundless. ~ A.A.D., 28 Aug 1852

R5. I held a curacy in a somewhat uncivilised and rough district in the north. I know that this belief existed among the poor of that district, and I have little doubt that the act itself had been occasionally been put into practice. One of my parishioners, then a young man of twenty-five, had a large scar on his cheek. Asking him how it occurred, he said he had been bitten by a mad dog and that the bitten flesh had been cut out. He added that notwithstanding this cautionary proceeding he had been seized with hydrophobia and owed his life to the determination and love of his father. He explained that, when all hope seemed over, a consultation was held by the neighbours at his bedside, which resulted in a decision to smother him to 'put him out of his misery'. The neighbours, he said, were restrained by his father, and by sheer force, from carrying out their purpose, and were finally persuaded to 'give the lad a chance'. The man who told me this story alluded to the proposed smothering as a matter of course, and a common practice. Whether he actually was seized by hydrophobia, or whether dread of the disease induced the symptoms, or the simulation of the symptoms, I had no means of ascertaining. ~ E.W., 25 Sep 1852

R6. In proof of the fact that the practice of smothering hydrophobic patients was certainly carried on within living memory, I may cite the experience of a clergyman, a friend of mine. A good many years ago he was conversing with one of his parishioners who had survived two or three husbands, and, having occasion to mention the particulars of their deaths, she said, 'My first died in such and such a manner, *and my second we smothered.*' My friend was a little startled at so quiet an avowal of murder, but it appeared, on examination, that the man had been seized with hydrophobia, and his widow evidently considered that he had met with the regular treatment for that malady. ~ H.W., 6 Nov 1852

R7. I forward the enclosed cutting from the *Irish Times* of Saturday 18 May 1861:

CASE OF HYDROPHOBIA – MELANCHOLY OCCURRENCE
A fatal case of hydrophobia is reported from the neighbourhood of Newport, County Tipperary, the victim being a fine young woman, the daughter of a farmer of that locality. It appears that, while engaged in some outdoor employment, a neighbour's dog attacked and bit her in the hand, and she soon evinced symptoms of the consequence. Hydrophobia in its most fearful aspect set in, and she became so hopelessly mad that it was found necessary to terminate her sufferings by smothering her between two beds. The dog was subsequently shot.

~ J.G.M., 15 June 1861

JIB, NOT LIKING THE CUT OF

N. 'The cut of the jib', or make and fashion of the foremost sail of a ship or other vessel, often indicates her character. At sea, especially in time of war, when every strange sail is anxiously and closely scanned, the peculiarities of rigging, the length and proportions of masts and yards, and the shape and disposition of sails are all carefully noted. When the result of such examination is unsatisfactory, the officer of the deck pronounces the stranger 'suspicious', while Jack expresses the same idea by telling his shipmates on the forecastle that he doesn't 'like the cut of that fellow's jib'. On shore he uses the phrase with a similar meaning, applying it to external peculiarities of countenance or expression, regarded as indications of character. ~ Vertaur, 16 Dec 1854

JUSTICE, POETIC

N. It has often been remarked that a kind of poetical justice has been manifested in the Nemesis which has overtaken those persons who have devised modes of punishment, torture, or death, for their fellow creatures. The Scriptures assure us that 'All they that take the sword shall perish with the sword' (Matthew 26:52); that 'Whatsoever a man soweth, that shall he also reap' (Galatians 6:7); and that 'Whoso diggeth a pit shall fall therein' (Proverbs 26:27). They afford us, moreover, an illustration in the case of 'the wicked Haman', who expiated his enmity to the Jewish people on the 'gallows, fifty cubits high, which he had made for Mordecai' (Esther 7:9).

In Shakespeare, too, the message of retributive justice recurs. In *Hamlet*, Act 3, scene 4, we read 'For 'tis the sport to have the engineer / Hoist with his own petar', while in *Macbeth*, Act 2, scene 7, we hear of 'Bloody instructions which, being taught, return / To plague the inventor. This even-handed justice / Commends the ingredients of our poisoned chalice / To our own lips.'

Turning to legend, that of Perillus of Athens at once suggests itself, for this artisan was condemned by the tyrant Phalaris to be roasted in the brazen bull which he had himself constructed for the torture of others.

In history, in the fifteenth century the following instance may be cited: 'The Bishop of Verdun was the inventor of the

A Petard

A small bomb; from the French *péter*, to break wind

iron cages in the time of Louis XI of France, and he himself became the very first tenant, being shut up in his own invention for eleven years.' (*Lambeth and the Vatican*)

Early in the sixteenth century we find the case of Ludovico Sforza, Duke of Milan, who, it is said, was crushed to death – he died in 1508 – in a collapsible metallic prison of his own invention.

Late in the seventeenth century we have the Parisian poisoner Sainte-Croix, who inadvertently let fall the precautionary glass mask which he was in the habit of wearing, and so lost his life through the noxious fumes of the destructive preparation he was compounding. His sudden fate led also to the downfall of that notorious participator in his crimes, his pupil and mistress, the Marquise de Brinvilliers.

In Italy we find another instance of death by poison with that infamous monster, Pope Alexander VI. According to Leopold von Ranke, in his *History of the Popes of Rome*, 'He once meditated taking off one of the richest of his cardinals by poison; his intended victim, however, contrived, by means of presents, promises, and prayers, to win over the head cook, and the dish which had been prepared for the cardinal was placed before the Pope. He thus died of the poison he had prepared for another.' Voltaire, however, throws discredit upon this legend, of which he gives a somewhat different version.

Our own history affords the next example: 'Richard Coeur de Lion, King of England, died of a wound received from a crossbow, while besieging a small castle in France. It has been remarked that he met his death by a weapon introduced into warfare by himself, much to the displeasure of the warriors of his time, who said that "Heretofore brave men fought hand to hand, but now the bravest and noblest might be brought down by a cowardly knave lurking behind a tree."' (*Saturday Magazine*, 30 March 1833)

Next we come to the notorious witchfinder, Matthew Hopkins. Bishop Hutchinson, in his *Historical Essay concerning Witchcraft* (1718), says that Hopkins went on seeking out supposed witches and putting them to trial by swimming 'till some gentleman, out of indignation at the barbarity, took him, and tied his own thumbs and toes, as he used to tie others; and when he was put into the water, he himself swam as they did. This cleared the country of him, and it was a great deal of pity that they did not think of the experiment sooner.'

Advancing to more recent history, and returning to France, the case of Dr Guillotin would serve me well – but truth is strong, and I must give it up. Neither did he invent the instrument which now bears his name, though he certainly recommended its adoption, nor did he become one of its victims, but died peaceably in his bed some twenty years later, his passing regretted by all who knew him. His character is represented as mild and benevolent. His unhelpful case notwithstanding, in no period, perhaps, is retributive fate more clearly to be discerned than in the ends which awaited the sanguinary leaders of the Revolution. The case of Danton, for one, may be cited, who was condemned by a decree of the Extraordinary Tribunal of which he was the originator.

I hope that these few instances strung together may serve sufficiently to point the moral of the poet: 'And thus the whirligig of time brings in his revenges...' (*Twelfth Night*, Act 5, scene 1) ~ William Bates, Birmingham, 27 Oct 1855

R. About thirty years ago a new city jail was built at Norwich. A gallows was made by a man of the name of Stratford, to be used when required over the gateway. Within a few years this Stratford was hung on it for poisoning. He thus became his own first victim. ~ J.S.M.M., Norwich, 12 Jan 1856

¶ John Stratford, the Norfolk Dumpling Poisoner, was a blacksmith who forged the ironwork of the gallows during the rebuilding of Norwich jail between 1824 and 1828. He was executed on 17 August 1829.

The tradition that Matthew Hopkins fell victim to his own 'sink and drown or swim and be proved guilty' test was firmly established by the time Samuel Butler wrote of him in the second part of *Hudibras* (1664): 'Who after prov'd himself a witch / And made a rod for his own breech.' However, there is no direct evidence of such a comeuppance, and, if it did occur, it does not seem to have proved fatal: fellow witch-hunter John Stearne recorded that Hopkins's end came 'after a long sick-nesse of consumption'. His burial is recorded in the register of Mistley with Manningtree, Essex, on 12 August 1647.

Matthew Hopkins
Witch Finder Generall

KANT'S WIG AND OTHER RELICS

N. I made the following cutting from a newspaper many years ago and am at fault in not having taken a note either of the date when, or the newspaper in which, the article appeared. It is, however, very curious.

ANTIQUITIES AND CURIOSITIES

The collectors of relics will perhaps feel interested in the subjoined statement of the prices paid within the last few years for various objects of historical curiosity.

- The Prayer Book used by King Charles I, when on the scaffold, was sold in London in 1825 for 110 guineas.

- A fragment of the coat worn by Louis XVI at the altar was announced in the catalogue of a sale in 1829, and would probably have fetched a very high price, but it was withdrawn.

- A tooth of Sir Isaac Newton was sold in 1815 for the sum of £330. The nobleman by whom it was purchased had it set in a ring, which he constantly wears.

- A propos teeth, it may be mentioned that, at the time when the bodies of Heloisa and Abelard were removed to the Petits-Augustins, an English gentleman offered 100,000 francs for one of Heloisa's teeth.[1]

- At the sale of the library of Dr Soarman at Stockholm in 1820 the skull of Descartes sold for a considerable sum.

[1] The celebrated twelfth-century lovers Heloise and Abelard were originally interred at the Paraclete, a convent founded by Abelard some sixty miles east of Paris. The subsequent history of their remains is uncertain and disputed, but during the French Revolution they were reputedly removed for protection to the convent of the Petits-Augustins in the capital.

- Voltaire's cane was some time ago sold in Paris for 500 francs.

- An old wig which had belonged to Kant, the German philosopher, was sold, after his death in 1804, for 200 francs.

- A waistcoat belonging to J. J. Rousseau was sold for 950 francs, and his metal watch for 500 francs.

- In 1822 Sterne's wig was sold at a public auction in London for 200 guineas.

- The hat worn by Napoleon at the Battle of Eylau was sold in Paris in 1835 for 1,920 francs. It was put up at 500 francs, and there were thirty-two bidders.

- There is at Pézanas an armchair which is said to have belonged to Molière. Its form bears evidence of its antiquity. [It] is now about to be sold in Paris, and will no doubt soon fill a place in some collection of curiosities.

~ G.N., 4 Sep 1858

R. On the matter of Kant's wig I offer the following from Victor Hugo's *Littérature et Philosophie Melées*: 'Kant's wig was sold for 30,000 florins at the time of his death, and no more than 1,200 crowns was paid for it at the last Leipzig fair. This proves, in my opinion, that the rage for Kant and his ideology is abating in Germany. This wig, in its changing price, may be considered a thermometer of the progress of Kantism.' The date of publication is April 1819, and it was reprinted eighteen years later without any appearance of joke or correction of error. Is the statement to be found elsewhere? In 1819 Victor Hugo was a young man and perhaps not very rigid in verifying historical facts. ~ H.B.C., United University Club, 11 Aug 1860

¶ Unfortunately no corroboration was forthcoming, but it is known that on Kant's death there was a brisk trade in mementoes: his silver hair was braided into rings and sold, and high sums were paid for his tobacco pouch, which he had used for twenty years, and for his three-cornered hat, which was purchased by an Englishman.

Immanuel Kant, worrying perhaps about
the future auction value of his wig

KETCH, JACK: His pay negotiations

N. In a collection of anecdotes, published anonymously and printed by Milner & Sowerby of Halifax, I lately found the following:

WAGES OF JACK KETCH

During the shrievalty of Sir Richard Phillips no execution
took place in London, but, on some culprits being ordered to
be whipped, Jack Ketch came to the sheriff and plainly told
him he might do it himself. 'What do you mean by such
conduct?' exclaimed the sheriff. 'Why, to tell your honour the
truth,' said Jack, 'you have made my place worth nothing at
all. I used to get a few suits of clothes after a sessions, but for
many months I have had no job but whipping, and that puts
nothing in a man's pocket.' 'Well, but Mr Ketch, you are paid
your salary of a guinea a week by the under-sheriffs, and this

seems sufficient, as your office is now become almost a sinecure.' 'Why, as to the matter of that,' said Ketch, 'do you see, sir, I've half a guinea a week to pay my man, and therefore only half a guinea for myself; and if it wasn't for a hanging job now and then in the country, where there's few in my line, I should lately have been quite ruined. I used to get clothes, and very often some gentleman would tip me a few guineas for civility, before he was turned off. Howsoever, I'll go on so no longer. So, if your honour won't raise my salary, I mean no offence, but you must perform this whipping yourself.' There was reason in the man's argument, and, as there seemed no alternative, the sheriff demanded his expectation. 'A guinea and a half, your honour. Without the customary perquisites, I can't fill the office for less; and no man knows his duty better. I've tied up many a good fellow in my time, and never had the least complaint.' 'Well, well, Mr Ketch,' said the sheriff, 'as I hope to be able to continue to deprive you of your favourite perquisites, you shall have the guinea and a half.' 'Then God bless your honour!' exclaimed the fellow; and he and his man began to prepare their whips in high spirits...

~ H. Martin, Halifax, 13 Oct 1855

¶ Jack Ketch became the common hangman of London at some point between 1666 and 1678, gaining particular notoriety from his botched executions of Lord Russell in 1683 and of the Duke of Monmouth two years later. In Monmouth's case, according to John Evelyn, Ketch took 'five chopps' before he had the head off, which 'so incens'd the people that, had he not been guarded and got away, they would have torne him to pieces'. In January 1686 Ketch was himself committed to Bridewell after falling out with the sheriff. He was released and reinstated in May, only to die later in the year.

There is a glancing contemporary reference to his successful pay negotiations in *Butler's Ghost* (1682) by Thomas D'Urfey:

> Till Ketch observing he was chous'd [cheated],
> And in his profits much abus'd,
> In open hall the tribune dunn'd,
> To do his office, or refund.

LEECHES: Can they predict the weather?

Q. In several large farmhouses in Lancashire they use the following as a weather indicator. A leech is put into a clear glass bottle full of water, the water being renewed every second day. If the day is to be wet, the leech lies close to the bottom of the bottle; if the day is to be showery, it occupies a place about the centre (upwards) of the bottle; but if the day is to be fine, the creeping thing lies on the surface of the water. A gentleman in this town tells me that he has tried this for the last seven months and found it accurately correct – ten times more so, he says, than any glass, patent or otherwise. Is this thing known and used elsewhere? ~ S. Redmond, Liverpool, 30 June 1860

R. I beg to refer your correspondent to a letter in *The Life and Posthumous Writings of William Cowper* by William Hayley. It is dated 10 November 1787 and is addressed to Lady Hesketh: 'Yesterday it thundered, last night it lightened, and at three this morning I saw the sky as red as a city in flames could have made it. I have a leech in a bottle that foretells all these prodigies and convulsions of nature... W.C.'

I have kept a leech in my room for three years past and have noticed the same results as mentioned by the poet Cowper. ~ Alfred Hill, 4 Aug 1860

R2. In the Great Exhibition of 1851 at the Crystal Palace was a 'Tempest Prognosticator, or atmospheric electromagnetic telegraph, conducted by animal instinct'. It was designed and invented by Dr George Merryweather, who also published an *Essay* explanatory of the contrivance by which leeches were induced to ring a bell as a signal of an approaching storm. ~ Joseph Rix, St Neots, 18 Aug 1860

¶ The happily named George Merryweather spent much of 1850 perfecting his Tempest Prognosticator, or Leech Barometer. It consisted of a dozen pint bottles arranged in a circle on a stand with a single large bell above them. Each bottle contained a leech and an inch and a half of rainwater and the bottles were placed close to each other so that the leeches would not feel, in Merryweather's words, 'the affliction of solitary confinement'. The theory was that, agitated by the electromagnetic changes in the atmosphere preceding a storm, the creatures would climb up the glass and try to escape from the bottles – at which point they would dislodge pieces of whalebone which were linked by wires to small hammers, and the hammers would then sound upon the bell. Merryweather dubbed his leeches 'a jury of philosophical councillors' – the more of them that climbed the glass to trigger ringing upon the bell, the greater the probability that a storm was on its way. He had high hopes for his device and tried to persuade the government to establish a series of leech warning stations around the coastline of Britain, to no avail.

With its ornate design inspired by Indian temples the original Prognosticator received considerable attention at the Great Exhibition. It has since disappeared, but two replicas exist: the first was made for the Festival of Britain in 1951 and is now in the Whitby Museum, of which Merryweather was curator, and a second has recently been made for display at Barometer World in Okehampton, Devon.

LIVERS, WHITE: A sign of murderers and cowards?

Q. Can any correspondent give some information as to the popular superstition of white livers? In a recent account of poisonings in France by a woman named Hélène Jegado, it is stated that, though for a long time she was not suspected to be an actual murderess, yet 'the frequency of deaths in the families by whom she was engaged excited a suspicion among the peasantry that there was something in her nature fatal to those that were near her; and they said that her liver was white, it being believed in that part of France that persons who are dangerous have white livers'. In the Midland counties here there is a similar saying among the lower classes, and I have heard it said, of an individual who had married and lost several wives by death, that he had a white liver. A young woman once told me that she had been advised not to marry a certain suitor because he had a white liver and she would be dead within a year, while 'white-livered rascal' is a common term of reproach in Gloucestershire. What is the origin and explanation of this? ~ Ambrose Florence, Worcester, 7 Feb 1852

R. The expression 'white-livered' has its origin in the auspices taken by the Greeks and Romans before battle, of which the examination of the liver and entrails of the animal victim formed an essential part. If the liver was the usual shape, and a blood-red colour, the omen was favourable; if pale or livid, it was an augury of defeat. The transposition from the victim to the enquirer was easy, and a dastard leader, likely to sustain disgrace, was called 'a man of a white liver'. ~ Richard F. Littledale, Dublin, 28 Feb 1852

R2. The superstition that a man or woman who survives several wives or husbands has a white liver is common among the lower orders in Lancashire. ~ P.P., 3 Apr 1852

¶ It is thought that the Brittany maidservant Hélène Jegado was responsible for over thirty arsenical poisonings between 1833 and her arrest in 1851. She was executed by guillotine in February 1852.

While ancient auspices explain the association between white livers and cowardice, the idea that it was dangerous to marry or be close to someone possessing such a liver may derive from another old belief, that the liver was the seat of love. In *The Merry Wives of Windsor*, Act 2, scene 1, Pistol speaks of Falstaff loving Mistress Ford 'with liver burning hot'. Conversely, someone with a cold, bloodless, un-Falstaffian liver might be considered deficient in human affection.

LONDON STREET CHARACTERS: What becomes of them?

Q. Mr Dickens's graphic description of the Court of Chancery in his new work, *Bleak House*, contains the following sketch:

> Standing on a seat at the side of the hall is a little mad old woman in a squeezed bonnet, who is always in court expecting some incomprehensible judgement to be given in her favour. Some say she really is, or was, a party to a suit: but no one knows for certain, because no one cares. She carries some small litter in a reticule which she calls her documents: principally consisting of paper matches and dry lavender.

There is a diminutive creature, somewhat answering this description, who limps on a stick and one leg that is shorter than the other, all the early morning in the still courts of the Temple. She seems to be waiting the result of some consultation, before she reappears, as is her wont, in Westminster Hall. The story commonly told of her is that she was ruined and crazed by the slow torture of a lawsuit. Is anything known of her real history?

What were the fortunes and fate of the poor female lunatic, who was called *Rouge et Noir* from her crape sables and painted cheeks, and who used to loiter every day about the Royal Exchange at four o'clock, and seemed to depend for subsistence upon the stray bounty of the money-changers? It was said that she had a brother who was hanged for forgery, and that this drove her mad.

About thirty years ago there might be heard any morning, in the smaller streets of the city, a cry of 'Dolls' bedsteads!' It came from a lean lame man on a crutch who wore an apron and carried miniature bedsteads for sale. Of this man it was generally reported that he was implicated in the Cato Street Conspiracy,[1] and had turned king's evidence.

Charles Lamb describes a character whom it is also impossible to forget: 'A well known figure, or part of the figure of a man, who used to guide his upper half over the pavements of London,

---

[1] A plot to murder Lord Liverpool's cabinet in February 1820.

wheeling along with most ingenious celerity upon a machine of wood... He was of a robust make, with a florid sailor-like complexion, and his head was bare to the storm and sunshine... The accident which brought him low took place during the riots of 1780.'[1] Is this all that is known of this half-giant?

When the old Houses of Parliament were standing[2] there used to be at one of the entrances a dwarf, long past middle age, who persisted in offering his services as a guide. His countenance was full of grave wisdom, quite Socratic in expression, but I believe he was an idiot. Does anything of interest attach to the remembrance of him?

And, lastly, what became of Billy Waters?

Do these street heroes die the death of common men, in bed, and with friends near them? Or do they generally find their fate at last in the workhouse or the gaol, and get buried no one knows when, or by whom, or where?

I cannot agree with Mr Dickens that 'no one cares'. Indeed, Mr Dickens's own philosophy and practice are at variance in this matter. He makes his own sketch of the 'little mad old woman' because he feels that it will interest. How much more would the original, could we get at it! But the truth is that these people are as mysterious as the fireman's dog. They 'come like shadows, so depart', leaving behind them on many minds ineffaceable impressions.[3] Indeed, some us could confess with

[1] The anti-Catholic Gordon Riots which lasted six days and caused widespread damage in London.

[2] Much of the Palace of Westminster was destroyed by fire in 1834.

[3] In the early 1830s a stray dog became famous for attending fires wherever they broke out across London, notably at Westminster in 1834. He was fed by firemen, who clubbed together to buy him a fine collar inscribed 'Stop me not, but onward let me jog, / For I am CHANCE, the London firemen's dog', but for all their kindness he would not stay with any of them for long. His death on 10 October 1835 was much lamented and his body, having been stuffed, was thereafter kept in a glass case in a place of honour in Watling Street fire station.

shame that the feathered cocked hat and fiddle of Billy Waters had survived the memory of a thousand things of real importance – which could hardly be, were there not some psychological force in these street characters, an inexplicable interest and attraction. ~ Alfred Gatty, 20 Mar 1852

R. I believe more than one of the courts to be haunted by persons who may have suggested Mr Dickens's 'little old lady'. Over twenty years ago a female of about fifty years was a constant attendant on the Court of Queen's Bench *in banco*: I never saw her at a *nisi prius* sitting.[1] She was meanly but tidily dressed, quiet and unobtrusive in manners, but much gratified by notice from any barrister. It was said she had been ruined by a suit, but I could not learn anything authentic about her, though I several times spoke and listened to her, partly from curiosity and partly from the pleasure which she showed at being spoken to. Her thoughts seemed fixed upon the business of the day, and I never extracted more than 'Will they take motions?' – 'Will it come on next?' – 'I hope he will bring it on today!' But who was 'he', or what was 'it', I could not learn, and when I asked she would pause as if to think, and, pointing to the bench, say, 'That's Lord Tenterden.' I have seen her rise, as about to address the court, when the judges were going out, and look mortified as if she felt neglected. I cannot say when she disappeared, but I do not remember having seen her for the last eight years.

I have heard that an old woman frequented Doctors' Commons[2] about seven years ago. She appeared to listen to the arguments, but was reserved and mopish if spoken to. She often threw herself in the way of one of the leading advocates, and always addressed him in the same words: 'Dr —, I am *virgo intacta.*'

[1] *In banco*: literally 'on the bench', used to indicate full sittings of superior courts. *Nisi prius*: literally 'unless previously', used to indicate civil trials in the crown court or assize court.

[2] The informal name for the College of Advocates and Doctors of Law, near St Paul's Cathedral, which housed the ecclesiastical and admiralty courts.

The sailor-looking man described by Charles Lamb lasted a long time. I remember him in Fleet Street and the Strand when I was a boy. His name was Samuel Horsey, and he was known as the King of the Beggars. Among the stories told of him one was that his ample earnings enabled him to keep two wives, and, what is more, to keep them from quarrelling. He presided in the evenings at a 'cadgers' club', planted at the head of the table, with a wife on either side. ~ H.B.C., United University Club, 17 Apr 1852

SAMUEL HORSEY

¶ Billy Waters was a celebrated black street singer and fiddler. With his wooden leg, military uniform, and hat decked with ribbons and feathers he was a familiar figure outside the Adelphi Theatre in the Strand. In 1822 he appeared there on stage as himself in *Life in London*, but he died penniless in St Giles's workhouse in the following year.

LOVELL, LORD: The mysterious fate of

Q. I find the following strange tale relating to Minster Lovell in Oxfordshire, the old seat of the Viscounts Lovell, in the *Monthly Magazine* for April 1812:

> Francis, the last lord of this family and chamberlain to King Richard III, was one of the noblemen who raised an army in the beginning of the reign of Henry VII to support the pretensions of the impostor Lambert Simnel. The decisive battle which gave security to Henry's usurpation was fought near the village of Stoke, on the banks of the River Trent in Nottinghamshire. The slaughter of the insurgent army was immense, especially among the officers, an uncommon proportion of whom were slain. The Lord Lovell, however, escaped by swimming his horse across the river and retiring, by unfrequented roads well known to him, into Oxfordshire.
>
> As the story proceeds, he took care to arrive at the gates of his castle in the dead of night and so disguised as to be known to no one except a single domestic on whose fidelity he could rely. Before the return of day he retired to a subterranean recess, of which the faithful servant retained the key, and there he remained for several months in safety and concealment; but, the estates being seized by the king's orders, the castle dismantled, and the inhabitants dispersed by authority, the unfortunate prisoner was left to perish from hunger in the place of his voluntary imprisonment.
>
> So late as in the last century, when the small remains of this once stately edifice were pulled down to make use of the materials, the vault was discovered, and the unfortunate nobleman in it, seated in a chair, as he had died. So completely had the external air been excluded by rubbish at the time of dismantling the building that his apparel, which was gorgeous in the extreme, and a prayer book lying before him upon a table, were discovered entire. On the free admission of air, it was said, the whole crumbled into dust. It is not improbable that the sanctuary was considerably profaned by the rude hands of the persons who discovered it...

Can this story be confirmed? And what was the exact date of the demolition of the old edifice?

It may not be uninteresting here to quote what Francis Bacon says concerning the fate of Lord Lovell, or Lovel, in his *History of King Henry VII* (1622): 'There went a report that he fled and swam over Trent on horseback, but could not recover the farther side by reason of the steepness of the bank, and so was drowned in the river. But another report leaves him not there, but [says] that he lived long after in a cave or vault.' ~ James Gairdner, 22 Mar 1856

R. In *The Last of the Plantagenets* (1829), William Heseltine gives a graphic description of the end of Francis, the ninth Lord Lovel, saying he had himself 'dressed in his armour as he was wont to be in the days of his power, and placed in a chair before a table, so that when they in after times shall haply find his wasted limbs and mouldered form in this secret place, which had been his cell and sepulchre, they may know who and what he was when living, nor confound the reliques of a Lovel and a soldier with the ashes of the ignoble dead!' The narrative adds that, being in a weak and exhausted state, he died soon after and was left in that position by his attendant, who escaped by a secret passage.

The book itself is a romance, but a note at page 215 says that the story of the body's discovery rests on the witness and authority of John Manners, third Duke of Rutland, as recorded in a letter from William Cowper, Esq., clerk of the parliament, dated Hertingfordbury Park, 9 August 1737. ~ Simon Ward, 1 Jan 1859

¶ Cowper's letter is given in Thomas Banks's *Dormant and Extinct Baronage of England*:

On the 6th of May 1728 the present Duke of Rutland related in my hearing that about twenty years then before, viz. in 1708, upon occasion of new laying a chimney at Minster Luvel, there was discovered a large vault or room underground, in which was the entire skeleton of a man, as having been sitting at a table, which was before him, with a book, paper, pen, etc., etc. In another part of a room lay a cap, all much mouldered and decayed. Which the family, and others, judged to be this Lord Luvel, whose exit has hitherto been so uncertain.

Banks accepts the story and adds that this strange death marked 'a melancholy period to the life and fortunes of one of the greatest and most active noblemen of the era wherein he lived. To complete the tragedy, King Henry VII, aspiring after the vast inheritance of this family, by an act of attainder confiscated the whole estate, then inferior to few or none in the kingdom.'

MARAT THE REVOLUTIONARY: Did he rob the Ashmolean?

Q. There is a tradition that this infamous revolutionary character was once French master at the Warrington Academy. Is there sufficient evidence of this? Is it alluded to in any life of Marat? There is a walk at Warrington called to this day Marat's Walk.
~ E.C.R.D., 9 Jan 1858

R. In the *Encyclopaedia Britannica* (8th edition, 1857) it is said of Marat: 'We find him in Edinburgh in 1774, supporting himself by giving lessons in French.' At about the same time his first publication, *The Chains of Slavery*, made its appearance, coming out anonymously in the same year. The title is very illustrative of the author's subsequent history and character: *The Chains of Slavery, a Work wherein the Clandestine and Villainous Attempts of Princes to ruin Liberty are pointed out, and the dreadful Scenes of Despotism disclosed, to which is prefixed an Address to the Electors of Great Britain, in order to draw their timely Attention to the Choice of proper Representatives in the next Parliament.* ~ G., Edinburgh, 16 July 1859

R2. I extract the following notice of M. Marat from the London *Star* newspaper of 4 March 1793. It is under the heading 'Glasgow' and may prove interesting to your readers:

From an investigation lately taken at Edinburgh it is said that Marat, the celebrated orator of the French National Convention, the humane, the mild, the gentle Marat, is the same person who, a few years ago, taught tambouring[1] in this city under the name of John White. His conduct while he was here was equally unprincipled, if not as atrocious, as it has been since his elevation to the legislatorship. After contracting debts to a very considerable amount he absconded, but was apprehended at Newcastle and brought back to this city, where he was imprisoned. He soon afterwards executed a summons of *cessio bonorum*[2] against his creditors, in the prosecution of which it was found that he had once taught in the Academy at Warrington; that he left Warrington for Oxford, where, after some time, he found means to rob the museum of a number of gold coins and medallions; that he was traced to Ireland, apprehended at an assembly there in the

---

[1] Embroidery using a circular frame called a tambour.

[2] A voluntary surrender of goods by a debtor to his creditors. Unless the property surrendered was sufficient it did not constitute a discharging of the debt, but it did secure the debtor from arrest.

character of a German count, brought back to this country, tried, convicted, and sentenced to some years' hard labour on the Thames. He was refused a *cessio*, and his creditors, tired of detaining him in gaol after a confinement of several months, set him at liberty. He then took up his residence in this neighbourhood, where he continued about nine months, and took his final leave of this country about the beginning of the year 1787. He was very ill-looked, of a diminutive size, a man of uncommon vivacity, of a very turbulent disposition, and possessed of a very uncommon share of legal knowledge.

It is not yet too late to prove the truth or falsehood of many of the accusations brought against Marat in this extract. ~ W.B.C., Liverpool, 24 Sep 1859

R3. I am happy to provide W.B.C. with a clue to further investigation. My grandfather, Edward Creswell, writing home from Christ Church, Oxford, thus mentions Marat (for so it is to be inferred after comparison with the extract from the *Star*), under the date of 12 February 1776:

I shall now tell you a piece of news respecting a robbery which was committed here lately. The particulars as I can learn are as follow. About a week ago a native of France, who calls himself M. Le Maitre and was formerly a teacher in the Warrington Academy, being invited here by a gentleman of this college to teach the French language, came over, and met with great encouragement in the university, but, happening to get acquainted with Mr Milnes, a gentleman of Corpus Christi College, who is the keeper of the museum and several other natural curiosities, he prevailed on him by repeated importunities to let him have a view of them. Accordingly they both went together, and, after M. Le Maitre had viewed them a great while, Mr Milnes, from the suspicions he entertained of his behaviour, under pretence of getting rid of him, told him that several gentlemen were waiting at the door for admittance, and that he must now go out immediately. But the Frenchman excused himself by saying he would retire into the other apartments, and, whilst the strangers that were admitted were surveying the curiosities with more than ordinary attention, this artful villain retired from them and concealed himself under a dark staircase that led into the street, where he stayed till the company were gone out. After which he stole away medals and other coins to the amount of £200 and upwards, and got clear off with his booty... I am sorry I have not time to tell you a few more particulars concerning this transaction, but shall defer it till I know further about it.

In an undated second letter, bound between two others dated 22 January 1777 and 5 March 1777 respectively, is the following: 'I shall now tell you a little Oxford news. The Frenchman who robb'd our museum was tried at our late assizes, and found guilty, and sentenced to work on the River Thames for five years.' ~ S. F. Creswell, The School, Tonbridge, Kent, 15 Sep 1860

R4. The following is extracted from a letter of Charles Harford, Esq., dated Stapelton, 26 November 1822, to the Rev. Samuel Seyer, author of the *Memoirs of Bristol*:

The infamous Marat, stabb'd by Charlotte Cordé, once disgraced this city,[1] and was unfortunately released from Newgate by the Society for Relief of Persons confined for Small Debts. This I know from the late Mr James Ireland of Brislington, who told my father that, being at Paris, I forget what year, he went to the National Assembly, and took his servant with him, who, on seeing Marat rise to speak, assured his master with astonishment the man was the very person to whom he had often taken money and victuals when a prisoner in Bristol gaol... I will add, my father saw this villain in 1772 at Warminster.[2] He afterwards was a hairdresser at Oxford; robbed the Ashmolean Museum; was taken in Dublin, but convicted at Oxford, and sent to Woolwich to the hulks. This I prove thus: in 1776 Mr Lloyd of Newbury and the late Mr J. S. Harford of Blaize Castle went to London, where, among other sights, they visited Woolwich; and Mr Lloyd recognised

[1] Bristol.

[2] This seems to be a slip or misreading for Warrington.

his Warminster tutor as one of the convicts wheeling a wheelbarrow and pointed him out to Mr Harford.[1]

~ C.J.P., 18 Oct 1862

¶ Jean Paul Marat was born in Switzerland in 1743 and, from the age of sixteen, travelled widely. By 1768 he was in London, lodging in St Martin's Lane, styling himself 'Doctor', and running into debt. Much of the next decade of his life is shrouded in uncertainty, but, in addition to spells in Edinburgh and Newcastle, it is known that he was in Dublin for a time and that, along with the works referred to in *N & Q*, he published medical essays on eye disease and gleets. On 24 June 1777 he was appointed to the medical staff of the Comte d'Artois in Paris and consequently returned to France, but he did not remain in the position for long and it is possible that, during the 1780s, he was again in England.

The Oxford theft of 1776 was widely noticed in contemporary newspapers, the perpetrator being described as 'a Swiss hairdresser' and 'Le Maitre, alias Mara'. The scene of the crime was the old Ashmolean in Broad Street, a building which now houses the Museum of the History of Science. The 'Mr Milnes' referred to by Edward Creswell was probably William Miles, who testified at the subsequent trial. Miles was not keeper of the museum but a 'servitor' or acting caretaker.

Le Maitre seems to have been fairly cunning. He waited for a Saturday evening, so that the loss would not be discovered until Monday morning, and fled to London on the Sunday. There he let it be known he was leaving for the Continent, but instead travelled to Norwich, where he disposed of some of the medals. Then he headed west, via Lichfield and Liverpool to Dublin, where he was arrested towards the end of February as a result of the circulation of his not-very-flattering description: 'a short thin man, squints very much, his black hair tied, marked with the smallpox, stoops a little'. This is not that far removed

[1] If the man recognised was the Ashmolean thief the visit must have taken place in 1777 or later.

from the description of Marat during his English years given in the diary of Joseph Farington: 'a little man, slender, but well made, of a yellow aspect and had a quick eye. He had a great deal of motion, seldom keeping his body or limbs still.'

Having spent a year in prison in Dublin and then in Oxford, Le Maitre was brought to trial at the Oxford assizes on 5 March 1777. He was convicted of grand larceny and sentenced to five years on the hulks lying off Woolwich dockyard, where, as his sentence records, he was to be 'kept to hard labour in the raising sand, soil, and gravel from and cleansing the River Thames'. He arrived on the hulks on the evening of 15 April, but may not have been there long, for within a few days an escape occurred, recorded in the *Annual Register* under 23 April 1777:

> One day last week the ballast lighter working on the Essex coast was drove over the river to Woolwich by the high wind, when fourteen of the convicts rose upon their keepers, cut one of them terribly in the shoulder, and made their escape. A naval officer, meeting them at Greenwich, persuaded eight to return to their duty, but the other six have not yet been heard of...

But was Le Maitre really the future revolutionary? The charge has been dismissed with scorn by Marat's defenders as a piece of scurrilous anti-Jacobin propaganda, just as it has been greeted with delight by his detractors, who have seen such a criminal history as being much of a piece with his later career. Few in either camp have bothered to sift the detail of the evidence. Perhaps the most careful and authoritative consideration remains that carried out by the historian J. M. Thompson in the *English Historical Review* in the early 1930s. He concluded that the scattered evidence proved 'beyond reasonable doubt that the Warrington tutor of 1772 was the Oxford thief and the Woolwich convict'. The difficulty then was to confirm the link between Marat and the Warrington Academy, but such confirmation had emerged in July 1922 – again in *Notes and Queries* – in the form of a letter from Andrew de Ternant:

My father, the late Victor de Ternant, about forty years ago purchased a copy of Marat's *Les Chaines de l'Esclavage* (Edinburgh, 1774, octavo) in a Lancashire town, with two letters addressed to Dr John Aikin inserted. In the letters Marat not only made proposals to Dr Aikin to become his authorised English translator, but also announced that his ambition was to become a naturalised Englishman, and a suitor for the hand of the doctor's sister...

Dr Aikin was at the time a young surgeon and had strong links to Warrington Academy – he had been a pupil there and his father was a senior tutor. As Thompson reasonably asked, 'How could Marat have become sufficiently acquainted with the Aikins to ask the brother to translate his books, and to suggest that the sister should become his wife, *except at Warrington*, during the years immediately preceding 1774?'

Unfortunately the de Ternant letters subsequently disappeared, and Thompson concluded that – for all the suggestive coincidences between the lives and movements of Marat and the Ashmolean thief – the final verdict had to be 'Not Proven'.

MARRIAGE 1: By proxy

Q. I find in William Stirling's *The Cloister Life of the Emperor Charles V* that Luis Mendez Quixada Manuel de Figueredo y Mendoza, the emperor's majordomo, was married to Donna Magdalena de Ulloa at Valladolid by proxy, he not being able to obtain leave of absence from Brussels. Are there any other instances of this in history? And is it allowed now in the Roman or Anglican churches? ~ Notsa, 21 Feb 1857

R. The historian Peter Heylin says that the Archduke Maximilian married Anne Duchess of Brittany by proxy, 'which marriage he consummated by a ceremony in those days unusual... For his ambassador, attended with a great train of lords and ladies, bared his leg unto the knee, and put the same within the sheets of the duchess, taking possession thereby of her bed and body.' But she afterwards married to Charles VIII, his divines holding 'that this pretended consummation was rather an invention of court than any way firm by the laws of the Church'. ~ R. W. Hackwood, 7 Mar 1857

¶ As a child Anne of Brittany (1476-1514) was promised by her father to the young Edward V, one of the Princes in the Tower, with a view to securing England as an ally in the long struggle to maintain Breton independence against French ambitions. Her proxy marriage to Maximilian of Austria, which took place at Rennes on 19 December 1490, was a later attempt in similar vein. It backfired dramatically: French troops advanced and laid siege to Rennes, where the 14-year-old Anne was, and Maximilian failed to come to her aid. As a result, and in the face of Austrian protestations, Anne married Charles VIII of France in the following year, thus bringing Brittany under the control of the French crown.

A few years later Prince Arthur, elder brother of Henry VIII, would go through three proxy marriages to Catherine of Aragon, with the Spanish ambassador representing Catherine, before his actual marriage to her in St Paul's in November 1501.

In May 1625 the marriage of Charles I of England to Henrietta Maria of France was celebrated in Paris with the Duc de Chevreuse acting as proxy for the bridegroom.

In March 1810 a proxy wedding took place at the church of St Augustine in Vienna between Marie Louise of Austria and Napoleon Bonaparte, who was busy elsewhere.

MARRIAGE 2: To the wrong heiress

Q. In the latter part of the last century Mr Haussoullier, a French Jew, married a Miss Trist of Totnes, an heiress. It appears, however, that he thought her to be the daughter of a gentleman of London of that name, and did not find out his error till after the marriage knot was tied. Where can I read the best account of this curious circumstance, and what became of the happy couple? ~ John Tuckett, Great Russell Street, 31 Jan 1863

R. Lewis John Marie Haussoullier was one of the fortune-hunters of the last century. He dined with others at Richardson's Coffee-house in Covent Garden, 18 January 1796, and drew a cheque for £21 upon Messrs Hammersley, for which Mr Richardson gave him the balance. This enabled him to set off with his most particular friend, Gilrary Pigott, to Bath, in pursuit of Miss Trist, the only child of a tailor in Surrey Street, Strand, supposed heiress to £40,000. On his arrival at Bath he carried off Miss Trist, and married her at Gretna Green; but on his return he found out that the young woman concerned was not the object of his pursuit, but Miss E. Ashford Trist, of Totnes, a young lady of good fortune, though not equal to that he had anticipated. He was naturalised in 1797, sold all her estates, broke her heart, and became as poor as ever. In 1811 he was stated to have been concerned in the poisoning of the horses at Newmarket. See 'An Act of Parliament for confirming and rendering effectual a Partition between Lewis John Marie Haussoullier, Esquire, and Tryphena Trist, Spinster, an Infant, of divers Manors, Boroughs, Lands, and Hereditaments, in the County of Devon, 1799.' The estates are very extensive and fully described. ~ Editor, 31 Jan 1863

R2. This ill-fated young lady died at Brighton on 5 March 1799, in the twenty-fourth year of her age, and was buried there. Her second name was not Ashford, but *Ayshford*, as descended from that very ancient family whose genealogical tree commences soon after the Conquest with Stephanus de Eisforde. ~ John A. C. Vincent, 3 Sep 1864

¶ Elizabeth Ayshford Trist was born on 31 January 1776, the eldest daughter of the Rev. Browse Trist. She had two younger sisters – Susanna, born *circa* 1780, and Tryphena, christened 15 July 1781 – but no brothers.

In 1791 Browse Trist died intestate having run up debts of nearly £9,000. His three young daughters inherited the debts and the family lands, but their aunt, Agnes Champernowne, was appointed their guardian and assumed control of the estate until they should come of age. Two years later Susanna Trist died aged only thirteen.

It was from this complicated family situation that the adventuring Haussoullier whisked Elizabeth away in 1796. The resulting marriage settlement brought him £10,000, raised by selling off her rights in much of her inheritance. A sizeable portion of this money was needed urgently to pay off his many creditors.

In 1797 Haussoullier became a British citizen, a step which, under the terms of the marriage settlement, made it possible for him to control his wife's estate. In the same year he and Elizabeth exhibited a bill in the High Court of Chancery against Agnes Champernowne and Tryphena Trist – so, almost as soon as she was married, Elizabeth was pitched into legal conflict with her aunt and younger sister.

The marriage produced two elaborately named children – Tryphena Angelica Elizabeth Trist Haussoullier, born *circa* 1797, and Guislain Walter Browse Trist Haussoullier, born *circa* 1798 – but Guislain died aged only six months and Tryphena, though still alive at the time of the Act of 1799, also died young.

As noted in *N & Q*, Elizabeth herself died early in 1799. In the same year – perhaps to boost his claim on what remained of her inheritance – Haussoullier assumed the name and arms of Trist and the melancholy saga drew to its close with the complicated private Act of Parliament which effected a final partition of the Trist estates between him and Tryphena, Browse Trist's only surviving daughter. The lands apportioned included an array of orchards, parks, moors, meadows, fields and quarry pits, amounting in all to something over 2,000 acres.

John Lewis Marie Trist (as he now was) returned to public notice in 1811. Lodging in Frith Street, Soho, he was rumoured to have conspired with Daniel Dawson to poison horses at Newmarket with a view to winning large sums on the Claret Stakes. Dawson was put on trial and condemned to death. Meanwhile Trist felt forced to issue a lengthy public denial

which was published in the *Sporting Magazine* of May 1812:
'My name has been dragged through almost every newspaper in
the kingdom,' he protested, 'as a participator in a deed which
from my soul I abhor.' He avoided prosecution, but Dawson
was hung on the drop of Cambridge Castle on 8 August 1812,
a crowd of over 12,000 flocking to the scene. On the scaffold,
according to the *Sporting Magazine*, the condemned man
'repeatedly declared that Mr Trist was innocent of all concern
in the business'.

MARRIAGE 3: Under the gallows

N. In *The Interesting Narrative of Olaudah Equiano, or Gustavus
Vassa, the African* (1789), it is stated that at New York, in 1784,
'A malefactor was to be executed on a gallows, but with a
condition that if any woman, having nothing on but her shift,
married the man under the gallows, his life was to be saved.
This extraordinary privilege was claimed; a woman presented
herself, and the marriage ceremony was performed.'

We find allusion to the same curious custom in a much
earlier work, Chastellain's *Chronique des Ducs de Bourgogne*. It
appears that in 1468 Hernoul, son of John de la Hamaide, lord
of Haudion and Mainvault, cruelly murdered a citizen because
a canon, the brother of the murdered man, had given an adverse
decision on a disputed point at a game of tennis. Charles the
Bold, Duke of Burgundy and Count of Flanders, caused Hernoul
to be arrested, and swore by St George that he should die for
his crime '*long ou court*'[1] – by the rope or axe. In spite of the most
powerful intercessions, Charles adhered to his resolution, and, at
the time when Bruges was crowded with visitors to witness the
arrival of Margaret of York, sister to our Edward IV, Hernoul
was led out to be executed. Chastellain, a contemporary and
probably an eyewitness of the scene, tells us that the criminal
was bound on a cart with cords and dressed as richly as if he

[1] Long or short.

were going to a wedding. The cart was followed by a great crowd, and, to use the chronicler's own words, 'Among others there was a crowd of poor mad women who followed him, and who shouted and cried piteously, demanding to have him in marriage...' ~ W. Pinkerton, Hammersmith, 6 Oct 1855

R. The Hon. Daines Barrington, in his *Observations on the more Ancient Statutes* (1769), included among a number of legal vulgar errors 'the notion that a woman's marrying a man under the gallows will save him from execution'. Be that as it may, it is certain that in the fifteenth century this exemption had a quasi legal existence in France. We read as follows in the *Journal d'un Bourgeois de Paris*: 'On 10 January 1430 eleven men were led out in the market of Paris and the heads of ten of them were cut off. The eleventh was a very handsome young man of about twenty-four years. He was stripped and ready to be blindfolded, when a young girl, born in the Halles district, came forward boldly and asked for him. He was led back to the Châtelet, and later they were married.'

There is also said to have been an amusing instance in which the alternative of marriage was offered to a criminal in Picardy, but the condemned was a philosopher and seems to have thought that even life might be purchased at too dear a rate. Having weighed up the pros and cons, and noted that the woman offered was lame, he turned to the executioner and said: '*Attaque! Attaque!*'

A similar tale is told of a Norman to whom the same proposition was made. Having examined the would-be bride in a manner befitting Lavater the physiognomist, he exclaimed, as he mounted the scaffold, '*Lèvres serrées, nez poinctu; / J'aime mieux être pendu!*' Of which couplet I attempt a translation: 'Thin lips, sharp nose – tho' sweet is life, / I'd rather swing than have such a wife!' ~ William Bates, Birmingham, 3 Nov 1855

R2. From Parker's *London News*, 7 April 1725: 'Nine young women dressed in white, each with a white wand in her hand, presented a petition to his majesty (George I) on behalf of a young man condemned at Kingston assizes for burglary, one of them offering to marry him under the gallows in case of a reprieve.' ~ W. J. Pinks, 29 Oct 1858

R3. John Manningham's *Diary* has the following entry on this subject under 12 December 1602:

> It is the custome (not the lawe) in Fraunce and Italy, that if anie notorious professed strumpet will begg for a husband a man which is going to execution, he shal be reprieved, and she may obteine a pardon, and marry him, that both their ill lives may be bettered by soe holie an action. Hence grewe a jeast, when a scoffing gentlewoman told a gentleman shee heard that he was in some danger to have been hanged for some villanie, he answered, 'Truely, madame, I was a-feard of nothing soe much as you would have begd me.' In England it hath bin used that if a woman will beg a condemned person for hir husband, shee must come in hir smocke onely, and a white rod in hir hand...

~ H. A. Kennedy, Gay Street, Bath, 13 Nov 1869

R4. Among the old Manx 'Temporary Customary Laws' of 1577 is the following: 'If any man take a woman by constraint, or force her against her will, if she be a wife he must suffer the law for her. If she be a maid or single woman, the deemster[1] shall give her a rope, a sword, and a ring; and she shall have her choice to hang with the rope, cut off his head with the sword, or marry him with the ring.' ~ J. M. Jeffcott, Isle of Man, 13 Nov 1869

R5. I have heard a different version and interpretation of the Manx law – viz. that the woman had the choice of the ring, the *knife*, or the halter. The ring in order that the base deceiver might have the chance of making the *amende honorable* by marrying her – that is, of course, if he were either a bachelor or a widower; but if either he would not or could not, then she might choose either the knife to punish the scoundrel by castration, and so prevent him ever doing the like again, or the halter to hang him. ~ James Brierley, Clerk, 11 Dec 1869

[1] Judge.

MARRIOT THE GREAT EATER

N. In that amusing and really instructive work, *The Life and Errors of John Dunton*, may be found the following: 'The air of New England was sharper than at London, which, with the temptation of fresh provisions, made me eat like a second Marriot of Gray's Inn.' Upon which Dunton's editor, Mr J. B. Nichols, has this note: 'Of this celebrated eater no other record, it is probable, now remains.'

Not so. In *The Obituary of Richard Smyth*, edited by Sir Henry Ellis, I find the following entry: '25 Nov. 1653, Old Marriot of Gray's Inn (ye great eater) buried.' Meanwhile Charles Cotton, Izaak Walton's associate in *The Compleat Angler*, has two verses on the Gray's Inn cormorant in his *Poems on Several Occasions*, one called 'On the Great Eater of Gray's Inn', the other 'On Marriot'. From the former we learn that he was spare and thin, 'approaching famine in thy physnomy'. The other has this line: 'Marriot the eater of Gray's Inn is dead.' ~ Peter Cunningham, 5 July 1856

R. I have before me a copy of a little tract entitled *The Grays Inn Greedy-Gut, or, the surprising Adventures of Mr Marriott, the famous glutton, with his receipts for many choice dishes* (1750). This is little better than a chap-book, and its contents are derived entirely from a quarto tract of forty or fifty closely printed pages, a copy of which is in the British Museum. I give its title at full length: *The Great Eater of Grayes Inne, or, the Life of Mr Marriot the Cormorant. Wherein is set forth all the Exploits and Actions by him performed, with many pleasant Stories of his Travells into Kent and other places. Also, a rare physicall dispensatory, being the manner how he makes his Cordiall Broaths, Pills, Purgations, Julips, and Vomits, to keep his Body in temper, and free from Surfeits. By G. F. Gent.* London: William Reybould, at the Unicorne in Pauls Church-Yard, 1652.

This tract consists of a number of chapters devoted to stories of his surprising feats of eating. It is evidently written by some enemy of the Gray's Inn lawyer. In addition to the sin of gourmandising, we learn that Marriot was apt to entertain himself rather at the expense of an unhappy friend or client than at his own, and even at times carried his meanness to the pitch of secreting portions of the feast in his sleeve, or in a bag which he carried with him. And we have the following sketch of his exterior: 'He walks in the street like Pontius Pilate, in robes of purple, but not like Dives in fine linnen; for he holds shirts unnecessary...'[1]

The Gray's Inn glutton may be well supposed to have been annoyed by this publication, but at about the same time there appeared, probably by the same hand, another quarto tract entitled *The English Mountebank, or, a Physical Dispensatory, wherein is prescribed many strange and Excellent Receits of Mr Marriot, the Great Eater of Grays Inn*. Among the delights listed are 'His pills to appease hunger', 'His strange Purgation, never before practised by any Doctor in England', and 'How to make his new Dish, called a Frigazee, the operation whereof expels all Sadness and Melancholy'. Prefixed to this we have a full-length portrait of Marriot, holding in one hand a large substance of pumpkin shape, which I take to be one of his 'pills', while on his arm hang three sheep's heads and seven large hearts of some animal – no doubt his usual dinner allowance. Out of his mouth issue the words, 'Behold the wonder of the age!'

How many of these characteristics of old Marriot were really true, and how far they were the invention of G. F. Gent. for the gratification of private animosity, the world will probably never know. These attacks were not, however, allowed to pass unchallenged, for an answer appeared about two months afterwards with the following title: *A Letter to Mr Marriot from a friend of his wherein His Name is redeemed from that Detraction G. F. Gent. hath indeavoured to fasten upon him, by a Scandalous and Defamatory*

---

[1] Dives, from the Latin for rich, was the name traditionally given to the rich man in the parable of Lazarus the beggar: 'There was a certain rich man, which was clothed in purple and fine linen, and fared sumptuously every day...' (Luke 16:19)

Libell. This has another full-length portrait of old Marriot beside a likeness of G. F. Gent. The latter is on his knees and performing an act of homage and apology towards the unbreeched and injured lawyer not to be described in the pages of *N & Q*. ~ W. Moy Thomas, 12 July 1856

R2. The following entry from the commonplace book of William Oldys is dated 1718:

Ben Marriot... Dy'd about forty years since, his appetite extraordinary from his birth, and suck'd his mother and half a dozen nurses dry, when if for no other reason they wean'd him, and no other of the children of which he was the youngest were treated with this voracity. The prudent mother took care that this young Benjamin had ten times as much as the rest, yet he practis'd the rule of physicians to rise with an appetite; as he encreas'd in years, so did his stomach, so that at fifteen he could master a Turkey at a meal, and proportionable bread.

~ Cl. Hopper, 6 June 1857

¶ There is some confusion as to Marriot's Christian name: he was admitted to Gray's Inn in 1605 and called to the Bar in 1611 as William, but in the pamphlets of 1652 he is referred to as John and in 1718 William Oldys referred to him as Ben.

It is thought that his antagonist 'G. F. Gent.' was George Fidge, a scurrilous pamphlet writer of the time. Whether Fidge acted from personal animus or for pecuniary reward is not known, but his accusations were certainly colourful: among other things Marriot was said to have eaten bitches and monkeys baked in pies.

The frontispiece of the defending *Letter to Mr Marriot*, referred to circumspectly in *N & Q*, shows Marriot side on and holding a whip above the head of his detractor, who is kneeling and preparing rather gingerly to kiss the great eater's backside.

On 4 February 1660, some six years after Marriot's death, Samuel Pepys was at Gray's Inn: 'I eat some bread and butter, having eat nothing all day, while they were by chance discoursing of Marriot the great eater; so that I was, I remember, ashamed to eat what I would have done.'

BENJ.ᴺ MARRIOT, the great Eater

A variant of the first portrait described in *N & Q*

MELANCHOLY: Does it cause waistcoat-bursting?

N. In the ballad of 'Annan Water', in Scott's *Minstrelsy of the Scottish Border*, is the following verse:

> O he has pour'd aff his dapperpy coat,
> The silver buttons glanced bonny;
> The waistcoat bursted aff his breast,
> He was sae full of melancholy.

A very unexpected effect of sorrow, but one that does not seem to be unprecedented. 'A plague of sighing and grief,' says Falstaff. 'It blows a man up like a bladder.' (*Henry IV part 1*, Act 2, scene 5)

A remarkable illustration of Falstaff's assertion, and of the Scottish ballad, is to be found in the *Saga of Egil Skallagrimson*. Bodvar, the son of Egil, was wrecked on the coast of Iceland. His body was thrown up by the waves. It was found by Egil and laid in the family tomb. The *Saga* continues: 'His hose were bound fast about his legs, and he had on a red linen kirtle, narrow above, and tied with strings at the sides. And men say that his body swelled so greatly that his kirtle burst from off him, and so did his hose.' ~ Richard John King, 28 Dec 1850

R. The general effect of melancholy is that digestion is imperfectly performed, and melancholy patients generally complain of being 'blown up'. Bodvar's 'blowing up', on the other hand, is the mere effect of the generation of gases in a dead body, well illustrated by a floating dead dog on the river side, or the bursting of a leaden coffin. ~ H.W.D., 22 Mar 1851

MPs' SALARIES: Payment with herrings

Q. Whatever estimate the people of the present day may put upon the elective franchise, it would seem that our ancestors held the privilege very lightly; for, although the wages to be received by Members of Parliament were fixed by law in 1323 at the low rate of 4 shillings a day for a knight of the shire and 2 shillings for a citizen or burgess, yet we are told by William Prynne, in his *Brief Register of Parliamentary Writs*, that many boroughs petitioned to be excused from sending members to parliament on account of the expense; and, in a note to Blackstone's *Commentaries*, we learn that from 1359, in the reign of Edward III, and uniformly through the five succeeding reigns, the sheriff of Lancashire returned that there were no cities or boroughs in his county that ought to or could, on account of their poverty, send any citizens or burgesses to parliament. There were some instances where even a lower sum than that established by statute was allowed, and it is on record that in 1463 Sir John Strange, the member for Dunwich, agreed to take a cade[1] and half a barrel of herrings as a composition for his wages.

The object of this note is to ask your readers at what time, and under what circumstances, the practice of paying members was discontinued. ~ D. M. Stevens, Guildford, 22 Feb 1862

¶ The Dunwich agreement stipulated that 'John Strange [is] granted no more taken for his wages than a cade full of herring and half a barrel full [of] herring, these to be delivered by Christmas next coming.' The number of herrings that made up the measures of cade and barrel changed over time, but Strange was probably entitled to 1,100: 600 for the cade and 500 for the half barrel.

From the sixteenth century onwards the medieval practice of constituencies paying their MPs – even with herrings – declined. In some cases, as at Dunwich, this reflected a lack of funds – even by 1463 a good part of the Suffolk town had disappeared under the North Sea, and many of its richer inhabitants had left. In other places competition among candidates led constituencies to bargain with them to reduce or eliminate costs. The result was that, by the 1660s, payment to members was limited to a handful of wealthy towns and cities, and even these had stopped paying by the end of the century. Samuel Pepys was one of many who worried as to the consequences: 'At dinner,' he wrote on 30 March 1668, 'all concluded that the bane of the parliament hath been the leaving off the old custom of the places allowing wages to those that served them... by which they chose

[1] Cask or barrel.

men that understood their business and would attend to it, and they could expect an account from, which now they cannot.'

Payment only returned in 1912, when a salary of £400 was introduced from central funds. This increased to £600 in 1937 and to £1,000 in 1946.

MICE: Fried and otherwise

N. My son falling ill of the whooping cough, 'I know,' said one of my parishioners, 'what would cure him, but m'appen you woudent believe me.' 'What is it, Mary?' I asked. 'Why, with mine I did everything that everybody told me. One teld me to get him breathed on by a piebald horse. I took him ever such a way, to a horse at —, and put him under the horse's mouth, but he was no better. Then I was teld to drag him backward through a bramble bush. I did so, but this didn't cure him. Last of all, I was teld to give him nine fried mice, fasting, in a morning, in this way: three the first morning; then wait three mornings, and then give him three more; wait three mornings, and then give him three more. When he had eaten these nine fried mice he became quite well. This would be sure to cure your child, sir.' ~ W.H.K., Drayton Beauchamp, 20 Apr 1850

R. I have often heard my father say that when he had the measles his nurse gave him a *roasted* mouse to cure him. ~ Scotus, 4 May 1850

R2. In the counties of Leicester and Northampton, nine roasted mice, three taken each third morning, constitutes the common charm for the whooping cough. ~ T.S., 1 June 1850

R3. Roasting mice for whooping cough is also very common in Norfolk. However, I am sorry to say that a more cruel superstitious practice is sometimes inflicted on the little animal, for it is not many years since I accidentally entered the kitchen in time to save a poor little mouse from being hung up by the tail and roasted alive as the means of expelling the others of its race from the house. I trust that this barbarous practice will soon be forgotten. ~ R.G.P.M., 24 Aug 1850

R4. An old woman lately recommended an occasional roast mouse as a certain cure for a little boy who wetted his bed at night. Her own son, she said, had got over this weakness by eating three roast mice. I am told that the Faculty employ this remedy, and that it has been prescribed in the Oxford Infirmary. ~ J.W.H., 30 Nov 1850

R5. Seeing some Queries and Replies on the medical use of mice I am induced to send you a few extracts from an old book in my possession, published in 1661. Its title is *Panzoologicomineralogia, or, a Compleat History of Animals and Minerals* by Robert Lovell, Christ Church, Oxon. It treats chiefly of the medicinal uses of the various objects. I am tempted to tell you the use of a 'unicorne', but confine myself to the mouse:

> The flesh eaten causeth oblivion, and corrupteth the meat; yet those of Chalecut eat them; it is hot, soft, and fattish, and expelleth melancholy... A mouse dissected and applied, draweth out reeds, darts, and other things that stick in the flesh... Mice bruised, and reduced to the consistence of an *acopon* (what's that?)[1] with old wine, cause hair on the eyebrows... Being eaten by children when rosted, they dry up the spittle. The magicians eat them twice a month against the paines of the teeth. The water in which they have been boiled helps against the quinsey. Being boiled and eaten, they help children's pissing in bed. The fresh blood kills warts. The ashes of the skinne, applied with vinegar, helps the paines of the head. The head worn in a cloth, helps the headach and epilepsy.

[1] 'A soothing salve; a poultice or plaster to relieve pain.' (*OED*)

The braine being steeped in wine, and applied to the forehead, helpeth the headach. Used with water, it cureth the phrensy. The heart, *taken out of a mouse WHEN ALIVE*, worne about the arme of a woman, causeth no conception. The fillet of the liver, drunk with austere wine, helpeth quartans.[1] The liver, rosted in the new of the moon, trieth the epilepsy. The dung is corrosive. Given in any liquor, it helpeth the collicke. It looseneth the body: therefore some nurses use it for children in suppositories. It helpeth the hollow teeth, being put therein.

There is more of the sort, to the extent of two and three-quarter closely printed pages. It should be added that the author quotes authorities, old and new, for the several facts he adduces. Pliny is a great authority with him, and Galen is often cited. ~ J.K., 26 July 1851

MINCE PIES: A seventeenth-century recipe

N.   TO MAKE MYNCE PYES, AD 1630

Take a phillet of veale or a leag of mutton, and, when it is parboyled, shred it very smalle, then put to it three pound of beefe suet shred likewise very smalle, then put to it three pound of Corinthes[2] well washt and pickt, and one pound of sugar beaten. Of nutmegs and synnamon of each an ounce; so put them in coffins[3] or pyes, and bake them. You must lay some of ye Corinthes at toppe of ye meat, when they bee made, and must not therefore mingle them all with the rest.

Thus did the learned Sir Roger Twysden at Christmas, and a right good receipt it seems to be. The moderns spoil their mince pies by putting in no meat. I think Sir Roger gives too much spice, and the addition of preserved citron (unknown in his days) would be a great improvement. ~ L.B.L., 15 Dec 1860

---

[1] Recurring fever.

[2] Currants, originally known as *raisins de Corinthe*.

[3] Dishes or pastry moulds for a pie.

MONKS, MUMMIFIED

Q. I remember having a conversation with a friend a few years ago respecting some bodies which he had seen preserved in the church of a town, of which I forget the name, on (I think) the Rhine. They consisted of about twenty monks ranged side by side in a vault which was open to the air. It was alleged that the peculiar character of the atmosphere had alone preserved them in their then state – namely, as soft to the touch as in life, the only peculiarity being the brownish hue of the faces, which caused my friend to suspect that they had been baked. Can any of your correspondents refer me to any information on the subject? ~ A.A., Abridge, Essex, 17 July 1852

R. These mummies are to be seen in the church at Kreutzberg, about a mile and a half from Bonn, on the Rhine. The church was formerly attached to a convent of Servites. ~ Viator, 31 July 1852

R2. In Mrs Trollope's *Belgium and Western Germany* (1834) the following passage is found touching the Kreutzberg monks:

The wonderful state of preservation in which these bodies remain, though constantly exposed to the atmosphere by being thus exhibited, is attributed by good Catholics to the peculiar sanctity of the place; but to those who do not receive this solution of the mystery, it is one of great difficulty. The dates of their interment vary from 1400 to 1713, and the oldest is quite as fresh as the most recent. There are twenty-six, fully exposed to view, and apparently many more beneath them. From the elder ones, the coffins have either crumbled away, or the bodies were buried without them. In some of these ghastly objects the flesh is still full, and almost shapely upon the legs; in others it appears to be gradually drying away, and the bones are here and there becoming visible. The condition of the face also varies very greatly, though by no means in proportion to the antiquity of each. In many the nose, lips, and beard remain, and in one the features were so little disturbed that 'All unruffled was his face, / We trusted his soul had gotten grace.' Round others the dust lies where it had fallen, as it dropped grain by grain from the mouldering cheeks, and the head grins from beneath the cowl nearly in the state of a skeleton. The garments are almost in the same unequal degree of preservation, for in many the white material is still firm, though discoloured, while in others it is dropping away in fragments. The shoes of all are wonderfully perfect.

The last person buried in this vault was one who acted as gardener to the community. His head is crowned with a wreath of flowers, which still preserves its general form; nay, the largest blossoms may yet be distinguished from the smaller ones; but the withered leaves lie mixed with his fallen hair on either side.

~ H.W.G., Elgin, 28 Aug 1852

R3. A far larger collection than that at Kreutzberg exists at a Capuchin convent near Palermo. Here the bodies are placed in a series of niches in a subterranean cloister, out of which they hang, horribly grotesque, in every variety of attitude. Besides the bodies of members of the order, there are those of others who have chosen to be buried in their habit; ladies too, dressed in every sort of finery, and carefully placed standing or lying behind glass or wires. In one place a number of children form a sort of cornice to the vault; in another they are preserved in glass cases like stuffed birds. Besides these, the floor is half covered with piles of coffins of all shapes and colours, duly ticketed with the names of the occupants. The process by which the bodies are preserved is said to be simply the enclosing them for six months in an airtight cell, after which period the cell is opened, and they are found completely mummified. ~ Cheverells, 2 Oct 1852

R4. I have recently seen seven bodies in St Michan's Church, Dublin, which are preserved solely by natural causes peculiar to the vaults of that church. The bodies are not soft but dry, and the skin rather hard like parchment, and of a brownish colour. ~ C.F.M., 2 Oct 1852

R5. Happening to be in Bordeaux on 22 September last, I was attracted to the church of St Michael by the following paragraph in Murray's *Handbook* for France:

Near the west end stands the elegant detached hexagonal belfry. In the vault beneath it are shown from forty to fifty human bodies. They were formerly buried in the churchyard which surrounded the belfry, but shortly before the Revolution the churchyard was closed and the bodies dug up. The bones and decayed bodies are in a vault beneath, but those shown were preserved by the dry and antiseptic qualities of the earth, until they are now like leather or salt fish – a disgusting sight.

The room in which these bodies are kept is a dry airy chamber on the ground floor of the tower, and is entered through the shop of a shoemaker, who exhibits them by the aid of a candle fastened to the end of a long stick. He states that there are sixty-three in number. They are ranged upright, round the sides of the room. The skins are like tough leather, which the guide evidences by poking them good-naturedly in the ribs with the end of the candle-stick. One unfortunate died with his tongue protruding, and this is duly wagged by the aid of the stick. So remarkably well are they preserved that the expression of face at the time of death is still easily discernible. Some have a quiet peaceful look, and others all the distortions which mark a violent death. On several the clothes in which they were buried are still perfect: the most remarkable of these is a priest, buried in his ecclesiastical vestments. A family of five, who died from eating mushrooms (at least so says the shoemaker), exhibit traces of having died in great agony, the faces being horribly distorted. The body of a boy, said to have been buried alive, bears evident testimony to the truth of the story, while the cut of a rapier is seen in the body of a man said to have been killed in a duel. All the bodies are dry and stiff, and I should think that the skin would do very well to bind a book, or for any purpose for which leather of the softer kind is required. There is no unpleasant or earthy smell, the room being dry and airy. ~ George W. Marshall, 23 Dec 1865

¶ The walls of the Capuchin catacombs in Palermo are lined with some 8,000 mummies dating from the sixteenth century through to 1920. Bodies were dried and some were then treated with vinegar. Among the most celebrated figures are those of an army officer in eighteenth-century uniform complete with a tricorn hat, and the two-year-old Rosalio Lombardo, whose lifelike appearance has led to her being known as the 'sleeping beauty'.

The bodies in the crypt of St Michan's, Dublin, are said to have inspired Bram Stoker to write *Dracula*: many of the Stoker family are buried in the church.

MOUSTACHES: Outlawed in Ireland

N. Among the statutes and ordinances of 1447 is the following enactment of the Irish parliament:

> *An Act that he that will be taken for an Englishman shall not use a beard upon his upper lip alone; the offender shall be taken as an Irish enemy*

For that now there is no diversity in array betwixt the English marchours[1] and the Irish enemies, and so by colour of the English marchours the Irish enemies do come from day to day into the English counties as English marchours, and do rob and pill[2] by the highways, and destroy the common people by lodging upon them in the nights, and also do kill the husbands in the nights, and do take their goods to the Irishmen. Wherefore it is ordained and agreed that no maner man that will be taken for an Englishman shall have no beard above his mouth, that is to say, that he have no hairs upon his upper lip, so that the said lips be once at least shavin every forthnight, or of equal growth with the neather lip. And if any man be found among the English contrary hereunto, that then it shall be lawful to every man to take them and their goods as Irish enemies, and to ransom them as Irish enemies.

This enactment remained in force for nearly 200 years, only being repealed by a statute of 1635. ~ F. A. Carrington, Ogbourne St George, 27 June 1857

R. The Act of 1447 was passed in a parliament held at Trim by John Talbot, Earl of Shrewsbury, then Lord Lieutenant. The Irish at this time were much attached to wearing mustachios, the fashion throughout Europe then and for more than two centuries after. As the unfortunate Irishman who became an enemy for his moustache could only be pardoned by the surrender of his land, the king was able to provide for his followers, many of whose descendants enjoy the confiscated properties to this

---

[1] Marchers; inhabitants of a border district.

[2] Pillage.

day. The effects of this statute became so alarming that the people submitted to the English razor, finding it more convenient to resign their moustaches than their lands. ~ J.Y., 1 Oct 1859

NELSON 1: Presented with his coffin

N. The subjoined extract, from Sir Nicholas Harris Nicolas's edition of Lord Nelson's *Dispatches and Letters*, may be interesting to some of your readers:

No present sent to Nelson after the Battle of the Nile was so extraordinary as that which he received from his gallant friend Captain Hallowell of the *Swiftsure*; and the idea could have occurred only to a very original mind. After *L'Orient* blew up, part of her mainmast was taken on board of the *Swiftsure*, and in May 1799 Captain Hallowell, fearing the effect of all the praise and flattery lavished on his chief, determined to remind him that he was mortal. He therefore ordered a coffin to be made out of part of *L'Orient*'s mast, and was so careful that nothing whatever should be used in its construction that was not taken from it that the staples were formed of the spikes drawn from the cheeks of the mast, which were driven into the edge of the coffin, and, when the lid was put on, toggles were put into the staples to keep it down so as to prevent the necessity of using nails or screws for that purpose. The nails in the coffin were likewise made from the spikes taken from the mast. A paper was pasted on the bottom, containing the following certificate:

'I do hereby certify, that every part of this coffin is made of the wood and iron of *L'Orient*, most of which was picked up by his majesty's ship under my command, in the Bay of Aboukir.

— *Swiftsure*, May 23rd, 1799.

Ben. Hallowell.'

This singular present was accompanied by the following letter:

'The Right Hon. Lord Nelson, KB

My lord,

Herewith I send you a coffin made of part of *L'Orient*'s mainmast, that when you are tired of this life you may be buried in one of your own trophies – but may that period be far distant, is the sincere wish of your obedient and much obliged servant,

Ben. Hallowell.

Swiftsure, May 23rd, 1799.'

The astonishment that prevailed among the crew of the *Vanguard*, Lord Nelson's flagship, when they were convinced it was a coffin which had been brought on board, will be long remembered by their officers. 'We shall have hot work of it, indeed!' said one of the seamen. 'You see the admiral intends to fight till he is killed, and there he is to be buried.'

Lord Nelson highly appreciated the present, and for some time had it placed upright, with the lid on, against the bulkhead of his cabin, behind the chair on which he sat at dinner. At length, by the entreaties of an old servant, he was prevailed on to allow it to be carried below.

When his lordship left the *Vanguard*, the coffin was removed into the *Foudroyant*, where it remained for many days on the gratings of the quarterdeck. While his officers were one day looking at it, he came out of his cabin: 'You may look at it, gentlemen,' said he, 'as long as you please, but, depend on it, none of you shall have it.' It is satisfactory to state that Nelson was actually buried in this coffin.

~ F. Phillott, 1 Mar 1856

R. I was intimate with Nelson's old valet, Tom Allen, and among many other interesting particulars which I have heard him relate of his brave master was the above fact. Tom added that at last he prevailed upon the hero to allow him to remove the coffin from the cabin: 'For, my lord,' said he, 'it always puts me in mind of a corpse.' ~ F.C.H., 16 July 1864

NELSON 2: His last signal

Q. Have there ever been doubts expressed as to the authenticity of Nelson's last order, 'England expects that everybody shall do his duty'? Is the version just quoted the only one? ~ H. Tiedeman, Amsterdam, 7 Mar 1868

R. Your correspondent may be satisfied with the account given of this glorious signal by the officer who made it, the late Rear Admiral John Pasco. Pasco acted as flag lieutenant on board the *Victory*, and his account appears in Nelson's *Dispatches and Letters*:

> His lordship came to me on the poop and, after ordering certain signals to be made, about a quarter to noon, he said, 'Mr Pasco, I wish to say to the fleet, England confides[1] that every man will do his duty; and,' he added, 'you must be quick, for I have one more to make, which is for close action.' I replied, 'If your lordship will permit me to substitute *expects* for *confides* the signal will soon be completed, because the word *expects* is in the vocabulary, and *confides* must be spelt.' His lordship replied with seeming satisfaction, 'That will do, Pasco, make it directly.' When it had been answered by a few ships in the van, he ordered me to make the signal for close action, and to *keep it up*. Accordingly I hoisted No. 16 at the top-gallant masthead, and there it remained until shot away.

[1] i.e. is confident.

In a note the editor, Sir Nicholas Harris Nicolas, gives the numbers of Sir Home Popham's telegraphic code of signals, by which Nelson transmitted his own spirit throughout the fleet:

Nos.	253	269	863	261	471	958	220
	England	expects	that	every	man	will	do

	370	4	21	19	24
	his	D	U	T	Y.

I hope my extracts will lead your correspondent to correct his own version of Nelson's words by substituting 'every man will' for 'everybody shall', and convince him that, although 'close action' was really Nelson's last order, there is no doubt about the authenticity of his memorable signal. ~ M., 21 Mar 1868

R2. In addition to the proof afforded by your correspondent M., I enclose the following extract from the *Memoirs* of Sir Samuel Burdon Ellis of the Royal Marines:

This glorious battle, which so greatly influenced the affairs of Europe, was one through which our ship passed with but little loss. As we neared the French fleet, I was sent below with orders, and was much struck with the preparations made by the blue-jackets, the majority of whom were stripped to the waist, a handkerchief was bound tightly round their heads and over the ears to deaden the noise of the cannon, many men being deaf for days after the action. The men were variously occupied; some were sharpening their cutlasses, others polishing the guns, as though an inspection was about to take place instead of a mortal combat; whilst three or four, as if in mere bravado, were dancing a hornpipe; but all seemed deeply anxious to come to close quarters with the enemy. It was at this time that Nelson's famous signal, 'England expects that every man will do his duty,' was hoisted at the masthead of the admiral's ship. These words were requested to be delivered to the men, and I was desired to inform them on the main deck. Upon acquainting one of the quartermasters of the order, he assembled the men with 'Avast there, lads, come and hear the admiral's words.' When the men were mustered, I delivered, with becoming dignity, the sentence, rather anticipating that the effect on the men would be to awe them by its grandeur. Jack, however, did not appreciate it, for there were murmurs from some, whilst others in an audible whisper muttered, 'Do our duty! Of course we'll do our duty. I've always done mine, haven't you? Let us come alongside of 'em, and we will soon show whether we will do our duty.' Still the men cheered vociferously – more, I believe, from love and admiration of their admiral and leaders, than from a full appreciation of this well known signal.

~ J.B., 10 Oct 1868

NEWTON'S APPLE: Did it exist?

N. I suppose all persons who are conversant with the history of science know that Newton's apple, if it was an apple, had little to do with his great discovery, but it may be worthwhile to make a note on the history of this tale.

Pemberton,[1] who received from Newton himself the history of his first ideas of gravity, does not mention the apple, saying only 'The first thoughts which gave rise to his *Principia* he had when he retired from Cambridge in 1666 on account of the plague. As he sat alone in a garden, he fell into a speculation on the power of gravity...' (*A View of Sir Isaac Newton's Philosophy*, 1728)

Voltaire says, 'One day in the year 1666, Newton retired to the country, and, seeing fruit fall from a tree, as his niece Madame Conduitt[2] has informed me, he entered a profound meditation on the cause which draws all bodies in a line which, if it were extended, would pass almost through the centre of the earth.' (*Eléments de la Philosophie de Newton*, 1738)

On the other hand the great German mathematician Carl Friedrich Gauss, according to his biographer, expressed himself

---

[1] Henry Pemberton (1694-1771), physician. Employed by Newton to oversee the 3rd edition of the *Principia Mathematica* (1726).

[2] Catherine Barton (1679-1739). She married John Conduitt in 1717.

quite indignant that the great discovery of the law of gravitation should be represented as the result of a trifling accident: ' "The history of the apple", he said, "is too absurd. Whether the apple fell or let it alone, how can anyone believe that such a discovery could in that way be accelerated or retarded? Undoubtedly the occurrence was something of this sort. There comes to Newton a stupid importunate man who asks him how he hit upon his great discovery. When Newton had convinced himself what a noodle he had to do with, and wanted to get rid of the man, he told him that an apple fell upon his nose; and this made the matter quite clear to the man, and he went away satisfied." ' ~ W., 17 Apr 1858

R. The following is Sir David Brewster's note upon the subject in his *Life* of Newton, published in 1855: 'Neither Pemberton nor Whiston,[1] who received from Newton himself the history of his first ideas of gravity, records the story of the falling apple. It was mentioned, however, to Voltaire by Catherine Barton, Newton's niece, and to Mr Greene[2] by Martin Folkes, the President of the Royal Society. We saw the apple tree in 1814, and brought away a portion of one of its roots. The tree was so much decayed that it was taken down in 1820, and the wood of it carefully preserved by Mr Turnor of Stoke Rocheford.'

First, was it an apple? This is very important. Voltaire only says *les fruits d'un arbre*. Folkes certainly says *pomum*, but this word is only some *round fruit*. Is it not Virgil who talks of the *poma* of the mulberry tree?

There is then nothing certain except that Newton's niece talked about some fall of fruit, and that we have recollections of her conversation by Voltaire and Folkes. If we remember how conversations grow by repetition, we may think it possible that Newton, in casual talk, mentioned the fall of some fruit as

[1] William Whiston (1667-1752), clergyman and scientist.

[2] Robert Greene (*c.*1678-1730), scientist and philosopher. Also slightly eccentric: in his will he directed that, after his body had been dissected, his skeleton should be hung up in the library of King's College, Cambridge.

having once struck his mind when he was pondering on the subject of the moon's motion, and that Mrs Conduitt made too much of it. Hence Greene's *pomum*, and its common rendering of *apple*, followed by the actual discovery that there *was* an apple tree at Woolsthorpe, and, it should seem, only one...
~ A. de Morgan, 28 Aug 1858

¶ The scepticism expressed in *N & Q* by the mathematician Augustus de Morgan was based on a rather partial consideration of the evidence. The first two printed references to the incident both appeared in 1727, the year of Newton's death. One comes in Robert Greene's *Principles of the Philosophy of the Expansive and Contractive Forces*, in which he gives Sir Martin Folkes as his source without adding any suggestion that Folkes was merely passing on a story told him by Catherine Conduitt; the other comes in an essay on epic poetry by Voltaire, who does explicitly refer to an apple: 'Sir Isaak Newton walking in his gardens had the first thought of his system of gravitation, upon seeing an apple falling from a tree.' Voltaire would go on to repeat the story in two later works (*Letters concerning the English Nation*, 1733, and *Eléments de la Philosophie de Newton*, 1738), and it is in those retellings that he uses the more general *'fruits'*.

There are also two other accounts dating from the same period: one, by John Conduitt, may well have derived from his wife Catherine, but the other, by William Stukeley, which was not published in full until 1936, is first hand and detailed:

On 15 April 1726 I paid a visit to Sir Isaac at his lodgings in Orbels buildings in Kensington... After dinner, the weather being warm, we went into the garden and drank tea, under the shade of some apple trees, only he and myself. Amidst other discourse, he told me he was just in the same situation when formerly the notion of gravitation came into his mind. It was occasion'd by the fall of an apple, as he sat in a contemplative mood. Why should that apple always descend perpendicularly to the ground, thought he to himself? Why should it not go sideways or upwards, but constantly to the earth's centre?

220

Assuredly, the reason is that the earth draws it. There must be a drawing power in matter: and the sum of the drawing power in the matter of the earth must be in the earth's centre.

Given that there are therefore at least three independent witnesses – Catherine Conduitt (as related by Voltaire), Sir Martin Folkes (as related by Greene), and William Stukeley (as related by himself) – it seems clear that in his last years, if not before, Newton did tell the apple story. However, room for scepticism remains on several counts. First, following Robert Hooke's accusation that in *Principia Mathematica* (1687) Newton had appropriated his ideas on gravitation, it was certainly helpful for Newton to be able to suggest that a great breakthrough in his thinking had occurred as early as 1666 and when he was quite alone. Second, the idea of a 'eureka' moment, in which gravity's secrets were illuminated by a sudden flash of genius, is not taken seriously by experts in the field, who point out that Newton's working notes from the period in question do not record any sudden advance in his thinking. Third, if Newton did only tell the story at the end of his life, it is a little surprising – even for so famously uncommunicative a man – that he had previously omitted to mention it for nearly sixty years.

NORTH SIDES OF CHURCHYARDS: The Devil's domain?

Q. In the West of England I have found an opinion to prevail in rural parishes that the north side of our churchyards was very commonly left unconsecrated in order that the youth of the village might have the use of it as a playground. I also found some reluctance in the people to have their friends buried north of the church.

Is there any ground for believing that our churchyards were ever thus consecrated on the south side of the church to the exclusion of the north? ~ J. Sansom, 22 June 1850

R. A portion of many churchyards is said to have been left unconsecrated, though not to be used as playground for the youth of the parish, but for the burial of excommunicated persons. This was not, however, always on the north side of the church, as is evident from the following extract from the register of Hart, Durham: 'Dec. 17th 1596, Ellen Thompson, Fornicatrix (and then excommunicated), was buried of ye people... at the entrance unto ye yeate or stile of ye churchyard, on the east thereof.'

Nor is the north side always the least favourite part for burial. I could name many instances where this is the only part used. The churchyard now within 200 yards of me contains an acre of ground, the large portion of which lies to the south of the church, but this has been very little used for sepulture till of late years, though the churchyard is very ancient. Even now the poor have an objection to bury their friends there. I believe the prejudice is always in favour of the part next the town or village, that on the other side being generally called 'the backside'. ~ W.H.K., 6 July 1850

R2. During a long series of years an average of about 150 corpses have been annually deposited in Ecclesfield Churchyard, which has rendered it an extremely crowded cemetery. Notwithstanding these frequent interments, my late sexton told me that he remembered when there was scarcely one grave to the north of the church, it being popularly considered that only suicides, unbaptised persons, and stillborn children ought to be buried there. However, when a vicar died about twenty-seven years ago, unlike his predecessors, who had generally been buried in the chancel, he was laid in a tomb on the north side of the churchyard, adjoining the vicarage. From this time forward the situation lost all its evil reputation amongst the richer inhabitants of the parish, who have almost entirely occupied it with family vaults. However, I suspect that, from inherited dislike, the poor are still indisposed towards it. When the women of the village have to come to the vicarage after nightfall they generally manage to bring a companion, and hurry past the gloomy end of the north transept as if they knew 'that close behind / Some frightful fiend did tread'. I cannot help fancying that the objection is attributable to a notion that evil spirits haunt the spot in which, possibly from very early times, there took place such interments as my sexton described. ~ Alfred Gatty, Ecclesfield, 20 July 1850

R3. The strong preference given to the south side of the churchyard is traceable to two principal causes: first and chiefly, because the churchyard cross was always placed here; second, because this is the sunny side of the churchyard. And, as the greater part of the congregation entered the church by the south and principal door, another cause of the preference was the hope that the sight of the resting-places of those who had died might remind their friends and neighbours to remember them in their supplications. ~ Arun, 17 Aug 1850

R4. The foregoing are not only meagre reasons, they are incorrect. The doctrine of the regions was coeval with the death of Our Lord. The east was the realm of the oracle: the especial throne of God. The west was the domain of the people: the Galilee of all nations was there. The south, the land of the midday, was sacred to things heavenly and divine. The north was the devoted region of Satan and his hosts: the lair of demons, and their haunt. In some of our ancient churches, over against the font, and in the northern walls, there was a Devil's door. It was thrown open at every baptism for the escape of the fiend, and at all other seasons carefully closed. Hence came the old dislike to sepulture at the north. ~ R. S. Hawker, Morwenstow, Cornwall, 14 Sep 1850

R5. I suspect Mr Hawker is nearest the truth, and the following, from Miles Coverdale on Praying for the Dead, may help to strengthen his conjecture: 'As men die, so shall they arise: if in faith in the Lord towards the south, they need no prayers: they are presently happy, and shall arise in glory; if in unbelief without the Lord towards the north, then are they past all hope.' ~ N.S., 26 Apr 1851

OMENS: In South Northants and a Cornish village

1. IN SOUTH NORTHANTS

Hares. Besides the ancient superstition attached to the crossing of the path by one of these animals,[1] there is also a belief that the running of one along the street or mainway of a village portends fire to some house in the immediate vicinity. ~ T.S., 4 Jan 1851

Magpies. To see one magpie alone bodes bad luck; two, good luck; three, a 'berrin'; four, a wedding. This is our version of the common saying. ~ T.S., 4 Jan 1851

Mice. A sudden influx of mice into a house, hitherto free from their ravages, denotes approaching mortality among its inhabitants. A mouse running over a person is considered to be an infallible sign of death, as is also the squeaking of one behind the bed of an invalid, or the appearance or apparition of a white mouse running across a room. To meet with a shrew-mouse, in going a journey, is reckoned ominous of evil. ~ T.Y., 10 Aug 1850

---

[1] Meeting a hare was considered an evil sign, so much so that the *Gospelles of Dystaves* (1507) advised returning home three times from the spot where the hare was seen: only then could you set out on your original journey 'withouten peryll'.

Robin Redbreast. The robin is considered a sacred bird: to kill one is little less than sacrilege, and its eggs are free from the destroying hand of the bird-nester. One cause for the veneration in which it is held may be the superstition which represents it as the medium through which mankind are warned of approaching death. Before the death of a person, a robin is believed in many instances to tap thrice at the window of the room in which he or she may be. ~ T.Y., 10 Aug 1850

Swallows et cetera. Omens of death and misfortune are also drawn from the howling of dogs, the sight of a trio of butterflies, and the flying down the chimney of swallows or jackdaws; and swine are sometimes said to give their master warning of his death by giving utterance to a certain peculiar whine, known and understood only by the initiated. ~ T.S., 4 Jan 1851

2. In a Cornish village

N. The place whose popular antiquities are here recorded is situated on the eminently romantic coast of the south-eastern part of Cornwall. In this quiet corner lurk many remnants of faded creeds and ancient usages which have vanished from districts more subject to mutation. Here are some of our superstitions connected with animals et cetera.

• The howling of dogs, the continued croaking of ravens over a house, and the ticking of the death-watch, portend death.

• The magpie is a bird of good or ill omen, according to the number seen at a time: 'One for sorrow; two for mirth; / Three for a wedding; four for death.'

• A crowing hen is a bird of ill luck. An old proverb in use here says: 'A whistling woman and a crowing hen are two of the unluckiest things under the sun.' The first is always reproved, and the latter got rid of without loss of time.

• Particular honour is paid to the robin and the wren. A local distich says: 'He that hurts a robin or a wren, / Will never prosper sea or land.'

• It is a very prevalent belief that a bed-pillow stuffed with the feathers of wild birds renders painful and prolonged the departure of the dying. Death is also thought to be delayed until the ebb of the tide.

• The killing the first adder you see predicts that you will triumph over your enemies. The slough of an adder, hung on the rafters, preserves the house against fire.

• Amongst other omens believed in I may farther mention that the breaking of a looking-glass entails 'seven years' trouble, but no want'; if you shiver, someone is walking over the spot destined to be your grave; and if your cheek burns, someone is talking scandal of you. I have frequently heard these lines spoken by the person whose cheek is burning:

> 'Right cheek! Left cheek! Why do you burn?
> Cursed be she that doth me any harm:
> If she be a maid, let her be slaid;
> If she be a widow, long let her mourn;
> But if it be my own true love – burn, cheek, burn!'

~ Thomas Q. Couch, Cornwall, 26 May 1855 & 21 Jul 1855

OWLS: Do they snore?

Q. A travelling party, whose destination was an old English mansion, being detained on the road, did not arrive till long after the household had retired for the night. On reaching their journey's end they pulled up at the ancient gateway of the mansion and for a long time knocked, rang, and shouted, without being able to rouse the inmates. What made their detention the more annoying was the audible snoring, as they thought, of some person or persons fast asleep almost close at hand, in fact so close that the sound seemed to proceed from immediately over the portals at which the party sought admission. Admitted at length, they asked with some impatience who were those obstinate sleepers that still snored and slumbered on, regardless of such loud appeals from benighted travellers. The reply was that the snorers were owls who built over the gateway.

Do owls snore? I was not aware of the fact, and I ought to know something about it. ~ Hibou, 15 Sep 1860

R. The snoring of owls is an article of popular belief, but we never enjoyed an opportunity of personally investigating this curious subject till the present season. Domiciled for a few weeks at a place called the Hall, which was once a splendid lordly residence, we stood after sunset in the porch on the evening of our arrival, when our attention was roused by a sound which issued from the trunk of a decayed but venerable elm not many paces distant, and which did certainly bear some resemblance to snoring. The sound was not indeed a snore, strictly speaking, but might easily be mistaken for one. Perhaps it rather resembled what in medical language is called 'stertorous breathing'. Still, as it was regularly repeated at short intervals, you would say that the party from which it proceeded, if not actually snoring, at any rate would begin to snore ere long, and no mistake. And coming as it did from an old elm in the still evening, and in a remarkably secluded and silent spot, with many solemn and medieval surroundings and the churchyard close at hand, the effect was very odd, and a little thrilling. We were informed on enquiry that a pair of owls had built in the elm, and that from them the sound proceeded.

Now as owls after sunset are usually wide awake, one had some difficulty in supposing that at such an hour they would be caught snoring. On reflection, therefore, we were led to think that the sounds which issued from the elm, and which subsequently we often heard repeated, were rather notes of menace, occasioned by our proximity to the nest, and designed to repel intrusion. Wishing, however, to obtain all the information we could, we at length consulted a venerable inmate of the Hall, who confidently maintains that the snoring (as *he* calls it) does not proceed from the owls at all, but from the owlets – it is their cry for food. We think this very likely, but perhaps some of our correspondents who have had more extended opportunities of investigation may be able to throw some further light upon this subject. ~ Editor, 15 Sep 1860

R2. Attending the afternoon service in a parish church of recent construction in Kent, the congregation was disturbed by a loud snoring during the sermon, which of course I attributed to someone on the other side of the aisle taking his nap instead of listening to the 'truths divine' which flowed from the preacher's lips. On the conclusion of the service I found that my opposite neighbours made the same charge against those on my side of the church, but, on enquiring among the congregation (by no means a large one), I could discover no one who would acknowledge himself or herself to be the delinquent. The minister on coming out solved the difficulty by saying that a colony of owls had established themselves in the roof of the church, and to them we owed the interruption. I do not say whether this was an excuse to avoid the discredit of preaching his congregation asleep, but certain it is that owls did congregate within the sacred precincts. ~ M.E.F., 29 Sep 1860

R3. We country folks well know, to our own inconvenience sometimes, that the young of the *Strix flammea*[1] are great snorers. I have many a time been kept awake by the snoring of owlets in the belfry of the church just opposite my bedroom window. So far as I have been able to observe, the owlets snore during the absence of the old birds in search of food, and, on the return of the old birds, sharpen the snore into a sort of hiss. ~ W.C., 29 Sep 1860

[1] Barn owl.

PARISIAN PUNISHMENTS: Tearing apart by horses and roasting in a cage

Q. What is the last instance in the history of France of a culprit being torn by horses? Jean Châtel, who attempted to assassinate Henri IV, suffered thus in 1595. ~ Ed. S. Jackson, 14 Dec 1850

R. This cruel death was suffered by François Ravaillac, who accomplished what Jean Châtel failed in doing. The execution took place on 27 May 1610 with the most atrocious severities of torture, of which the drawing by horses was but the last in a scene that continued for many hours. The day before he had been racked to the very extremity of human suffering. The horses dragged at the wretch's body for an hour in vain. At length a nobleman who was present sent one of his own, which was stronger, but even this would not suffice. The executioner had to sever the mangled body with his knife before the limbs would give way. I could add more of these details, but the subject is intolerable.

This form of execution was repeated with the utmost exactness, but with more cruelty, if possible, in the case of Robert François Damiens, sentenced for an attempt on Louis XV, who suffered in the Place de Grève on 28 March 1757. The frightful business lasted from morning till dusk! Here again the knife was used before the body gave way, the horses having dragged at it for more than an hour first, the poor wretch living, it is said, all the while. I believe this was the last instance of the punishment in France, if not in Europe. ~ V., Belgravia, 28 Dec 1850

R2. In the case of Damiens the awful penalty of the law was carried out in complete conformity with the savage precedents of former centuries. Not one of the preparatory barbarities of question, ordinary and extraordinary, or of the accompanying atrocities of red-hot pincers, melted lead, and boiling oil, was omitted. The agony of the wretched man lasted for an hour and a half, and was witnessed, as Louis-Sébastien Mercier informs us, by all the best company in Paris. The men amused their leisure with cards while waiting, as Mercier says, for the boiling oil, and the women were the last to turn their eyes from the hideous spectacle. Your correspondent may be glad to be informed that the same punishment was inflicted on Poltrot de Méré in 1563, for the murder of the Duke of Guise; on Salcède in 1582, for conspiring against the Duke of Alençon; on Brilland in 1588, for poisoning the Prince de Condé; on Bourgoing, Prior of the Jacobins, in 1590, as an accessory to the crime of Jacques Clément; as well as on Ravaillac in 1610 for the murder of Henry IV. These, with the case of Jean Châtel, are all of which I am aware.

As I am upon the subject of judicial horrors, I would ask whether any of your correspondents can supply me with a reference to the case of a woman executed, in Paris I think, for a systematic series of infanticides. She was put to death by being suspended over a fire in an iron cage, in which a number of wild cats were shut up with her. I read the story many years ago, and for some time have been vainly endeavouring to recover it. ~ J.S., 1 Feb 1851

R3. An account of this affair will be found in *Wonders of the Universe, or, Curiosities of Nature and Art* (1827). The culprit was named Louise Mabrée, a midwife in Paris. The corpses of no fewer than sixty-two infants were found in and about her house, and she was sentenced to be shut up in an iron cage with sixteen wild cats and suspended over a slow fire. When the cats became infuriated with heat and pain they turned their rage upon her, and, after thirty-five minutes of the most horrible sufferings, put an end to her existence – all the cats dying at the same time, or within two minutes after. This occurred in 1673. ~ J. S. Warden, Balica, 10 Jan 1852

PIGS: Playing on the church organ in Leicestershire?

Q. I should be much obliged by any of your correspondents favouring me with their opinions as to the origin of the saying, 'Hogs Norton, where pigs play upon the organs', which was in vogue in the middle of the seventeenth century. A. B. Evans, in his *Leicestershire Words, Phrases and Proverbs* (1848), says: 'The true name of the town is Hocks Norton, but vulgarly pronounced Hogs Norton. The organist to this parish church was named Piggs.' However, organs were not common in parish churches in the seventeenth century, and I do not know which of the many Nortons in England is referred to.

The only instance that I can recollect of pigs being connected with an organ is in that curious freak recorded of the Abbé de Baigne, *maître de musique* to Louis XI, when he made a hog-organ by enclosing pigs of various ages and pitches of voice in a kind of chest. The older ones were placed on the left hand for the bass, the younger on the right for the treble, and over all these was suspended a keyboard, which, when played on, pressed long needles into the pigs' backs. The result is left to the imagination. ~ Thos. Lawrence, Ashby-de-la-Zouch, 13 Mar 1852

R. Your correspondent may be surprised to find that Hog's Norton is almost in his own immediate neighbourhood. From John Curtis's *Topographical History of the County of Leicester* (1831) it appears that Norton juxta Twycross was in other days

'Nortone, Hoggenortone, Hog's Norton'. There is, then, no doubt as to which of the many Nortons in England is Hog's Norton. But whether there is now, or ever was, an organ in the church, or whether a Mr Piggs, or any number of *pigs*, played on one there, I know not. ~ S.S.S., 27 Mar 1852

¶ Another possible explanation of the saying was suggested by Sir Thomas Cave and quoted in the *Gentleman's Magazine* of June 1813: 'Looking for antiquities about this church, I found in a corner an old piece of a pair of organs, upon the end of every key whereof there was a boar cut, the earls of Oxford sometime being owners of land here.' The crest of the De Veres, earls of Oxford from 1156 to 1703, famously features a blue boar.

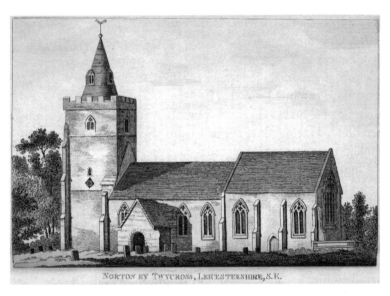

NORTON BY TWYCROSS, LEICESTERSHIRE, S.E.

POCKET-HANDKERCHIEF: Evolution of

Q. The compound structure of this word invites an enquiry into its etymology. Can any of the readers of *N & Q* suggest why it is that the English language does not afford a term for the item in question so simple as the word *mouchoir*? Is it to be inferred that so indispensable an article of the toilet came later into use with us than with the French? ~ H.N., New York, 11 Dec 1858

R. The component parts of this word are four, viz. *pocket*; *hand*; *ker*, cur, or cover, from *couvre*; *chief*, from *chef*, head; that is, pocket-hand-cover-head. Hence the transitions that have taken place in the use of this article of dress: first worn on the *head*, then carried in the *hand*, and lastly in the *pocket*. The word *mouchoir* is not the translation of it, unless *de poche* be added: for the French have *mouchoir de tête*, *mouchoir de cou*, as well as *mouchoir de poche*. In fact, *mouchoir* has, like handkerchief, deviated from its original meaning. First confined to the use of the *nose*, as the verb *moucher*[1] implies, it has passed from that organ to the *head*, from the head to the *neck*, and from the neck to the *pocket*. ~ G. de Chaville, Parkstone, Poole, Dorset, 1 Jan 1859

R2. Commencing with *kerchief*, or 'coverchief' as it is called by Chaucer in *The Wife of Bath's Tale*, it simply meant a square of cloth, linen or silk for the head. In Shakespeare's time its use must have extended, for in *The Merry Wives of Windsor*, Act 4, scene 2, he makes Falstaff 'put on a hat, a muffler, and a kerchief'. Having thus slipped from the head to the neck, it applied to any square of material, and therefore, when carried in the hand for the purpose of wiping the face et cetera, it became *hand*kerchief. In proof of this Shakespeare uses it some twenty-six times or more in *Othello*. The best example occurs in Act 3, scene 3, where Iago says 'such a handkerchief... did I today / See Cassio wipe his beard with...' And the final step came when, being carried in the pocket, it assumed its full form of 'pocket-handkerchief'. ~ T. W. Wonfor, Brighton, 29 Jan 1859

R3. H.N. is not correct in supposing that the English language is so poor as to possess no equivalent of *mouchoir*. *Muckender* is a good old word to express the same thing – though now, on the score of gentility, discarded from colloquial use. Like the French *mouchoir*, or the corresponding Spanish *mocudero*, it involves a reference to the use of the article to which, in

[1] To wipe or blow.

England at least, it is not generally held necessary to direct attention. ~ R.S.Q., 29 Jan 1859

R4. Your correspondents on the Pocket-Handkerchief Question do not seem aware that in the northern parts of North Britain the word is unknown. Drop your *mouchoir* into the salmon-pool, as I am ever doing – a grief of no small moment for a snuff-taker – and your gillygaffer will exclaim, 'Ye hae droppit yer pookeit napkin.' ~ G.H.K., 12 Mar 1859

Understandably confusing to a man without pockets

POLPERRO: Some unusual words from

N. My late friend Thomas Bond, Esq., in his *Sketches of Looe* (1823), says: 'I have been informed that, about a century ago, the people of Polperro had such a dialect among them that even the inhabitants of Looe could scarce understand what they said. Of late years, however, from associating more with strangers, they have nothing particularly striking in their speech.'

To collect and fix, before it is too late, those dying modes of expression, several years ago I adopted the practice of making a note of words and phrases which appeared to be unusual, and I offer below a selection of them arranged into alphabetical order.

Arymouse, the common name for a bat, signifying a mouse that flies in the air.

Braggaty, mottled, like an adder, with a tendency to brown.

Cawdle, entanglement, confusion. A line or thread so entangled as not to be separated is said to be 'all in a *cawdle*'.

Click-handed, left-handed.

Clopp, to walk lame, and with jerks; *clopping*, walking in this manner.

Cockle, to assume to be 'cock of the walk'; to *cockle over* anyone is to assume superiority over him, chiefly by speech.

Cribbage-faced, having a face that is thin and emaciated.

Crowd, a fiddle; *crowder*, a fiddler. We have a proverb 'If I can't *crowdy*, they won't dance,' meaning they will take no notice of me when I have no power to feast or entertain them.

Dafter, daughter.

Drang, a narrow passage, whether between houses or between deep rocks in or near the sea. There is a place near Polperro called Sylly Cove Drang, from this cause.

Duggle, to walk about like a very young child, with effort and care.

Dwalder, to speak tediously and confusedly.

Escaped, a person is said to be just escaped when his understanding is only just enough to warrant his being kept free from constraint or the tutelage of his friends.

Fenigy, to run away secretly, or to slip off as to deceive expectation; deceitfully to fail in a promise. It is most frequently applied to cases where a man has shown appearances of courtship to a woman, and then has left her without any apparent reason, and without any open quarrel.

Flickets, flashes of colour; usually applied to sudden and rapid changes of colour in the face from the alternations of fever.

Forthy, officious; too much disposed to push himself forward.

Gaddle, to drink eagerly and much; to swallow fluid voraciously.

Gigglet, one who shows her folly by a disposition to grin and laugh for no cause. It is used as a term of slight contempt, and commonly to a young girl.

Glaze, to stare.

Goody, to *goody* is for an animal to fatten, thrive, improve in quality.

Gribble, the young stock of a tree on which a graft is to be inserted; chiefly applied to the apple.

Grizzle, to grin.

Havage, a comprehensive word applied to the lineage of a person, his family, and companions. It thus marks the race from which he has sprung, and his station in society.

Lasher, a large thing of any sort. The meaning appears to be that this thing beats or excels every other.

Louster, to work hard, but clumsily. We have a proverb which says that 'Such as cannot skill must *louster*.'

Mulligrubs, gripings of the bowels.

Nattled, starved to so thin a condition as almost to be seen through. The *nattlings* are the small intestines.

Nibby gibby, a very narrow escape. 'It was *nibby gibby* with him,' that is, he had a very narrow escape from injury.

Niddick, the pit of the neck behind, where the head is joined to it.

Peendy, meat which has begun to suffer a change in smell or taste; a peculiar taste or smell short of decay or decomposition.

Plum, soft. Bread is said to be *plum* when it is well fermented, and consequently has sprung up well. Any substance, such as fur or a cushion, is *plum* when it is soft and yielding.

Poddle, to move about with the feet irregularly.

Pots, the bowels. The idea corresponds with a vessel fit to hold something.

Purt, a sharp displeasure, smart resentment. A common phrase is, such a one 'has taken a *purt*'.

Rodling, wandering in the mind; beginning to be mad.

Sabby, moist, only a little wet.

Sclow, to scratch with the nails, as a cat does. It is most commonly applied to the action of little children, when they scratch each other with their nails.

Sconce, understanding, intellect, the faculty of comprehension.

Sych, the edge or foaming border of a wave, as it runs up a harbour or on the land.

Tail-on-end, a proverbial phrase to describe a person standing full of expectation, and ready to act or snatch an advantage.

Tiddy, a mother's milk. To *give tiddy* is to suckle the child. It is no doubt connected with the word *teat*.

Totelish, foolish, like an idiot.

Vogget, to hop on one leg.

Voitch, to tread on by trampling; to trample on a thing over and again.

Wang, to hang about a person in a tiresome manner. Children are said to be *wanging* about their mother when they hold and drag themselves by her garments wherever she goes.

Whinnick, to cheat in a cunning way.

Whisht, melancholy. A place or person is said to be or to look *whisht* when it has a gloomy appearance.

Yolky, dirty, unclean, from habitual neglect. Wool is said to be *yolky*, and *in the yolk*, when in the state in which it is sheared from the sheep.

Zacky, imbecile. Very deficient in understanding.

~ Video, 2 Sep to 16 Dec 1854

POPE THE POET: What became of his skull?

Q. Can any correspondent throw light upon a story, which was formerly current in the neighbourhood of Twickenham, as to the desecration of Pope's grave and the removal of his skull? This is said to have taken place about twenty years since, when an eminent distiller, having died in that parish, was buried in Pope's grave in Twickenham Church. It used to be reported that, on opening the grave, the only part of the remains discovered was the skull of the poet, and that that was then removed. If so, where was it removed to, and is it known to be now in existence? ~ P.S., 25 Nov 1854

R. The following, from William Howitt's *Homes and Haunts of the British Poets* (1847), throws some light upon the subject of P.S.'s Query:

> By one of those acts which neither science nor curiosity can excuse, the skull of Pope is now in the private collection of a phrenologist. The manner in which it was obtained is said to have been this. On some occasion of alteration in the church, or burial of someone in the same spot, the coffin of Pope was disinterred and opened to see the state of the remains. By a bribe to the sexton of the time, possession of the skull was obtained for the night, and another skull returned instead of it. I have heard that £50 was paid to manage and carry through this transaction.

~ R.V.T., 9 Dec 1854

R2. That the grave of Pope has been disturbed I have no doubt, for about twenty or twenty-five years ago an old gentleman, who is since dead, told me he had himself seen the bones of Pope the poet when the vault or grave was opened. Besides this, I was once a member of a literary and scientific institution which met in Hackney Road, where a lecture was given on phrenology. The lecturer, whose name I forget, was showing that the parts of the cranium where the most exercised organs were situated became thinner, and vice versa. 'Now,' said the lecturer, holding up 'The dome of thought, the palace of the soul,' as Byron finely expresses it, and placing it near the light, 'you will perceive that the *os frontis* is here nearly transparent, while the back part has twice the substance, showing the person to whom it belonged must have passed his life in continual study and contemplation. This, ladies and gentleman, is the skull of Pope the poet!' The sensation caused by this announcement was such that at the conclusion of the lecture there was a general rush to view it more closely, as it lay for a few minutes on the table before being put away. I have never seen or heard of it from that time, some twelve or fifteen years to the present. ~ W.B., Dalston, 16 Dec 1854

QUARRELSOME, CARELESS AND HAIRY: Some nicknames of kings and others

N. Nicknames are as old as the most venerable of chronicles, for even thundering Jove had no better name at Rome than Pistor the Baker, while kings, great captains, divines and statesmen have received from malice, humour, or revenge a sportive title which will cling to them to the end of time, be it drawn from singularity in address, habit, or gesture, or some accident or circumstance of life. I shall give just a few of the many examples:

> Albert I of Brandenburg – the Bear
> Alfonso II of Portugal – the Fat
> Alfonso IV of León – the Monk
> Bermudo II of León – the Gouty
> Boleslav III of Poland – Wrymouth
> Bolelsav IV of Poland – Curlypate
> Boleslav V of Poland – the Chaste

Charles I of France – the Bald
Charles II of Naples – the Lame
Charles VIII of France – the Affable
Charles XII of Sweden – the Madman of the North
Childeric III, King of the Franks – the Stupid
Clodius, King of the Franks – the Hairy
Erik III of Denmark – the Lamb
Ethelred II of England – the Unready
Garcia II of Navarre – the Trembler
Henry II of Bavaria – the Quarrelsome
Henry IV of Castile – the Impotent
Ivan IV of Russia – the Terrible
Pope John XII – the Infamous
Ladislaus I of Poland – the Careless
Louis II, King of the Franks – the Stammerer
Louis V of France – the Lazy
Louis X of France – the Headstrong
Mary I of England – Bloody
Pedro I of Portugal – the Cruel
Pope Sergius IV – Hogsnout
Sweyn I of Denmark – Forkbeard
William I of Sicily – the Wicked

There was also a French general of the fourteenth century well known as *Gnaw-crust*. ~ Mackenzie Walcott, 4 Apr 1857

¶ Among many names which could be added to Mackenzie Walcott's list are:

Alfonso IX of León – the Slobberer
Bernard II, Count of Auvergne – Hairyfoot
Blot-Sweyn of Sweden – the Sacrificer
Cadafael, King of Gwynedd – the Battle-shirker
Charles VI of France – the Silly
Erik II of Denmark – the Memorable
Erik II of Norway – the Priest-hater
Frederick III, Elector of Saxony – the Hesitater
Fyodor I of Russia – the Bell-ringer

Charles the Bad meets an Unhappy End

Charles II, King of Navarre from 1349 to 1387, earned his sobriquet by shameless manoeuvring between the French and English during the Hundred Years War and a regrettable inclination to murder people (he poisoned one of his victims with a crystallised pear). In his last years he became afflicted with great pain in his limbs and a trembling coldness. As a remedy he had a basin of hot coals laid beneath his bed to make him sweat, which seemed to help. One night, however, according to Froissart's *Chronicles*, 'as God wished, or the Devil, a burning flame took in the sheets, in such manner that, before he could be rescued, he was burnt to the bowels... He lived fifteen days after in great pain and misery, and then he died.'

Joanna of Castile – the Mad
Justinian II, Byzantine emperor – Split-nosed
Otto IV, Duke of Austria – the Jolly
Pedro IV of Aragon – the Ceremonious
Rudolf III of Burgundy – the Sluggard
Sancho I of Portugal – the Populator
Vlad III of Wallachia – the Impaler

RAIN: A device for the prevention of

N. The surprising announcement in the accompanying newspaper cutting is surely worthy of being embalmed in your miscellany as an example of the 'wonders' of the age:

NO MORE RAIN

There is now before the Academy of Science at Paris a wonderful invention of Mons. Helvetius Otto of Leipzig, by which he promises to ensure fine weather – in fact, by making use of his invention, rain cannot fall unless desired. His plan is simple enough. He erects a platform at a considerable height in the air, on which he places a 'propeller', or huge bellows, worked by steam. With these bellows, which are very powerful, he blows away the clouds as they gather; and, as rain comes from the clouds, it must necessarily follow that where clouds are not allowed to gather there can be no rain. He maintains that if a certain number of his 'Rain Propellers', or 'Pluvifuges' as he has named them, are placed at intervals over the city, he can provide for the inhabitants a continuance of fine weather, and a certain protection from sudden showers and muddy streets, so long the terror of fair pedestrians. The Academy have received the proposition of Mons. Otto with acclamation, so we trust it will soon be put into execution. The invention is scarcely more wonderful than Franklin's discovery of lightning conductors, and, as the American succeeded by attraction, why should not Mons. Otto by repulsion?

~ Credat Judaeus, 15 Sep 1860

RATS 1: Deserting a sinking ship

Q. Do they? And where do they go to? ~ Job J. Bardwell Workard, 21 Dec 1861

R. I forward the following extract, which throws some light upon this enquiry:

> At the beginning of our voyage an incident occurred which had considerable influence on the men's cheerfulness. This was the jumping overboard of a rat, just as we were getting well out to sea, which, after swimming round a circle two or three times, struck out in the direction of the shore. I believe it went over to escape from the pigs, for these animals seemed to have a great taste for rats. I had myself seen them wrangling over one not long before, and I told the men so, but they preferred to believe that the act was a voluntary one on the part of the rat, and indicative of misfortune to the ship.
>
> (*Leisure Hour*, 16 January 1862)

~ Vedette, 25 Jan 1862

R2. When the water rises in a ship's ceiling, rats are obliged to leave, or they would be drowned: hence sailors infer the ship is not seaworthy, or wants good pumping, when this occurs.

It reminds me of a cunning plan of a Welsh captain whose ship was infested with rats some years ago in Liverpool. He found out there was a cheese ship in the basin. Getting alongside it about dusk, he left all hatches open, kept watch, saw the rats over onto his neighbour, and then slipped his moorings.
~ George Lloyd, Thurstonland, 12 Apr 1862

RATS 2: In military operations

Q. Charles James, in his *Military Dictionary* (1816), has stated that 'rats are sometimes used in military operations, particularly in enterprises for the purpose of setting fire to magazines of gunpowder. On these occasions a lighted match is tied to the tail of the animal. Marshal Vauban recommends, therefore, that the walls of powder magazines should be made very thick, and the passages for light and wind so narrow as not to admit them.'[1]

Can any instances be given of powder magazines having been exploded in the manner described? Doubtless they did occur, or Marshal Vauban would not have recommended that such precautions should be taken in their construction. ~ W.W., Malta, 18 Apr 1857

¶ No instances of the use of living rats were forthcoming in *N & Q*, but during the Second World War the Special Operations Executive famously planned to use dead rats to conceal plastic explosive. The official guide to devices listed them as follows:

Rats, Explosive. A rat is skinned, the skin being sewn up and filled with P.E. to assume the shape of a dead rat. A Standard No. 6 Primer is set in the P.E. Initiation is by means of a short length of safety fuse… The rat is then left amongst the coal beside a boiler and the flames initiate the safety fuse when the rat is thrown on the fire.

They were never used: the first consignment was discovered by the Germans, who were fascinated, exhibited them at their military schools, and spent a great deal of time searching for dead rats. An SOE report concluded that 'The trouble caused to them was a much greater success to us than if the rats had actually been used.'

---

[1] Sebastien le Prestre de Vauban (1633-1707), marshal of France from 1703, was the foremost military engineer of his day and the author of celebrated treatises on siegecraft and fortification.

REMEDIES: For ague, plague, et cetera

Ague 1

N. One of my parishioners, suffering from ague, was advised to catch a large spider and shut him up in a box. As the creature pines away, the disease is supposed to wear itself out. ~ ⊃, L— Rectory, Somerset, 27 July 1850

R. In the Fens of Huntingdonshire the spider was considered an infallible curer of the ague. It was swallowed *alive*, wrapped up, pill-fashion, in paste. I have been told of many cases cured by this Arachnidaian recipe. ~ Cuthbert Bede, 27 June 1857

R2. I find the following in the Diary of Elias Ashmole, under 11 April 1681: 'I took early in the morning a good dose of elixir, and hung three spiders about my neck, and they drove my ague away. *Deo gratias!*'[1] ~ F. Phillott, 1 Sep 1860

Ague 2

N. Being afflicted two years since with a severe tertian ague, I was solicited by a lady, after the usual medical treatment had failed, to take as much of the snuff of a candle as would lie on a sixpence, made into an electuary with honey. I complied, and, strange to say, a complete cure was effected. Whether the nausea consequent on such an unpleasant remedy had any effect on the spasmodic nature of the malady I cannot say, but the fact is certain, and it is esteemed a sovereign specific by the Norfolk rustics. ~ E. S. Taylor, Martham, Norfolk, 26 July 1851

[1] Living spiders were worn about the neck in a nutshell until they died. As in the case cited by ⊃, the 'remedy' relied on the operation of sympathy between spider and disease.

R. The benefit derived by Mr Taylor was owing to the minute quantity of creosote contained in each dose. Dr Elliotson tried the same nauseous remedy with partial success at St Thomas's Hospital some years since. ~ J.N.T., 9 Aug 1851

R2. The cure mentioned by Mr E. S. Taylor has been practised with much success by some lady friends of mine for some years past amongst the poor of the parishes in which they have lived. From the number of cures effected by them, I have sent the same application (with the exception of using ginger instead of honey) to a relative of mine in India, who has been suffering from ague acutely, and am anxiously waiting to hear the result. ~ W.H.P., 4 Oct 1851

Baldness and Tired Feet

N. In his *Bulwark of Defence against all Sickness* (1562) William Bulleyn says 'The beare is a beaste whose flesh is good for mankind: his fat is good, with laudanum, to make an ointment to heale bald headed men to receive the haire againe. The grease of the beare, the fatte of a lambe, and the ointment of the fox, maketh a good ointment to anoint the feete against the paine of travell or labour of footemen.' ~ F. J. Furnivall, 15 June 1872

Fits

N. The following disgusting case of superstition is chronicled by the *Stamford Mercury* of 8 October this year. It ought to be perpetuated in *N & Q*: 'A collier's wife recently applied to the sexton of Ruabon Church for ever so small a piece of a human skull for the purpose of grating it similar to ginger, to be afterwards added to some mixture which she intended giving her daughter as a remedy against fits, to which she was subject.' ~ K.P.D.E., 25 Dec 1858

Gout

N. From the *Calendar of State Papers*, Domestic Series: '1619, June 12. The king killed a buck in Eltham Park, and bathed his bare feet and legs in the blood as a cure for the gout.' ~ Cuthbert Bede, 8 July 1871

Lethargy in the Head

N. The following is extracted from *The Queen's Closet Opened, comprehending several hundreds of Experienced Receipts, and Incomparable Secrets, in Physick, Chyrurgery, Preserving, Candying, Cookery, etc.*, printed in 1684:

> *For the Lytargie in the Head in the hinder part, which maketh for it to shake*

Take a pure blacke cat, and flea her, and pull out her bowels, and picke away the fat from the guttes, and put them into the body againe, and fill the body full of musterdseede, well steeped in the juice of nep,[1] and sage, and then sow the body up, and rost it upon a spit, till it be so dry that it drop no more moisture, then take the dripping that commeth therof, and put it in bladders, and, when you will occupy[2] it, shave the patient in the neck, and anoint him by the fire in the joint next to the head, and it shall help the grieved.

~ H.B., Warwick, 25 Oct 1856

Plague et cetera

N. Among the many curious books of combined cookery and chemistry which were common amongst our ancestors of the seventeenth and eighteenth centuries, one was called *The Lady's Cabinet enlarged and opened*, by 'the late Right Honourable and Learned Chymist, the Lord Ruthven'. I have an imperfect copy of the 4th edition, printed by G. Bedel and T. Collier at the Middle Temple Gate in Fleet Street, 1667. It contains many strange things. A peculiar oil of cream is recommended by his lordship as a cure for 'the gout in a hawk's leg', while to have a sovereign remedy 'for all aches' we are advised to take 'two dozen or twenty swallows out of the nest', add rosemary leaves, lavender, cotton, and strawberry leaves, stamp them all together, and fry them all in May butter or salad oil. Other articles in Lord Ruthven's pharmacopoeia include 'worms of the earth' (good for

[1] Catmint.

[2] Make use of.

bruises), deer's suet, hen's and duck's grease, the pith of an ox's back, goose dung, the lungs of a fox, an ox's paunch, frogs, eyes of crabs, droppings from a candle, mice dung, and the skins of snakes and adders. I close by extracting one of a number of plague recipes:

> Take a live frog, and lay the belly of it next the plague sore; if the patient will escape, the frog will burst in a quarter of an hour: then lay on another; and this you shall do till[1] more do burst, for they draw forth the venom. If none of the frogs do burst, the party will not escape. This hath been frequently tried. Some say a dried toad will do it better.

~ John Bruce, 5 Upper Gloster Street, 4 Oct 1856

R. The Queen's Closet Opened (1684) offers the following alternative remedy for the plague:

> When the sore doth appeare, then to take a cock-chick and pull it; and let the rump be bare, and hold the rump of the said chick to the sore, and it will gape and labour for life, and in the end die; then take another, and the third, and so long as any one so die; for when the poison is quite drawn out the chick will live, the sore presently will asswage and the party recover. Mr Wintour proved this upon one of his own children: the thirteenth chick died, the fourteenth lived, and the party [was] cured.

~ H.B., Warwick, 25 Oct 1856

Rheumatism

N. The right forefoot of a hare, worn constantly in the pocket, is considered a fine amulet against the 'rheumatiz'. ~ T.S., 15 June 1850

Whooping Cough

N. There is a superstition in Cheshire that whooping cough may be cured by holding a toad for a few moments with its head within the mouth of the person affected. I heard only the other day of a cure by this somewhat disagreeable process: the toad was said to have caught the disease, which in this instance proved fatal to it within a few hours. ~ A.H.H., 5 Apr 1851

---

[1] For as long as.

RHINOCEROS: The first in England?

Q. In the *London Gazette* of October 1684 there is an advertisement of a rhinoceros, 'the first that ever was in England'. Can any of your readers help me to any further account of this arrival? ~ H.E., 17 Feb 1866

R. From the *Diary* of John Evelyn: '1684. Oct. 22nd. I went with Sir William Godolphin to see the rhinoceros, or unicorn, being the first that I suppose was ever brought into England. She belonged to some East India merchants, and was sold (as I remember) for above £2,000.' ~ Edw. Marshall, 10 Mar 1866

R2. This was probably the animal concerning which Roger North relates the following anecdote in *Lives of the Norths*:

It fell out thus. A merchant of Sir Dudley North's acquaintance had brought over an enormous rhinoceros, to be sold to showmen for profit.[1] It is a noble beast, wonderfully armed by nature for offence, but more for defence, being covered with impenetrable shields, which no weapon would make any impression upon, and a rarity so great that few men in our country have in their whole lives opportunity to see so singular an animal. This merchant told Sir Dudley North that if he, with a friend or two, had a mind to see it, they might take the opportunity at his house before it was sold. Hereupon Sir Dudley North proposed to his brother, the Lord Keeper,[2] to go with him upon this expedition; which he did, and came away exceedingly satisfied with the curiosity he had seen. But the very next morning a bruit went forth all over the town and in a very short time, viz. that his lordship rode on the rhinoceros – than which a more infantine exploit could not have been fastened upon him. And most people were struck with amazement at it, and [many ran] here and there to find out whether it was

[1] Sir Dudley North (1641-1691), merchant, financier, and government official.

[2] Francis North, Baron Guilford (1637-1685), Keeper of the Great Seal and Lord Chancellor.

thus or no, and soon after dinner some lords and others came to his lordship to know the truth from himself; for the tellers of the lie affirmed it positively, as of their own knowledge. I never saw him in such a rage, and to lay about him with affronts as then, for he sent them away with fleas in their ear. And he was seriously angry with his own brother, Sir Dudley North, because he did not contradict the lie in sudden and direct terms, but laughed...

~ B. Blundell, 10 Mar 1866

¶ The first rhinoceros seen in Europe since Roman times was shipped from India to Lisbon in 1515 as a gift to Dom Manuel I of Portugal. During its brief sojourn in Portugal it was pitched in public battle against an elephant, which fled ignominiously, and became the subject of a celebrated woodcut by Albrecht Dürer, who did not see the creature in the flesh but worked from a sketch sent to him in Germany. At the end of 1515 the rhinoceros was despatched to Rome as a gift to Pope Leo X – Manuel wishing to outdo the elephant he had sent the year before – but in January 1516 the ship carrying it was wrecked off the coast of northern Italy, and, hampered by its chains, the creature drowned.

The first rhinoceros seen in England was brought from Golconda, near Hyderabad, in the summer of 1684. A newsletter of 23 August records that 'On board one of the East India ships is come a rhinincerous valued at £2,000 at the Customes House, and will be sold next weeke by inch of candle.'[1] On 25 August the animal was sold at auction to John Langley, a London merchant, for the substantial sum of £2,320. However, a newsletter of 30 August reports that 'Mr Langley, who bought the rhinocerus, not being able to raise the money, forfeited the £500 he paid in hand, and this evening the owner put up the beast to sale again by inch of candle for £2,000, but noe person bid a farthing so [it] lies upon their hands.'

---

[1] The auctioneer would light a one-inch tallow candle on top of his desk and accept bids only as long as the flame continued.

It seems likely that the merchants who had brought the animal to England decided to put it on show themselves. Hence the advertisement in the *London Gazette* of 16 October 1684: 'A Very Strange Beast called a Rhynoceros, brought from the East Indies, being the first that ever was in England, is daily to be seen at the Bell Savage Inn on Ludgate Hill, from nine a clock in the morning till eight at night.'

Visitors were charged a shilling to look at the animal and two shillings to ride on its back. It was reported that takings ran to £15 a day.

The rhinoceros reappears in another advertisement in the *London Gazette*, dated 22 March 1686: 'These are to give notice, that this strange beast, called the Rhynoceros, will be sent beyond sea, and therefore will not be seen in this city after the 14th of April next, which it may be in the mean time at the Bell Savage on Ludgate Hill.' The animal's death is recorded in a newsletter of 28 September in the same year: 'Last weeke died that wonderfull creature the Rhynocerus... The several proprietors having ensured £1,200 on her life, the ensurers are catched for much money.'

RICHELIEU, CARDINAL: A serpentine letter from

N. I do not recollect seeing, among the literary curiosities preserved in *N & Q*, a specimen of a 'serpentine' or double-faced letter. One such lies before me in a work entitled *A Short Account of Scotland* (1702) by the Rev. Thomas Morer. When visiting the college of Edinburgh he was shown this remarkable production, Englished as follows, in which the great Cardinal Richelieu introduces a Benedictine friar to the French ambassador at Rome in Jesuitical fashion. The letter is, your readers will see, to be read as the friar understood it in the two columns together; but, as the cardinal meant it, we are to read the first column only. ~ J.O., 24 Mar 1855

Master *Compy, a SAVOYARD* Friar of the Order of St BENNET is to be a BEARER to you of this Letter. He is one of the most Vicious Persons that I ever yet knew, and has earnestly desired me to give him a LETTER of Recommendation, which I granted to his importunity. For, believe me, sir, I would be sorry you should be mistaken in not KNOWING him, as many OTHERS have been, who are my best FRIENDS. Hence it is, that I desire to advertise you to take special NOTICE of him, and say NOTHING in his Presence in any SORT. For I may and do assure you, there cannot be a more Unworthy PERSON in the World I KNOW that as soon as you shall be ACQUAINTED with him you will thank me for this ADVICE. CIVILITY doth hinder me to say more upon this subject.

NEWS from me by Means of DISCREET, WISE, and Least among all I have CONVERST with to write to you in his FAVOUR, CREDENCE with some pressing MERIT I assure you rather than he deserves infinitely your Esteem, and wanting to oblige him by your being I should be afflicted if you were so, on that Account who now esteem him and from no other MOTIVE that you are obliged more than any to afford him all imaginable Respect that may OFFEND or DISPLEASE him truly say I love him as my self, and convincing ARGUMENT of an than to be capable of doing him injury. cease to be a stranger to his Virtues, and will LOVE him as well as I, and The assurance I have of your great write further of him to you, or to

I am, sir,
Your affectionate friend,
JEAN ARMAND DE PLESSIS

Paris, 23 November 1638.
For the Ambassador of France
at Rome

RIDING WHIP: Found inside a fish

N. James S. M'Intire, of the United States Army, advertises in the *Francisco Herald* a lady's riding whip that he found in a sturgeon, weighing seventy-five to one hundred pounds, which he had caught at Benecia. The whip is 21½ inches long, and silver mounted. ~ W.W., Malta, 8 Sep 1855

ROYAL POSITIONS: Some curious

Whipping Boy

Q. Will any correspondent inform me when ceased the custom of male heirs apparent to the throne of England having whipping boys? When and why it originated? What remuneration such boys received? And whether our queens had during their state of pupillage any such kinds of convenience? I have only met with the names of two whipping boys: Brown, who stood for Edward VI, and Mungo Murray, who did the like for Charles I. ~ Thos. Lawrence, Ashby-de-la-Zouch, 15 May 1852

¶ Edward VI's whipping boy is usually named as Barnaby Fitzpatrick (*c.*1535-1581). In England the practice of exempting the royal backside from punishment died out at the end of the seventeenth century as adherence to the doctrine of the divine right of kings declined and monarchs and their progeny came increasingly to be seen as ordinary mortals.

Cock-crower

N. During Lent an officer, denominated 'The King's Cock-crower', crowed the hour every night within the precincts of the palace, instead of proclaiming it in the ordinary manner. On the first Ash Wednesday after the accession of the House of Hanover, as the Prince of Wales, afterwards George II, was sitting down to supper, this officer suddenly entered the apartment and proclaimed, in a sound resembling 'the cock's shrill clarion', that it was past ten o'clock. Taken thus by surprise, and very imperfectly acquainted with the English language, the prince mistook the tremulation of the assumed crow as some mockery intended to insult him, and instantly rose to resent the affront. With some difficulty he was made to understand the nature of the custom, and that it was intended as a compliment and accorded with court etiquette, but from that period the custom has been discontinued. ~ Notsa, 24 Jan 1857

¶ From the *Gentleman's Magazine*, May 1785: 'The intention was undoubtedly to remind waking sinners of the august effect the third crowing of the cock had on the guilty apostle St Peter. The adaptation to the precincts of the court seems also to have had a view, as if the institutor (probably the royal confessor) had considered that the greater and more obdurate sinners resided within the purlieus of the palace.'

Ratcatcher

N. A pamphlet published in 1813, giving 'Directions how to kill all sorts of animals, insects, and vermin', has a portrait of the Royal Ratcatcher prefixed. ~ William Kelly, Leicester, 16 May 1863

Joculator

Q. In *Specimens of Early English Metrical Romances*, George Ellis says of minstrels: 'They were obliged to adopt various modes of amusing, and to unite the mimic and the juggler. Their rewards were in some cases enormous, and prove the esteem in which they were held – though this may be partly ascribed to the general thirst after amusement, and the difficulty of the great in dissipating the tediousness of life.' He then states that William the Conqueror assigned three parishes in Gloucestershire as a gift for the support of his *Joculator*, and adds: 'This may, perhaps, be a less accurate measure of the minstrel's accomplishments than of the monarch's power and of the insipidity of his court.'

Three parishes in Gloucestershire must at any time have been an immense donation for almost any services one can imagine, and I should be much obliged to any reader of *N & Q* who can point out which these three parishes were, and the name of the fortunate joculator, if it has descended to posterity. ~ Λ, 9 Aug 1856

R. I beg to inform Λ that the name of William the Conqueror's joculator *has* descended to posterity. It was *Berdic*. The particulars will be found in the first volume of Domesday Book on the first page relative to the county of Gloucester: '*Berdic joculator regis habet iii villas et ibi v carucas, nil reddit.*' That is, he not only had three towns, but also five carucates of land, and all rent free.[1] It does not appear what were the names of his towns. ~ W.H.W.T., Somerset House, 21 Feb 1857

Keepers of the Cormorants

N. Among the documents in the State Paper Office is a petition 'of Robert Wood, John Wood, and two others, Keepers of His Majesty's Cormorants', to the Commissioners for the funeral of James I, praying that they may have mourning weeds. ~ M.N.S., 4 June 1859

Yeomen of the Mouth

Q. In the cemetery attached to Morden College, Blackheath, is a stone commemorating John Thompson, who died in 1708 and was 'Yeoman of the Mouth in the Kitchen' to Charles II. Can anyone give me information either of this person or the nature of his office? ~ H. S. Richardson, Greenwich, 22 Sep 1866

R. This officer is thus noticed in the Northumberland Household Book of 1512: 'Furst, a Yoman Cooke for the mouth, who doith hourely attend at the kitching at the haistry for roisting of meat at braikefestis and meallis.' To this passage Bishop Percy has added the following note: 'This officer attended hourly in the kitchen at the *haistry* i.e. the fireplace, to see the roasting of the meat used at breakfast and other meals.' At a later period we find this officer in attendance at the royal table, and he was probably the one frequently designated as the *Taster*. In Queen Elizabeth's Household Book in the forty-third year of her reign we read of 'Yeomen at the Mouth two. They have 100*s.* a-yeare a-peece, and there is two messes of meate of three dishes a-peece allowed for them and the rest of the officers of the pantry.' In the establishment of William and Mary in 1689, Ulrick Horitiner was Yeoman of the Mouth: wages £5; board-wages £45. The husband of the witty dramatist, Mrs Centlivre, was Yeoman of the Mouth to Queen Anne. ~ Editor, 22 Sep 1866

---

[1] A carucate was an area of land equivalent to that which could be ploughed in a year by a single plough and eight oxen.

I AM THE ONLY RUNNING FOOTMAN

RUNNING FOOTMEN

N. The following description of this now extinct class of retainers is extracted from a volume of manuscript 'Notes on Old Plays', in the handwriting of the Rev. George Ashby, Rector of Borrow in Suffolk, and Fellow of Trinity College, Cambridge. The notes appear to have been written in about 1780 and seem to me so characteristic of a bygone state of society as to deserve a corner in *N & Q*.

The running footmen drank white wine and eggs. One told me, fifty years ago, that they carried some white wine in the large silver ball of their tall cane or pole, which unscrews; that they could easily keep ahead of the coach and six in uphill and down countries (N.B. bad roads), but that in the plain they were glad to sign to the coachman with the pole to pull in, as they could not hold out. I have often wondered how he came to tell us little schoolboys at Croydon thus much. Since the roads have been made good, the carriages and cattle lightened, we have little of them; yet I remember he told us of vast performances, threescore miles a day, and seven miles in an hour. The last exploit of one of them that I recollect was, the late Duke of Marlborough drove his phaeton and four for a wager from London to Windsor against one, and just beat him, but the poor fellow died soon. They wore no breeches, but a short silk petticoat, kept down by a deep gold fringe.

In these long poles of the running footmen we have, I presume, the origin of the long silver-headed canes carried by the footmen of many families at the present day.

I have been told that the late Duke of Queensbury was the last nobleman who kept running footmen and that he was in the habit, before engaging them, of trying their paces by seeing how they could run up and down Piccadilly, he watching and timing them from his balcony. They put on his livery before the trial. On one occasion a candidate presented himself, dressed, and ran. At the conclusion of his performance he stood before the balcony. 'You'll do very well for me,' said the duke. 'Your livery will do very well for me,' replied the man, and gave the duke a last proof of his ability as a runner by then running away with it. ~ Editor, 5 Jan 1856

R. It was stated in the public journals, early in 1851, that on the opening of one of the assize courts in the North of England (Carlisle, I believe) the sheriff and judges were preceded by two running footmen. I recollect that, nearly forty years ago, a very old man was residing at Lyndhurst who had been a running footman. It was his boast of having run from London to Lyndhurst (about eighty-six miles) in one day. If I mistake not, he was employed in the after part of his life by the gentlemen of the New Forest Hunt in attending to some of their matters on the chase, for which his fleetness and strength of constitution well adapted him. No doubt there are persons now living in Hampshire who remember a tall, white-haired man, attired in a faded scarlet hunting coat and velvet jockey cap, frequenting the Forest Courts, even when unable to do more than walk out for recreation. That man was poor old Choats, the running footman. ~ Henry Edwards, 26 Jan 1856

R2. I was in Dresden on a hot day in July 1845, during the lifetime of the late king, when his travelling coach and four passed me on the road to the palace at Pillnitz. I recollect vividly how startled I was at the running footmen, three in number, who preceded it, dressed and accoutred as I had never seen mortal man. First, in the centre of the dusty *chaussée*, about thirty yards ahead of the foremost horses' heads, came a tall, thin, white-haired old man; he looked six feet high, about seventy years of age, but as lithe as a deer; his legs and body were clothed in drawers or tights of white linen, his jacket was like a jockey's, the colours blue and yellow, with lace and fringes on the facings; on his head a sort of barret-cap, slashed and ornamented with lace and embroidery, and decorated in front with two curling heron's plumes; round his waist a deep belt of leather with silk and lace fringes, tassels, and quaint embroidery, which seemed to serve as a sort of pouch to the wearer. In his right hand he held a staff about two feet long, carved and pointed with a silver head, and something like bells or metal drops hung round it, that jingled as he ran. Behind him, one on each side of the road, dressed and accoutred in the same style, came his two sons, handsome, tall young fellows of from twenty to twenty-five years of age; and so the king passed on.

From the gallery of the dining hall at the palace at Pillnitz I saw his majesty the king at dinner (a strange but very ancient custom), and the white-haired old footman waited behind the king's chair in full running costume, all except the staff. ~ C. D. Lamont, 1 Mar 1856

R3. The following extract relating to one of these retainers in Ireland is from the autobiography of the playwright John O'Keeffe. He was born in 1747 and is speaking of mansion houses near Dublin during his early years.

My lord's or the squire's was called the Big House, and had its privileged fool or satirist, its piper, and its running footman. The latter I have often seen skimming or flying across the road. One of them I particularly remember, his dress a white jacket, blue silk sash round his waist, light black-velvet cap with a silver tassel on the crown, round his neck a frill with a ribbon, and in his hand a staff about seven feet high with a silver top. He looked so agile, and seemed all air like a Mercury. He never minded roads, but took the shortest cut, and, by the help of his pole, absolutely seemed to fly over hedge, ditch, and small river. His use was to carry a letter, message, or despatch, or, on a journey, to run before and prepare the inn or baiting-place for his family or master, who came the regular road in coach and two, or coach and four, or coach and six. His qualifications were fidelity, strength, and agility.

~ Robert S. Salmon, Newcastle-on-Tyne, 5 Apr 1856

R4. Peter Beckford, in his *Familiar Letters from Italy*, writes thus from Piacenza:

It was from hence, in the spring of 1766, that I sent my running footman with a letter to Mantua. He could not have set out before six o'clock in the morning, for till that time the gates were not open. The answer was dated Mantua, two o'clock at noon.[1] I received it early the next morning before I was up, and he made many excuses for not returning the same day. It is wonderful what these fellows are capable of doing, but it is cruel to put it unnecessarily to the trial.

The distance between Piacenza and Mantua appears from the map to be exactly sixty miles as the crow flies, and the road by no means direct. ~ J.F.M., 31 May 1856

[1] i.e. after noon.

RURAL NUTRITION: Snails and roasted hedgehogs

N. In Surrey, and probably in other counties where shell-snails abound, children amuse themselves by charming them with a chant to put forth their horns. Of this I have only heard the following couplet, which is repeated until it has the desired effect, to the great amusement of the charmer: 'Snail, snail, come out of your hole, / Or else I'll beat you as black as a coal.' ~ S. W. Singer, 22 Feb 1851

R. The practice of *eating*, if not of *talking to*, snails seems not to be so unknown in this country as some of your readers might imagine. I was just now interrogating a village child, in reference to the address to snails quoted in your previous issue, when she acquainted me with the not very appetising fact that she and her brothers and sisters had been in the constant habit of indulging this horrible *Limacotrophy*: 'We hooks them out of the wall (she says) with a stick, in winter time, and not in summer time (so it seems they have their seasons); and we roasts them, and, when they've done spitting, they be a-done; and we takes them out with a fork, and eats them. Sometimes we has a jug heaped up, pretty near my pinafore full. I loves them dearly.' ~ C.W.B., 15 Mar 1851

R2. Your correspondent C.W.B. does not seem to be aware that 'a ragout of boror' (snails) is a regular dish with English gypsies. He has clearly not read Mr George Borrow's remarks on the subject in *The Zincali: An Account of the Gypsies of Spain*: 'Know then, O Gentile, whether thou be from the land of Gorgios (England) or the Busné (Spain), that the very gypsies who consider a ragout of snails a delicious dish will not touch an eel because it bears a resemblance to a snake, and that those who will feast on a roasted hedgehog could be induced by no money to taste a squirrel!'

Having tasted of roasted *hotchiwitchu* (hedgehog) myself among the 'gentle Romanys', I can bear witness to its delicate fatness; and though a ragout of snails was never offered for my acceptance, I do not think that those who consider – as most 'Gorgios' do – stewed eels a delicacy ought to be too severe on 'Limacotrophists'! ~ Hermes, 22 Mar 1851

R3. Perhaps you will permit me to remark, in reference to the communication of C.W.B., that snails are occasionally taken medicinally, and are supposed extremely strengthening. I have known them eagerly sought after for the meal of a consumptive patient. As a matter of taste, too, they are by some considered quite epicurean. A gentleman whom I used to know was in the constant habit, as he passed through the fields, of picking up the white slugs that lay in his way and swallowing them with more relish than he would have done had they been oysters.

That snails make a not inconsiderable item in the bill of fare of gypsies and other wanderers, I proved while at Oxford some time ago. Passing up Shotover Hill, in the parish of Headington, I unexpectedly came upon a camp of gypsies who were seated round a wood fire enjoying their Sunday's dinner. This consisted of a considerable number of large snails roasted on the embers, and potatoes similarly cooked. On enquiry I was told by those who were enjoying their repast that they were extremely good, and were much liked by people of their class, who made a constant practice of eating them. I need hardly say that I received a most hospitable invitation to join in the feast, which I certainly declined. ~ L.J., 22 Mar 1851

R4. This practice is very general in Italy. One day, while residing near Florence, I happened to meet the *contadina* coming out of my garden with a basket on her arm. From her shy, conscious manner, and an evident wish to avoid my seeing the contents, I rather suspected she had been making free with my peaches. To my surprise, however, I found that she was laden with about three quarts of large brown snails, carefully removed from their shells, which lay in a ditch nearby. I asked her what in the world she intended to do with them, and, with a look of amazement at my question, she informed me that her brother and his wife had come to visit and that, with my kind permission, she would treat them to '*una bellissima cena*'. The large brown kind only are eaten, and are reputed to be marvellously nutritious. ~ Nocab, 26 Apr 1851

RUSSIA, THE FIRST ENGLISH AMBASSADOR TO, or, How to Handle Ivan the Terrible

Q. Sir Jerome Bowes was ambassador from Queen Elizabeth to the then Tsar of Muscovy, Ivan the Terrible. A very remarkable anecdote was once in existence of his reply to that despot, on refusing, with Roman haughtiness, to pay a slavish obeisance to the barbarian, for which he was well nigh having his hat nailed to his head. Can any of your readers give me a copy of his heroic answer, or direct me where to search for it? ~ A.B., 12 Aug 1854

R. In the *Quarterly Review* of July 1817 we find the following notice:

On entering the presence chamber [at Moscow] the ambassador was desired by the emperor to take his seat at ten paces distance and to send to him her majesty's letters and present. Sir Jerome, thinking this not reasonable, stepped forwards towards the emperor, but was intercepted by the chancellor, who would have taken his letters; to whom the ambassador said that her majesty had directed no letters to him, and so went forward and delivered them himself to the emperor's own hands. In the course of his mission, however, he offended the emperor, because he would not yield to everything he thought fit, who, with a stern and angry countenance, told him that he did not reckon the Queen of England to be his fellow. Upon which Sir Jerome boldly told him to his face that the queen his mistress was as great a prince as any was in Christendom, and well able to defend herself against the malice of any whomsoever. The emperor on this was so enraged that he declared, if he were not an ambassador, he would throw him out of doors. Sir Jerome replied coolly that he was in his power, but that he had a mistress who would revenge any injury done unto him. The emperor, unable to bear it longer, bade him 'Get home', when Sir Jerome, with no more reverence than such usage required, saluted the emperor and departed.

~ W. Beaumont, Warrington, 9 Sep 1854

R2. The anecdotes after which A.B. enquires may be found in Dr Samuel Collins's *Present State of Russia* (1671):

This Ivan Vasilyevich nailed a French ambassador's hat to his head. Sir Jerome Bowes, a while after, came as ambassador, and put on his hat and cocked it before him; at which he sternly demanded how he durst do so, having heard how he chastised the French ambassador. Sir Jerome answered, 'He represented a cowardly King of France, but I am the ambassador of the invincible Queen of England, who does not veil her bonnet, nor bare her head, to any prince living; and if any of her ministers shall receive any affront abroad, she is able to revenge her own quarrel.' 'Look you there,' quoth Ivan Vasilyevich to his boyars, 'there is a brave fellow indeed, that dares do and say thus much for his mistress. Which whoreson of you all dare do so much for me, your master?' This made them envy Sir Jerome, and persuade the emperor to give him a wild horse to tame, which he did, managing him with such rigour that the horse grew so tired and tamed that he fell down dead under him. This being done, he asked his majesty if he had any more wild horses to tame. The emperor afterwards much honoured him, for he loved such a daring fellow as he was, and a mad blade to boot.

~ C. H. Cooper, Cambridge, 9 Sep 1854

R3. There is some difference between the accounts A.B.'s query has called forth, so may I be permitted to call your readers' attention to John Milton's account of Bowes in his *Brief History of Moscovia*? He tells us that Ivan Vasilyevich, having sent his ambassador, Feodor Andrevich, to England touching matters of commerce, the queen (Elizabeth) sent Sir Jerome Bowes to Russia. The Dutch at this time had intruded themselves into the Muscovy trade, which had been granted to the English by privilege long before, and had made friends with one Shalkan, the emperor's chancellor, who 'so wrought' that Bowes was badly treated. Like a true Englishman, however, Bowes asserted his rights, and with such success that the emperor openly preferred him, and loaded him with marks of distinction. Unfortunately the emperor then died. Shalkan became the chief power in the state, and imprisoned Sir Jerome in his own house for nine weeks, and afterwards sent him away 'with many disgraces'.

In addition, Pepys's *Diary*, under 5 September 1662, has the following entry:

To Mr Bland's the merchant, where I find all the officers of the customs, very grave fine gentlemen... And, among other discourse, some was of Sir Jerome Bowes, ambassador from Queen Elizabeth to the Emperor of Russia – who, because some of the noblemen there would go up the stairs to the emperor before him, he would not go up till the emperor had ordered those two men to be dragged downstairs, with their heads knocking upon every stair, till they were killed. And when he was come up, they demanded his sword of him before he entered the room. He told them, if they would have his sword, they should have his boots too; and so caused his boots to be pulled off and his nightgown and nightcap and slippers to be sent for, and made the emperor stay till he could go in his night dress, since he might not go as a soldier. And lastly, when the emperor, in contempt, to show his command of his subjects, did command one to leap from the window down, and broke his neck in the sight of our ambassador, he replied that his mistress did set more by, and did make better use of, the necks of her subjects: but said that, to show what her subjects would do for her, he would, and did, fling down his gauntlet before the emperor, and challenged all the nobility there to take it up in defence of the emperor against his queen. For which, at this very day, the name of Sir Jerome Bowes is famous and honoured there.

~ J. Virtue Wynen, 1 Portland Terrace, Dalston, 23 Dec 1854 & 11 Aug 1855

¶ Sir Jerome Bowes was sent to Russia in the autumn of 1583 with the challenging task of securing valuable trading privileges from Ivan the Terrible without having anything to offer in return. Starting on 18 October that year Bowes had fourteen audiences with Ivan and his ministers and seems to have bluffed and braved his way as best he could, thus inspiring the range of stories related in *N & Q*. Finally, on 14 February 1584, he was sent away empty-handed: 'Since you came to us with nothing,' Ivan remarked, 'we will send you back with what you brought us.'

The idea that the mission failed because of Ivan's death, which occurred on 19 March, may have been promoted by Bowes to exculpate himself. Certainly his bravado had antagonised Ivan's ministers, and, still being in Russia on the tsar's death, he was placed under house arrest for some weeks before finally being allowed to leave. Later that year Ivan's successor, Fyodor the Bell-ringer, wrote to Elizabeth I to complain about her envoy's behaviour: 'When Sir Jerome was with our father he spake many unseemly words, not meet for an ambassador before high princes; and of our nobles he made false reports, as that they spake different words to our father and to himself...'

SALTING THE BODIES OF THE DEAD

Q. I desire to draw the attention of the reader to a curious mode of preserving the bodies of the dead that is mentioned by Turpin in his *History of Charles the Great*. He says that the Christians, being without a sufficient supply of aromatic drugs wherewith to embalm the dead, disembowelled them, and filled them up with salt. Does any other author but Turpin mention this 'salting', or rather 'pickling', of the dead? ~ W. B. MacCabe, 5 July 1851

R. An amusing instance of this custom – perhaps even now, under certain circumstances, prevalent in parts of England – occurs in Mrs Bray's *Letters* on the superstitions of Devonshire.

A traveller, while passing over one of the large unenclosed tracts of land near Tavistock, was overtaken by a violent snow-storm which compelled him to seek a night's shelter from the inhabitants of a lonely cottage on the moor. In the chamber assigned for his repose he observed a curiously carved oak chest of antique appearance: 'He made some remarks upon it to the old woman who had lighted him upstairs. There was something he thought shy and odd about the manner of the woman when he observed the chest, and after she was gone he had half a mind to take a peep into it...' After a while he did, and *horribile dictu!* a human corpse, stiff and cold, lay before his sight! After a night spent in the most agonising apprehensions he descended to breakfast, and his fears became somewhat lightened by the savoury fumes of the morning meal: 'Indeed so much did he feel reassured that, just as the good woman was broiling him another rasher, he out with the secret of the chest, and let them know that he had been somewhat surprised by its contents, venturing to ask, in a friendly tone, for an explanation of so remarkable a circumstance. "Bless your heart, your honour, 'tis nothing at all," said her son; " 'tis only fayther!" – "Father! Your father!" cried the traveller; "what do you mean?" – "Why, you know, your honour," replied the peasant, "the snaw being so thick, and making the roads so cledgy like, when old fayther died, two weeks agon, we couldn't carry un to Tavistock to bury un, and so mother put un in the old box, and salted un in. Mother's a fine hand at sulting un in."'

In connection with this subject you will perhaps permit me to observe that the custom of placing a plate of salt on the body is still retained in many parts of the country. An instance of its use in the metropolis came under my notice only last week. The reason assigned for this is that it prevents the spread of any noxious vapours. ~ Speriend, 19 July 1851

¶ The *Gentleman's Magazine* of October 1785 noted another explanation: 'A pewter plate, well filled with coarse salt, laid on the corpse... is still the custom in several counties of England... the intent to prevent air getting into the bowels, and so swelling up the belly as to occasion either a bursting, or at least a difficulty in closing the coffin'.

SCHOOLMASTER'S CAREER: Total canings et cetera

N. In Thomas Frognall Dibdin's *Bibliomania* I find the following, to which I call your attention as being a curious result of the diligence of a calculator and the cruelty of a schoolmaster:

A German magazine recently announced the death of a schoolmaster in Swabia, who, for fifty-one years, had super-intended a large institution with old fashioned severity. From an average, inferred by means of recorded observations, one of the ushers had calculated that in the course of his exertions he had given 911,500 canings, 121,000 floggings, 209,000 custodes,[1] 136,000 tips with the ruler, 10,200 boxes on the ear, and 22,700 tasks by heart. It was further calculated that he had made 700 boys stand on peas, 6,000 kneel on a sharp edge of wood, 5,000 wear the fool's cap, and 1,700 hold the rod. How vast (exclaims the journalist) the quantity of human misery inflicted by a single perverse educator!

~ Henry Kensington, 19 Jan 1856

[1] Presumably detentions (cf. custodial sentences).

SEDAN CHAIR: Unusually long journey in a

N. The following, from the *Post Boy* of 13 April 1728, records a whimsical journey which commenced on that date and terminated on 19 April:

> On Saturday the Princess Amelia set out for the Bath, whither her highness is to be carry'd in a sedan chair by eight chairmen, to be relieved in their turns, a coach and six horses attending to carry the chairmen when not on service. Her highness dined the same evening at Hampton Court, being accompany'd by the Princess Royal and the Princess Carolina. Sunday morning her highness set out thence for Windsor, where she was to be entertained in the evening; and yesterday morning proceeded to Dr Freind's house near Reading, in Berkshire. A party of the Horse Guards escorted her highness to Hampton Court, relieved next day by a party of the Blue Guards...

~ Alexander Andrews, 3 May 1856

¶ The journey of the 17-year-old daughter of George II began at St James's Palace and has been described as 'perhaps the longest journey ever performed in a sedan'. Early on her progress she was encountered by Mary Pendarves, better known as Mrs Delany, who recalled the scene in a letter to her sister Ann Granville:

> Last week, as we were sauntering agreeably in the King's Road to take a little air, we met Princess Amelia in her way to the Bath. She is carried in a chair, not being able to bear the motion of a coach. Our coach was very close to her, and she looked smiling and pretty, bowed to us all, and asked who we were. I wish the Bath may do her good, for she has lived hitherto a life of misery, and everybody commends her temper...

SERMON: An unusually short

N. The late Dean Kirwan was one of the most eloquent preachers who ever adorned a pulpit. He was once pressed, while suffering from a very severe cold, to preach in St Peter's Church in Dublin, I believe for the orphan children in the parish school. He tried to excuse himself, but at last yielded, ill as he was. After mounting the pulpit, while the church was crowded to suffocation, and having given out the text, he merely pointed with his hand to the orphan children in the aisle, and said, '*There they are.*' It is said the collection on that occasion exceeded all belief. ~ Y.S.M., 24 Mar 1855

¶ Walter Blake Kirwan (1754-1805) officiated at St Peter's, Dublin, from 1787 and was Dean of Killala from 1800. According to an anonymous sketch of his life published in 1815, his eloquence was such that whenever he preached 'such multitudes assembled that it was necessary to defend the entrance of the church by guards and palisadoes'. Collections repeatedly exceeded £1,000 – a considerable sum at the time – and, not content with emptying their purses into the plate, 'his hearers... sometimes threw in jewels or watches as earnest of further benefactions'.

SIC TRANSIT GLORIA MUNDI: A rite to humble popes

Q. Can anyone tell me whence the phrase *Sic transit gloria mundi* is derived? ~ R.H., 31 July 1852

R. Cardinal Wiseman, in his *Recollections of the Last Four Popes* (1858), describing the Pope's coronation in St Peter's, mentions the striking ceremony of the smoking flax, a warning against self-applause in the new pontiff:

> And wherefore this pause in the triumphant procession towards the altar over the Apostle's tomb, and to the throne beyond it? It is to check the rising of any such feeling, if it present itself, and to secure an antidote to any sweet thought which humanity may offer, so that the altar may be approached in humility and the throne occupied in meekness. A clerk of the papal chapel holds up right before the Pope a reed surmounted by a handful of flax. This is lighted: it flashes up for a moment, dies out at once, and its thin ashes fall at the pontiff's feet, as the chaplain, in a bold sonorous voice, chants aloud: '*Pater Sancte, sic transit gloria mundi.*' 'Holy Father, thus passeth away the world's glory.' Three times is this impressive rite performed in that procession, as though to counteract the earthly influence of a triple crown.[1]

Philo of Alexandria tells us that flax was an old Jewish symbol of the Earth. Speaking of the Curtains of the Tabernacle he says, 'Flax is an emblem of the Earth, for the flax grows out of the Earth,' while the French poet Guillaume Du Bartas uses 'th'azure-flowred flax' as an emblem of transitoriness.

How far back can this striking ceremony be traced? Filippo Picinelli mentions a device of Martin V, Pope from 1417 to 1431, which, encircled with the motto *Sic transit gloria mundi*, is depicted in George Wither's *Collection of Emblemes* (1635). Over the emblem are the lines: 'Even as the smoke doth passe away; / So, shall all worldly pompe decay.'

---

[1] Since at least the fourteenth century the papal tiara has boasted three crowns, symbolic of earthly and spiritual power. The particular significance of the respective crowns is moot.

Since writing the above I met with, in a country farmhouse, a dilapidated little book, lacking the title page, but apparently printed in the last century and consisting of a treatise by one W. Mason. I accidentally lighted on the following passage: 'It was a custom in Rome, when the emperor went on some grand day in all his imperial pomp and splendour, to have an officer go before him with smoking flax, crying out "*Sic transit gloria mundi*": "So passeth away the glory of the world." This was to remind him that all his honour and grandeur passed away just like the nimble smoke and burning flax.' If this writer be correct, the ceremony at the Pope's coronation is a relic of imperial Rome. ~ Eirionnach, 14 Sep 1861

¶ According to the eleventh-century cleric Pietro Damiani, during his lifetime it was the custom in Byzantium for an acolyte to present the newly elected emperor with linen flax, which, when set on fire, was rapidly consumed by flames.

It is not known when such a ceremony became part of papal coronations, but the first eyewitness account is provided by the Welsh chronicler Adam of Usk on 11 November 1404. He records a ceremony more or less identical to that described by Cardinal Wiseman 450 years later, and compares it to an analogous custom in ancient Rome: 'In the same manner, at the coronation of the emperor, in the very noontide of his glory, stone-cutters would present him with stone of every kind and colour, calling to him, "Most excellent prince, of what kind of stone do you wish us to make your tomb?"'

SLEEPERS IN CHURCH: How to waken them

Q. I remember many years ago attending the church at Dunchurch, Warwickshire, where an excellent sermon was preached. Notwithstanding this, the weather being very hot, there were several parties fast asleep in different parts of the building. A respectable-looking man, who had very much the air of a churchwarden, bearing a long stout wand with, I believe, a fork at the end of it, at intervals stepped stealthily up and down the nave and aisles, and, whenever he saw an individual whose senses were buried in oblivion, he touched the sleeper with his wand so effectually that the spell was broken. I watched as he mounted with wary step into the galleries. At the end of one of them there sat in the front seat a young man who had very much the appearance of a farmer, with his mouth open and his eyes closed, a perfect picture of repose. The official marked him for his own, and, having fitted his fork to the nape of his neck, he gave him such a push that, had he not been used to such visitations, it would probably have produced an ejaculatory start highly inconvenient on such an occasion.

Now, sir, I am curious to know whether the custom still exists in that parish, and whether any of your correspondents have witnessed it practised elsewhere? ~ R.W.B., 4 Oct 1856

R. I recall reading that at a certain church the beadle was accustomed to go round during service carrying a long staff, at one end of which was a fox's brush, at the other a knob. With the former he gently tickled the faces of those sleepers who were of the female sex, while on the heads of their male compeers he bestowed with the knob a sensible rap. And often in country churches, where the children of the national schools sit in the aisles, the beadle may be seen rapping those who fall asleep, as well as those who are disorderly, with a cane. I have seen it done at Little Hampton Church, Sussex. ~ Threlkeld, Cambridge, 27 Dec 1856

SPUR MONEY

Q. Two or three years ago a party of sappers and miners was stationed at Peterborough, engaged in the trigonometrical survey, when the officer entered the cathedral with his spurs on and was immediately beset by the choristers, who demanded money of him for treading the sacred floor with armed heels. Does anyone know the origin of this singular custom? I enquired of some of the dignitaries of the cathedral, but they were not aware even of its existence. The boys evidently have more tenacious memories, at least where their interest is concerned, yet we must not look to them for the origin of a custom that appears to have long existed. In the *Memorials of John Ray* there is the following entry in his second Itinerary: 'July the 26th, 1661, we began our journey northwards from Cambridge, and that day, passing through Huntingdon and Stilton, we rode as far as Peterborough, twenty-five miles. There I first heard the cathedral service. The choristers made us pay money for coming into the choir with our spurs on.' ~ East Winch, 6 Apr 1850

R. The following note from my *Book of the Court* will serve to illustrate the curious custom referred to by our correspondent:

> In the time of Ben Jonson, in consequence of the interruptions to divine service occasioned by the ringing of the spurs worn by persons walking and transacting business in cathedrals, and especially in St Paul's, a small fine was imposed on them, called 'spur money', the exaction of which was committed to the beadles and singing-boys. This practice still obtains, at least did till very lately, in the Chapel Royal and other choirs. Our informant himself claimed the penalty, in Westminster Abbey, from Dr Fisher, Bishop of Rochester, and received from him an eighteenpenny bank token as the fine. He likewise claimed the penalty from the King of Hanover (then Duke of Cumberland), for entering the choir of the Abbey in his spurs. But his royal highness, who had been installed there, excused himself with great readiness, pleading his right to wear his spurs in that church, inasmuch as it was the place where they were first put on him.

~ Editor, 6 Apr 1850

R2. Although I used often, twenty years ago, when a chorister at the Chapel Royal, to take part in levying a fine on all who entered that place with spurs on, I was not aware of its origin till I saw it explained in your interesting publication. There was a custom, however, connected with this impost, the origin of which I should be glad to learn. After the claim was made, the person from whom it was sought had the power to summon the youngest chorister before him and request him to 'repeat his gamut'[1] – and, if he failed, the spur-bearer was entitled to exemption. ~ E.J.H., 11 May 1850

R3. In a curious tract, published in 1598 under the title *The Children of the Chapel stript and whipt*, we have the following

---

[1] Complete musical scale.

passage: 'Wee think it very necessarye that every quorister sholde bringe with him to churche a Testament in Englishe, and turne to everie chapter as it is daily read, or som other good and godly prayer-booke, rather than spend their time in talk and hunting after spur money, whereon they set their whole mindes, and do often abuse divers if they doe not bestowe somewhat on them.'

In 1622 the dean of the Chapel Royal issued an order by which it was decreed 'That if anie knight, or other persone entitled to weare spurs, enter the chappell in that guise, he shall pay to ye quiristers the accustomed fine; but if he command ye youngest quirister to repeate his gamut, and he faile in ye so doing, the said knight, or other, shall not pay ye fine.' This curious extract I copied from the ancient cheque-book of the Chapel Royal.

Within my recollection his grace the Duke of Wellington (who, by the way, is an excellent musician) entered the Chapel Royal 'booted and spurred', and was, of course, called upon for the fine. However, his grace calling upon the youngest chorister to repeat his gamut, and the 'little urchin' failing, the impost was not demanded. ~ Edward F. Rimbault, 25 May 1850

R4. This custom is a very ancient one, royalty even not being exempt, for one of the items in the Privy Purse Expenses of Henry VII is as follows: '1495. Oct. 1. To the children, for the king's spoures, 4*s*.' A similar entry occurs thrice in the reign of Henry VIII in the year 1530.

Within my recollection a person applied to the magistrates at Hereford for redress, the choristers having decamped with his hat on his refusal to pay the customary fine. The magistrates decided in favour of the boys. ~ J. Woodward, Shoreham, 21 Sep 1861

STAGECOACH TRAVEL: Some miseries of

N. There being persons who seriously lament the good old time of coaches, when they could travel leisurely and securely, see the country and converse with the natives, it may be well to register some of their miseries before they are altogether effaced from the memory.

1. Although your place has been contingently secured days before, and you have risen with the lark, yet you see the ponderous vehicle arrive full – full – full.

2. At the end of a stage, beholding the four panting, reeking, foamy animals, which have dragged you twelve miles, and the stiff, galled, scraggy relay crawling and limping out of the yard.

3. Being politely requested, at the foot of a tremendous hill, to ease the horses – mackintoshes, vulcanised Indian rubber, gutta percha, and gossamer dust-coats then unknown.

4. Finding to your consternation that an outside passenger, resolving to endure no longer 'the pelting of the pitiless storm', takes refuge within with dripping hat, saturated cloak, and soaked umbrella.

5. Being set down with a promiscuous party to a meal bearing no resemblance to that of a good hotel, except in the charge, and having no time to enjoy it.

6. Being closely packed in a box, 'cabined, cribbed, confined, bound in', with five companions morally or physically obnoxious, for two or three comfortless nights and days.

7. During a halt, overhearing the coarse language of the ostlers and tipplers at the roadside pot-house[1] and being besieged by beggars exposing their mutilations.

8. Being roused from your nocturnal slumber by the horn or bugle, the lashing and cracking of whip, turnpike gates, a search for parcels under your seat, and solicitous drivers.

9. Discovering at a diverging point in your journey that the Tally-ho[2] runs only every other day or so, or has finally stopped.

10. Clambering from the wheel by various iron projections to your elevated seat.

11. After threading through the narrowest streets of an ancient town, entering the inn yard by a low gateway, to the imminent risk of decapitation.

12. Seeing the luggage piled 'Olympus high', so as to occasion an alarming oscillation.

13. Having the reins and whip placed in your unpractised hands while coachee indulges in a glass and a chat.

14. Being exposed to piercing draughts owing to a refractory glass, or, contrariwise, being in a minority, feeling compelled, for the sake of ventilation, to thrust your umbrella accidentally through a pane.

15. At various seasons, being suffocated with dust and broiled by a powerful sun – or petrified with cold – or torn by fierce winds – or cowering under an umbrella in a drenching rain – or struggling through snow – or wending your way through perilous floods.

16. Perceiving that a young squire is receiving an initiatory practical lesson in the art of driving, and that a jibbing horse, or a race with an opposition, is endangering your existence.

---

[1] Small tavern.

[2] One of the faster stagecoach services.

17. Losing the enjoyment or employment of much precious time, not only on the road, but also from consequent fatigue.

18. Being interrupted before the termination of your hurried meal by your two rough-coated, big-buttoned, many-caped friends, the coachman and guard – who hope you will remember them. Although the gratuity has been repeatedly calculated in anticipation, you fail in making the mutual remembrances agreeable.

~ C.T., 16 Aug 1856

R. I am one of those who well remember the journeys to and from home in our schoolboy days, when a week or more was deducted from the holidays for the time necessarily passed in travelling. There are, doubtless, many others who equally well recollect Collier's and Rogers's long coaches from Southampton to London. Then came the adventurous expedition to York by 'Nelson' or 'Highflyer', occupying two days and the intervening night. On the fourth day I reached the domestic hearth, but only when the season was summer. Never shall I forget the delays and *circumbendibuses*[1] of a winter's journey in a deep snow. Nor shall I ever forget, when very young, and easily alarmed by stories of hobgoblins and highwaymen, what horrible tales of murder and robbery were inflicted by coachee and guard on my shuddering ears when we came in sight, on some desolate moor, of the remains of some desperate villain hanging in chains. But, without further preface or remark, let me proceed to mention two coach miseries not included in your catalogue, respecting which I may say with truth, *Experto crede.*[2]

19. Arriving at daybreak, more than half famished, after an excessively cold winter's night ride on the box, with fingers too benumbed to assist you in partaking of the solids of the breakfast table, and receiving the summons of 'Now gentlemen! Coach is waiting!' just as the prospect of returning circulation gives you the hope of getting a meal.

[1] Roundabout routes.

[2] Believe one who has had the experience.

20. Being prepared against 'the pelting of the pitiless storm' with wraps and waterproofs, cape, apron, etc., only to find that, from a point of your female neighbour's umbrella, which continually tickles your ear, and threatens to upset your hat, a regular stream is conducted down your neck, common politeness forbidding you to remonstrate.

~ N.L.T., 18 Oct 1856

SUICIDE: Encouraged at Marseilles but discouraged among the Milesian virgins

Q. In the *Lancet* of 30 November 1839 it is stated that anciently, in Marseilles, persons having satisfactory reasons for committing suicide were supplied with poison at the public expense. What authority is there for this? I should also like to be informed what was the occasion on which a suicidal propensity in the Milesian ladies was corrected by an appeal to their posthumous modesty? ~ Elsno, 19 Feb 1853

R. In Book 2, Chapter 3 of Montaigne's *Essays* I find the following:

> In former times there was kept, in our city of Marseilles, a poison prepared out of hemlock, at the public charge, for those who had a mind to hasten their end, having first, before the Six Hundred, which were their Senate, given an account of the reasons and motives of their design; and it was not otherwise lawful than by leave of the magistrates, and upon just occasion, to do violence to themselves. The same law was also in use in other places.

This, however, is not the original authority required by your correspondent.

In the earlier part of the same chapter Montaigne makes the following statement, his authority being Plutarch's *On the Virtuous Deeds of Women*:

The Milesian virgins, that by an insane compact hanged themselves, one after another, until the magistrate took order in it, enacting that the bodies of such as should be found so hanged should be drawn by the same halter, stark naked through the city.

~ J.P., Birmingham, 26 Mar 1853

R2. The original authority for the custom at Marseilles is Valerius Maximus, Book 2, Chapter 6. ~ Zeus, 21 May 1853

¶ In his *Facta et Dicta Memorabilia* (Memorable Deeds and Sayings) the first-century Roman writer Valerius Maximus claimed that the practice had been introduced to Marseilles from the Greek island of Ceos, and that he had himself seen a high-ranking woman of that island plead successfully with her fellow citizens for the right to end her life with poison on the grounds of extreme old age.

In *De Mulierum Virtutibus* (On the Virtuous Deeds of Women), Plutarch gives the following account of the melancholy events in the city of Miletus in Asia Minor:

Once upon a time a dire and strange trouble took possession of the young women in Miletus for some unknown cause. The most popular conjecture was that the air had acquired a distracting and infectious constitution, and that this operated to produce in them an alteration and derangement of mind. At any rate, a yearning for death and an insane impulse toward hanging suddenly fell upon all of them, and many managed to steal away and hang themselves. Arguments and tears of parents and comforting words of friends availed nothing, but they circumvented every device and cunning effort of their watchers in making away with themselves. The malady seemed to be of divine origin and beyond human help, until, on the advice of a man of sense, an ordinance was proposed that the women who hanged themselves should be carried naked through the market-place to their burial. And when this ordinance was passed it not only checked, but stopped completely, the young women from killing themselves.

SUNDIAL MOTTO AT THE TEMPLE:
Serendipitous history of

N. Many persons now living must remember the vertical sundial, with a very remarkable motto, which was on the front of a building at the Temple in London before the edifice in question was rebuilt a few years ago. But most have probably never heard of the following curious tradition, probably a true one, respecting the motto.

When the sundial was put up the artist enquired whether he should, as was customary, paint a motto under it. The Benchers assented, and appointed him to call at the library at a certain day and hour, by which time they would have agreed upon the motto. It appears, however, that they had totally forgotten this, and when the artist called at the library at the time appointed he found no one but a cross-looking old gentleman poring over some musty book. 'Please, sir, I am come for the motto for the sundial.' 'What do you want?' was the pettish answer; 'why do you disturb me?' 'Please, sir, the gentlemen told me I was to call at this hour for a motto for the sundial.' '*Begone about your business!*' was the testy reply. The man, either by design or by mistake, chose to take this as the answer to his enquiry, and accordingly painted in large letters under the dial '*BEGONE ABOUT YOUR BUSINESS.*'

The Benchers, when they saw it, decided that it was very appropriate, and that they would let it stand – chance having done their work as well as they could have done it for themselves. ~ Anon., 14 Apr 1860

¶ According to John Timbs, in his *Curiosities of London*, the dial was on an old brick house at the east end of the Inner Temple terrace and was removed in 1828.

SURNAMES 1: Curious American

N. The following may perhaps be of interest to your readers.

Two merchants trading under the name of Swindler and Co. dissolved partnership in Columbia, South Carolina, about ten years ago. It is more surprising that the partnership was ever formed.

A Mr Gambler has been nominated a director of the public schools, and a Mr Gobble was plaintiff in an action of eject-ment brought in Centre County, Pennsylvania, a few years ago.

Colonel Pancake was a military man of some note here shortly after the Revolution, while General Quattlebum was recently a member of the South Carolina legislature.

Mr Pickup is the proprietor of an omnibus line in this city, while Henry Moist was a waterman here not many years ago. Meantime Mr Violet Primrose is a respectable saddler, and we also have Mr Rees Wall Flower, who at one time lived in Garden Street.

John Thunder and Son were tailors in this city a few years ago; at a later date a Mr Thunder was an organist in one of our churches, and a Mr Loud was organist in another.

Dr Toothaker is a physician in this city.

Rev. Mr Slicer was one of the chaplains to Congress a few years ago.

Mr Gagger was a lawyer in Albany, New York, in 1852.

Nicholas Dabb is a painter in New Jersey.

John C. Copper is an engraver in this city.

Messrs Gutelius and Slink were officers of the Pennsylvania legislature in 1849.

Pope and Dryden kept adjoining stores in Baltimore not long ago.

The Rev. Jesse Boring, from Georgia, died at St Louis in 1850. His death was announced by Bishop Capers.

Mr Failing keeps a hotel at Canandagua, New York, and a Mr Owings was an insolvent debtor lately, as might have been expected.

Amongst other appropriate names we may include those of Doctor Physic, an eminent practitioner of medicine here, and Messrs Law and Lex of the Philadelphia Bar. We cannot say the same of Dr Slaughter, a physician here in 1830, or of Mr Whale, who has been a dancing-master for many years.

Occasionally we find that a French name is translated. One of two brothers living near this city is known as Mr La Rue, his brother as Mr Street.
~ Uneda, Philadelphia, 22 July 1854 & 21 July 1855

R. Add, on the authority of a person well acquainted with Philadelphia, a legal firm bearing the ominous title of Katchum and Cheatum. The unfortunate owners were compelled to dissolve partnership. ~ O. Φ., 11 Aug 1855

R2. You might add Mr Preserved Fish, who managed the secretariat of the Baptist Board of Foreign Missions, Boston, some years ago. ~ J.O., 11 Aug 1855

R3. Ketchum and Cheatum were not Philadelphians but New York lawyers. Preserved Fish was also a New Yorker, a foundling left upon the steps of a Mr Fish, who adopted him and gave him the name Preserved with reference to that circumstance. He became an eminent merchant and a very popular man. On one occasion he showed a strong American spirit, which gave great satisfaction to the majority of his countrymen. At a public dinner of the New York merchants, about twelve years ago, a toast in honour of Queen Victoria was received with cheers, and one in honour of the President of the United States almost in silence, upon which Mr Fish got up, put on his hat, and retired.
~ D.W., Philadelphia, 17 Nov 1855

R4. The enclosed notice, which I have cut from a local paper of 5 December 1855, may be of interest: 'Died, at the residence of his son-in-law Mr A. Curtis, in North Dorchester, on the 29th Nov., Preserved Fish, aged 83 years.' ~ Thomas Hodgins, Toronto, Canada, 2 Feb 1856

SURNAMES 2: Curious English et cetera

N. I learn that your correspondent Mr Lower has on the stocks a systematic Dictionary of Surnames, and trust that his etymological research will be successfully exercised on such names as Nettleship, Moneypenny, Peabody, Sidebottom, Sheepshanks, Snodgrass, Wiggins, Figgins, Higgins, Wigglesworth, Pocock, Locock, etc.[1] Let me also bring under his notice the singularly unattractive name of *Suckbitch*. It is used by more than one branch of a respectable and ancient family in the West of England, and I have traced its existence for at least five centuries. Instead of availing themselves of the recent opinions of some great lawyers, that a surname may be changed at will, this family rather pride themselves on a name that can boast an antiquity probably not surpassed by that of any family in England. ~ E.S., 1 May 1852

R. On arriving here a few days since I was particularly struck with the singularity of the surnames of tradesmen and others. I noted a few at the time, the equal of which I think it would be hard to find during an hour's stroll in any other town of 13,000 inhabitants in England. The following is the list:

Bugg, Boby, Bear, Shave, Sneezum, Flint, Steel, Cobbell (shoemaker), Balaam, Grief, Death, Nunn, Guy, Ion, Tubbs, Plane, Last, Hoy, Glew, Quant, Image, Prigg, Pyman, Crick, Sore, Stiff, Crack, Scotcher, Simper, Catchpole, Gathercole, Mothersole, Mulley, Ramsbottom, Rainbird, Middleditch, Sitwell, Nice, Stotter, Seakens, Wing, Perfect, Boore. ~ James Pitt, Bury St Edmunds, 29 Aug 1863

R2. Quaint surnames seldom mean what they seem. Such names as Balaam and Sneezum are compounded of *ham*, meaning a dwelling-place. Death is from De Ath in France. Stiff is from Stephen, Simper from St Pierre, and Rainbird from Rambert, the inverse of Bertram. Tubb and Tubbs may, like the Cornwallian Tubby, be nicknames of Thomas, and Cobbell is

---

[1] M. A. Lower's *Patronymica Britannica: A Dictionary of Family Names of the United Kingdom* was published in 1860.

a diminutive of Cobb. To illustrate further, among very many names apparently relating to the medical world we have Bark, Bowell, Brain, Fever, Gumboil, Lance, Lancet, Morter, Pestel, Physick, Pill, Plaster, and Truss. However, of these Bowell is probably corrupted from Powell or Howell; Brain is corrupted from an Irish name; Fever is the same as the French name Le Fevre, 'the smith'; Gumboil is corrupted from the German name Gumpold or Gumbold; Pill is the same as the Pecksniffian name Peel, signifying a fortification; and Truss is probably from Theresa. ~ R. S. Charnock, 24 Oct 1863

R3. Blood, Fury, and Death, were at one time seen together in a market town in Ireland, while Blood and Thunder were on the plates of two doors adjoining each other in Gloucester Street, Dublin. In this town we have Dodge and Wynne, attorneys at law; a Sheepwash for hair dressing; and a Half-penny who once carried parcels for a penny. In Bristol there was once a Rod that kept a school. ~ W.B., Liverpool, 24 June 1865

R4. A curious combination of names formerly appeared on three adjoining shops in St Clement's, Oxford: Wise – Parsons – Hunt. This afforded much amusement to the undergraduates of that day. ~ Thomas E. Winnington, 16 Sep 1865

R5. I have for several years been in the habit, when I have come upon an odd surname, of making a note of it. As I think it a pity that my collection, gathered by way of friends from all parts of England, should 'waste its sweetness on the desert air', I beg to present it to the readers of *N & Q*:

Alabaster, Apothecary, Ancient, Allgood, Allfree, Allchin.

Beadle, Body, Budge, Beetle, Bottle, Boots, Bodily, Basket, Blossom, Bolster, Blight, Baby, Brain, Blood, Bellringer, Birdseye, Bible, Barefoot, Breeks, Boatman, Brush, Bishoprick, Bray, Breeze, Boiling, Butter, Beggar, Brothergood, Bodkin.

Cant, Cherry, Crackle, Christmas, Cowmeadow, Curate, Cage, Coffee, Cakebread, Chataway, Camomile, Cleverly, Candle, Crowfoot, Cutbush (a florist), Chant, Curds, Cobble-dick, Cushion, Crush, Chicken, Craze, Challenger, Cockle.

Death, Deadman, Dust, Drought, Drawwater, Drinkwater, Drinkall, Drawbridge, Dainty, Dearlove, Delight, Dodge, Ditch, Daggers, Dollar, Dudgeon, Dinner.

Eighteen, Eatwell, Earthy.

Frizzle, Freshwater, Fish, Faultless, Friday, Fudge, Folly, Flippant, Fury, Forecast, Foreigner, Farthing, Friendship, Fright.

Goose, Goosey, Gosling, Gossip, Greedy, Graygoose, Game, Greenhorne, Greengrass, Goodenough, Goodfellow, Goodchap, Goodbody, Gotobed, Gallop, Going, Giggle, Gush, Ginger, Guinea, Golightly, Grief, Governor, Griffinhoofe, Galilee, Ghost, Gammon, Goat, Garlick, Gallant, Greenland.

Honey, Honeybone, Hornbuckle, Hornblower, Herod, Horseshoe, Hazard, Hurry, Hamper, Holyland, Handsome-body, Hasluck, Haddock, Haggis, Hole, Halfhide, Hailstone, Heaven, Hollowbread, Haggard, Herbage, Hogsflesh, Hatfull.

Innocent, Irishman, Ironmonger, Idle.

Jolly, Jelly, Jabberer, Jump, Joy, Jealous, Jingle, Juniper, January.

Kiss, Kindness, Kettle, Kite, Knocker, Kneebone, Kitchen.

Leatherbarrow, Lovely, Lively, Leapingwell, Limb, Large, Littleproud, Legal, Ledger, Lunch, Lovelock, Longcake, Lash, Lavender, Littleboy, Lambswool.

Mackerel, Mutton, Mustard, Mercy, Moneypenny, Manifold, Mummery, Milestone, Marriage, Meanwell, Muddle, Menlove, Midwinter, Manhood, Monument, Mamon.

Nice, Nurse, Nodding, Nephew.

Old, Odd, Organ, Others, Oysters.

Pigeon, Peppercorn, Pickles, Pheasant, Physick, Pain, Precious, Punch, Puncher, Parsonage, Prettybody, Pagan, Prophet, Pilgrim, Paradise, Prudence, Patent, Playfoot, Pitchfork, Pinches, Pickup, Pluckrose.

Quickfall.

Rawbone, Rasberry, Rainbow, Rust, Rant, Reason, Roadknight.

Shove, Slaughter, Shave, Swine, Sheepshanks, Spice, Swearer, Stirrup, Slipper, Stocking, Sword, Sleep, Silversides,

Sowerbutts, Sermon, Snowdrop, Snowball, Smite, Screech, Stutter, Steptoe, Swiggs, Sturdy, Smallbones, Sweetlove, Sweetapple, Spry, Sly, Sunshine, Snake, Sneezum, Seefar, Showers, Sheepwash, Skill, Snipe, Saveall, Sanctuary.

Truelove, Thirst, Twiddle, Twaddle, Twopeny, Tart, Trot, Treasure, Tongue, Tinker, Thoroughgood, Toogood, Thick, Trusty, Tartar, Tarbox, Treble, Trick, Tiger, Thunder, Titmouse, Toy, Tantrum, Tattoo, Thirdborough, Tingle.

Vicarage, Virgin, Vile, Valentine.

Whistler, Whalebelly, Whalebone, Whip, Whackum, Whereat, Wailing, Whisker, Waistcoat, Weekly, Wellbeloved, Walklate, Window, Wager, Wisdom, Wizard, Waterfall, Wildgoose, Worship, Whitehair, Why.

Younghusband, Yes.

~ Jonathan Bouchier, 2 Stanley Villas, Bexley Heath, 2 Aug 1873

R6. If Mr Bouchier should ever visit the parish church of Heacham, King's Lynn, he will find a black marble slab in the floor to the memory of a Mr Pig, with a coat of arms attached.

~ W.M.H.C., 30 Aug 1873

R7. Sometimes the occupation associates very peculiarly with the name: we have known apothecaries and surgeons of the surnames of Littlefear, Butcher, Death and Coffin; Pie, a pastry-cook; Rideout, a stable-keeper; Tugwell, a dentist; Lightfoot, a dancing-master; Mixwell, a publican; and two hosiers of the names of Foot and Stocking.

I add the following, from Reuben Percy's *Relics of Literature*: A more fatal equivoque[1] was, perhaps, never produced by surnames than the following. Count Valavoir was a general in the French service, and distinguished himself under the great Turenne.[2] It happened that, while they were lying encamped before the enemy, the count one evening attempted to pass one of the sentinels after sunset. The sentinel challenged

[1] Ambiguity.

[2] The celebrated military commander Henri de la Tour d'Auvergne, Vicomte de Turenne (1611-1675).

him, and the count answered '*Va-la-voir*,' which literally signifies 'Go and see.' The soldier, who took the word in this sense, indignantly repeated the challenge, and was answered in the same manner, when he fired; and the unfortunate count fell dead upon the spot – a victim to the whimsicality of his surname.

~ Fredk. Rule, 30 Aug 1873

SWANS: Do they only hatch during thunder?

Q. The fable of the singing of swans at death is well known, but I recently heard a bit of folklore as to the birth of swans quite as poetical, and probably equally true. It is this: that swans are always hatched during a thunderstorm. I was told this by an old man in Hampshire who had been connected with the care of swans all his life. He, however, knew nothing about their singing at death. Is this opinion as to the birth of swans common? ~ Robert Rawlinson, 28 Dec 1850

R. Some years ago I purchased a pair of swans and, during the first breeding season, they made a nest in which they deposited seven eggs. After they had been sitting about six weeks I observed to my servant, who had charge of them and the other waterfowl, that it was about the time for the swans to hatch. He immediately said that it was no use expecting it till there had been a rattling peal of thunder to crack the eggshells, as they were so hard and thick it was impossible for the cygnets to break them without some such assistance. Perhaps this is the reason why swans are said to be hatched during a thunderstorm. I need only say that this is a popular fallacy, as swans regularly hatch after six sitting weeks, whether there happens to be a thunderstorm or not. ~ Henry E., 25 Jan 1851

SWEARING: An Act of Parliament against

Q. I have a small volume entitled *A short and modest Vindication of the common Practice of Cursing and Swearing, occasioned by a new Act of Parliament against the said Practice.* By a Gentleman. Printed for J. Robinson, at the Golden Lion, in Ludgate Street. No date. Was the custom of profane swearing ever really so bad in England that it required an Act of Parliament to put it down? ~ S. Wmson, Glasgow, 16 Oct 1852

R. An Act against swearing and cursing was passed in 1623, and another, for the more effectually suppressing cursing and swearing, in 1694. Both these, however, were repealed by the Profane Oaths Act 1745, introduced 'more effectually to prevent profane swearing', which was ordered to be read quarterly in all parish churches and public chapels. ~ Editor, 16 Oct 1852

R2. Our countrymen appear to have been addicted to profane swearing from an early date. Of this the trial of Joan of Arc in 1431 affords us a distinct proof. One of the witnesses, Colette, being asked who 'Godon' was, made answer that the term was not the designation of any particular individual, but a nickname generally applied to the English on account of their continual use of the exclamation 'G–d d—n it.' ~ W.B.M., Deeside, 13 Nov 1852

¶ The fine for swearing under the 1623 Act was one shilling. If anyone could not pay they were set in the stocks, or, if under twelve years of age, whipped. In June 1650 the Rump Parliament passed 'An Act for the better preventing and suppressing of the detestable sin of prophane swearing and cursing'. In keeping with the times, penalties were now graduated according to rank: a lord had to pay 30 shillings, a baronet or knight 20 shillings, an esquire 10 shillings, a gentleman 6*s.* 8*d.*, and those of inferior status 3*s.* 4*d.* All fines were doubled for any second offence.

Under the 1694 Act there were only two rates: one shilling for servants, labourers and common soldiers and seamen, two shillings for everyone else. The Profane Oaths Act 1745 retained these fines and introduced a higher rate of five shillings for gentlemen and above. It was only formally repealed in 1967.

SWOT

Q. I have often heard military men talk of *swot*, meaning thereby mathematics, and persons eminent in that science are termed *good swots.* As I never heard the word except amongst the military, but there almost universally in 'free and easy' conversation, I am led to think it a cant term. At any rate I shall be glad to be informed of its origin – if it be not lost in the mists of soldierly antiquity. ~ Cantab, 30 Mar 1850

R. Swot is, as the querist supposes, a military cant term, and a sufficiently vulgar one too. It originated at the great slang-manufactory for the army, the Royal Military College, Sandhurst. You may depend upon the following account of it, which I had many years ago from the late Thomas Leybourne, FRS, Senior Professor of Mathematics in that college.

One of the professors, Dr William Wallace, in addition to being a Scotchman, had a bald head and an exceedingly 'broad Scotch' accent, besides a not very delicate discrimination in the choice of his English terms relating to social life. It happened on one hot summer's day, nearly half a century ago, that he had been teaching a class, and had worked himself into a considerable effusion from the skin. He took out his handkerchief, rubbed his head and forehead violently, and exclaimed in his Perthshire dialect, *'It maks one swot.'* This was a Godsend to the gentlemen cadets, wishing to achieve a notoriety as wits and slangsters, and mathematics generally ever after became *swot*, and mathematicians *swots.* I have often heard it said 'I never could do *swot* well, sir,' and 'These dull fellows, the *swots*, can talk of nothing but triangles and equations.'

I should have thought that the *sheer disgustingness* of the idea would have shut the word out of the vocabularies of English *gentlemen.* It remains nevertheless a standard term in the vocabulary of an English soldier. It is well, at all events, that future ages should know its etymology. ~ T.S.D., 6 Apr 1850

TAXES: On beards et cetera

Beards

Q. I find the following entry in the burghmote books of the city of Canterbury under the year 1549: 'The sheriff and another person pay their fines for wearing their beards – viz. ¾ and ⅛.' One would look with greater interest on the flowing beards depicted in the portraits of that period on knowing that they were paid for, and it would be interesting to know how they were assessed, as the rate is not the same in all cases.
~ Quercubus, 25 May 1867

¶ The beard-sporting Henry VIII introduced a tax on beards in 1535, and under Elizabeth I the annual levy was 3*s*. 4*d*. on all beards of above a fortnight's growth.

Another notable beard-taxer was Peter the Great. Convinced by a visit to Europe that some western customs were superior to those of Russia, in 1698 he ordered his courtiers and officials to wear European clothes and shave off their voluminous beards. Failure to comply resulted in a tax of 100 roubles a year. Beard-retainers also had to wear a medal proclaiming that 'Beards are a ridiculous ornament.'

Chimneys and Hearths

Q. In Pepys's *Diary*, under the date 3 March 1662, there is the following entry: 'I am told that this day the parliament hath voted two shillings per annum for every chimney in England, as a constant revenue for ever to the crowne.' Can any of your readers inform me how long this tax continued to be levied?
~ Libya, 27 Feb 1858

R. The chimney tax, or hearth money, was so peculiarly odious to the poor during the reigns of Charles II and James II that it was abolished soon after the Revolution by order of William and Mary. It was not only considered as a great oppression to the poorer classes but a badge of slavery upon the whole people, exposing every man's house to be entered and searched at pleasure by persons unknown to him. The tax was farmed, and a farmer of taxes is, of all creditors, the most rapacious. ~ Editor, 27 Feb 1858

¶ The tax was introduced to meet some of the costs of running the reinstated royal household following the Restoration. In June 1662 Pepys noted that the people 'clamour against the chimny-money and say they will not pay it without force'. It was abolished in 1689.

Clocks and Watches

N. In a printed receipt for a half-year's taxes due from a small farmer in Essex, dated 10 April 1798, there occurs the item: 'For clocks and watches, 5*s.* 7½*d.*' It was a novelty to me that the owners of clocks and watches had been liable to taxation for the luxury at so recent a period. ~ E.L.C., 24 Feb 1855

¶ The tax on clocks and watches was introduced in 1797 at the rate of 2*s.* 6*d.* for a basic watch rising to ten shillings for a gold one. As a result people stopped buying clocks and watches and many clockmakers went out of business. The tax was repealed within a year.

Hair-powder

N. Mr Pitt, in his budget of 23 February 1795, laid a tax of £1 1*s.* per head on hair-powder. ~ M.M., 13 Jan 1855

¶ The tax effectively ended the fashion for wigs and powder. Nonetheless, it lingered on the statute book until 1869.

Windows

Q. In a manuscript chronicle now before me, compiled by an inhabitant of Norwich named Nobbs and relating events from the earliest period to the year 1716, there occurs the following passage under 1696: 'This year the parliament made an Act for remedying the coin of the nation, which was generally debased by counterfeits, and diminished by clipping, and laid a tax upon glass windows.' Is it generally known that this tax originated in this year and this manner? ~ Cowgill, 7 June 1851

¶ Window tax began as part of the 1696 Act for Making Good the Deficiency of the Clipped Money. Cottages were exempt. Otherwise the original rates ranged from two shillings for houses with fewer than ten windows up to ten shillings for those with more than twenty. The threshold of ten windows was adjusted to seven in 1766 and to eight in 1825. The tax led to the bricking in of windows and to many new houses being built with only as many windows as could be enjoyed without cost. The tax was finally abolished in 1851 but in its heyday produced considerable sums: £2 million in 1815, for example.

The window tax and the other taxes cited in *N & Q* were part of the long-running effort by British governments to raise public money without resorting to the extreme and feared measure of income tax. In the latter stages of this effort William Pitt the Younger, faced with the rising costs of war with France, introduced taxes on everything from dogs to armorial bearings. Finally, in 1799, he resorted to income tax as a temporary measure with a top rate of ten per cent. In 1816, with Napoleon defeated, it was repealed, only to be reintroduced by Robert Peel in 1842.

THAMES, THE RIVER: Frost Fairs upon

N. The following is from the *Express* of 11 January 1861 and is worth preserving in *N & Q*:

The Thames was frozen for fourteen weeks in 1063, and below bridge to Gravesend from 24 November to 10 February in 1434.

In 1515 carriages passed over from Lambeth to Westminster, and fires and diversions were witnessed in 1607.

In 1684 the river was covered with ice eleven inches thick, and nearly all the birds perished.

In 1716 a fair was held, and oxen were roasted; this frost continued from 24 November to 9 February.

A frost in 1740 lasted nine weeks, when coaches plied upon the Thames and festivities of all kinds were celebrated upon the ice.

From November to January, in 1789, the river was passable opposite the Custom House, and in 1814 booths were erected.

The present frost has lasted about fourteen days, and, if it continues for the same period longer, the scenes of the Serpentine may be transferred to our great metropolitan river.

~ Grime, 2 Feb 1861

R. In a Bible of 1660 in my possession, at the back of the Old Testament title page, is pasted a paper:

Mrs — —

Printed on the Frozen-THAMES,

February the 5th, 168¾.

~ Joseph Rix, St Neots, 16 Feb 1861

R2. I possess a sheet of paper about four inches long by three wide. After the last line of poetry a wide space is left for the insertion of a name:

Upon the Frost in the Year 1739-40

Behold the Liquid Thames now frozen o'er!

That lately Ships of mighty Burden bore.

Here you may Print your name tho' cannot Write,

'Cause numb'd with cold: 'Tis done with great Delight,

And lay it by; that Ages yet to come
May see what Things upon the Ice were done.

. . . .

Printed on the ice upon the Thames at Queen Hithe,
February the 8th, 1739-40.

~ Edward Peacock, 16 Mar 1861

R3. I find the following among some old family papers:

Elizabeth Pomeroy,
Printed upon the Thames when frozen, 12th Jan. 1740.

I may add that I walked across the Thames near Blackfriars
Bridge in January 1814. ~ R.W., 16 Mar 1861

¶ Another great frost, that of 1564-5, is recorded in Holinshed's
Chronicles:

On new yeares even, people went over and alongst the Thames
on the ice from London Bridge to Westminster. Some plaied
at the football as boldlie there as if it had been on the drie
land; diverse of the court, being then at Westminster, shot
dailie at pricks[1] set upon the Thames; and the people, both
men and women, went on the Thames in greater numbers
than in anie street of the citie of London.

The diarist John Evelyn gives perhaps the best description of
the frost of 1684:

24th January. The frost continuing more and more severe,
the Thames before London was still planted with boothes in
formal streetes, all sorts of trades and shops furnish'd and full
of commodities, even to a printing presse, where the people
and ladyes tooke a fancy to have their names printed, and the
day and yeare set down when printed on the Thames. This
humour tooke so universally that 'twas estimated the printer
gain'd £5 a day, for printing a line onely, at sixpence a name,
besides what he got by ballads etc. Coaches now plied from
Westminster to the Temple, and from severall other staires to
and fro, as in the streetes; also sleds, sliding with skeetes, a

---

[1] Archery targets.

bull-baiting, horse and coach races, puppet plays and interludes, cookes, tipling, and other lewd places, so that it seem'd to be a bacchanalian triumph, or carnival on the water, whilst it was a severe judgment on the land, the trees not onely splitting as if lightning-struck, but men and cattle perishing in divers places, and the very seas so lock'd up with ice that no vessells could stir out or come in. The fowles, fish, and birds, and all our exotiq plants and greenes universally perishing. Many parks of deer were destroied, and all sorts of fuell so deare that there were greate contributions to preserve the poore alive.

Among those taken by the printing humour was Charles II, who visited the fair at the end of January and had his name printed with those of his wife and children on a small card.

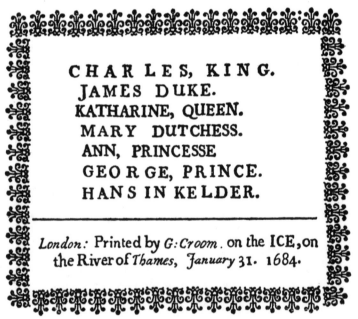

CHARLES, KING.
JAMES DUKE.
KATHARINE, QUEEN.
MARY DUTCHESS.
ANN, PRINCESSE
GEORGE, PRINCE.
HANS IN KELDER.

London: Printed by *G:Croom*. on the ICE, on the River of *Thames*, *January* 31. 1684.

'Hans in Kelder', or 'Jack in the Cellar', was the king's playful reference to the pregnancy of his daughter Anne. The child would be stillborn in the spring.

Printing returned to the Thames in 1716. According to *Dawks's News-Letter* of 14 January:

The Thames seems now a solid rock of ice, and booths for the sale of brandy, wine, ale, and other exhilarating liquors have been for some time fixed thereon; but now it is in a manner like a town; thousands of people cross it. On Thursday a great cook's shop was erected, and gentlemen went as frequently to dine there as at any ordinary.[1] Over against Westminster, Whitehall, and Whitefriars, printing presses are kept upon the ice, where many persons have their names printed, to transmit the wonders of the season to posterity.

In 1814, when R.W. crossed the Thames at Blackfriars, a plumber called Davis was not so fortunate: having ventured to cross at the same spot with lead in his hands, he sank through the ice and was not seen again. Meanwhile swings and merry-go-rounds did brisk business and a sheep was cooked over a coal fire inside a tent. People paid sixpence to see the sight and a shilling for a slice of the delicate meat, sold as Lapland mutton.

The Thames has not frozen over between Westminster Bridge and Tower Bridge since that time, not least because, since the replacement of the narrow-arched medieval London Bridge in the 1820s, the river has flowed more freely. During the cold weather of 1861, which prompted the *N & Q* correspondence, thermometers in London fell to 17 degrees below freezing but conditions soon eased.

[1] An eating-place (restaurant, public house, etc.) where regular meals were available at a fixed price.

TOAD-EATERS AND TOADIES

Q. Will any of your readers be kind enough to explain the origin of the word 'toady', which is constantly used in conversation when speaking of a sycophant? ~ F.M., 1 May 1852

R. From John Ogilvie's *Imperial Dictionary*:

Toady, or *Toad-eater*, a vulgar name for a fawning, obsequious sycophant, was first given to a gluttonous parasite, famous for his indiscriminate enjoyment and praise of all viands whatever set before him. To test his powers of stomach and complaisance, one of his patrons had a *toad* cooked and set before him, which he both ate and praised in his usual way.

~ Editor, 1 May 1852

R2. In *The Adventures of David Simple* (1744), a novel by Sarah Fielding, sister of the celebrated Henry Fielding, the hero of the tale asks the meaning of this term and the following answer is given:

'It is a metaphor taken from a mountebank's boy's eating toads, in order to show his master's skill in expelling poison. It is built on a supposition (which I am afraid is too generally true), that people who are so unhappy as to be in a state of dependence are forced to do the most nauseous things that can be thought on, to please and humour their patrons.'

This seems to give the exact meaning of the term as now used. The expression also occurs in the works of Thomas Brown. In his 'Satire upon an ignorant Quack' (1704), he says, 'Be the most scorn'd Jack-pudding in the pack, / And turn toad-eater to some foreign quack.' In addition, in pretended letters Brown wrote in the *persona* of Joe Haines, a celebrated mountebank and fortune-teller who had died in 1701, Haines tells his friends: 'I intend to build a stage and set up my old trade of fortune-telling; and I shall have occasion for some understrapper to draw teeth for me, or to be my toad-eater, upon the stage.' ~ E.β.E., 15 Feb 1862

R3. The French say *avaler un crapaud*, or swallow a toad – a stronger expression than merely *to eat* a toad. In the same vein they say *avaler des couleuvres* – literally to swallow adders. Indeed, if it be true that a language often points to the habits of the people by whom it is spoken, we should, I think, be entitled to conclude that the French are a very humble and submissive nation, continually swallowing a great many disagreeable things, for they constantly apply to sorrows, vexations, affronts, insults, et cetera, verbs which signify *to eat* and *to drink*. Thus they say *Manger des douleurs, Dévorer des chagrins, des dégoûts, des affronts, des injures*, et cetera.

Whilst I am upon the subject of toads, perhaps I may be allowed to ask whether the Latin name for these animals, *bufo*, is not related to *buffoon*. In Middle Latin the two words are spelt in precisely the same manner, viz. *buffo*, while in Italian *bufone* means a toad and *buffone* a buffoon. *Buffoon* is generally derived from the French *bouffer*, to blow or put out the cheeks, because, so it is said, buffoons were in the habit of blowing out their cheeks, either in their violent explosions of laughter, or in order that slaps upon their faces might produce a louder noise, or simply for the purpose of making themselves ridiculous. At all events the word is considered to involve the notion of *blowing* or *swelling up*, of inflation or tumidity. Now is not the toad noted for swelling up its body? Has not Dryden the line, 'The hissing serpent, and the *swelling* toad'? ~ F. Chance, 5 Apr 1862

¶ The *Oxford English Dictionary* supports the mountebank's boy derivation of toad-eater, rather than the parasite story given in Ogilvie's *Dictionary*, and traces the term back to the early seventeenth century. In the eighteenth century the word came to be applied more generally to compliant sycophants, and by the nineteenth century it was being shortened: 'You know what a toadey is?' asked the young Disraeli in *Vivian Grey* (1826). 'That agreeable animal which you meet every day in civilised society...'

As for buffoon, modern dictionaries concur with the view that it originated in imitation of puffing up, and it seems likely that F. Chance was correct in his suggestion that the Latin for toad originated in the same way.

TRAFALGAR: Remarkable *sang froid* at

N. The historic importance attaching to any incident connected with the Battle of Trafalgar must be my apology for offering your readers the following brief extract from the Journal of HMS *Leviathan*, recording a remarkable act of British heroism. The *Leviathan*, after helping to disable the French admiral's ship and the four-decker *Santissima Trinidada*, closed with the enemy's ship *Augustin*, which she soon took:

> While this was doing, a shot took off the arm of Thomas Main, when at his gun on the forecastle. His messmates kindly offered to assist him in going to the surgeon, but he bluntly said, 'I thank you, stay where you are. You will do more good there.' He went down *by himself* to the cockpit. The surgeon, who respected him, would willingly have attended him in preference to others whose wounds were less alarming, but Main would not admit it, saying, 'Avast, not until it comes to my turn, if you please.' The surgeon soon after amputated the shattered part of the arm near the shoulder, during which, with great composure, smiling, and with a steady clear voice, he [Main] sang the whole of *Rule Britannia*!

~ F. Phillott, 6 Dec 1856

TRAVELLERS: Some eccentric

Q. I have somewhere heard or read of an Englishman who went abroad with the design of making an extensive tour on the Continent, but who was diverted from his purpose by finding himself so comfortable on board a certain canal-boat, or *trekschuit*, in Holland or Belgium, that he went no further, preferring to be a daily passenger in the boat, which went and returned between certain limits on alternate days. When and where was this, if there is any truth in the story? ~ B.M., 16 Feb 1861

R. We believe this story to be founded on fact. It seems to be agreed that the gentleman started on his intended tour in 1815, the year of the Battle of Waterloo; that he landed at Ostend with the design of pushing on to Brussels; and that the canal-boat which arrested his progress was one that plied between Bruges and Ghent. It is said that he went abroad not merely to see foreign lands, but in the hope of meeting illustrious personages and distinguished characters, which will account for his making for Brussels in 1815. Finding, however, that on board the *trekschuit* he not only fell in with many persons worth meeting, but had the opportunity of sitting down with them to the *table d'hôte*, he thought he could not do better, and went backwards and forwards, never getting further than Ghent. Mr Thackeray, in *Vanity Fair*, gives a somewhat different version of the story, saying that the traveller in question 'went backwards and forwards from Ghent to Bruges perpetually until the railroads were invented, when he drowned himself on the last trip of the passage-boat'. ~ Editor, 16 Feb 1861

R2. To stories of eccentric travellers may be added that of the Englishman who is said to have made a bet that van Amburgh, the lion tamer, would be eaten by his ferocious pupils within a given time, and who followed him about the continents of Europe and America in the hope of seeing him at last devoured, and so winning his stake. The Russians also have a story of an eccentric traveller, of course an Englishman, who posted overland and in the depth of winter to St Petersburg, merely to see the famous wrought-iron gates of the Summer Garden. He is said to have died of grief at finding the gates superior to those at the entrance to his own park at home. Add to this the lying traveller who boasted that he had been everywhere, and who, being asked how he liked Persia, replied that he scarcely knew *as he had only stayed there a day.* ~ George Augustus Sala, Clement's Inn, 23 Feb 1861

¶ Isaac van Amburgh was the most celebrated wild animal trainer of his day. In 1833 he caused a stir in New York by entering a cage occupied by lions, leopards and a panther, and in 1838 he travelled to Europe, where the young Queen Victoria was among his many fans: she attended his performance at the Drury Lane Theatre six times in as many weeks, went on stage after one performance to see the animals being fed, and commissioned Sir Edwin Landseer to paint his portrait.

Van Amburgh was reputedly the first man to put his head into a lion's mouth – voluntarily at least – and his exploits inspired a popular song called 'The Menagerie':

Van Amburgh is the man who goes to all the shows,
He goes into the lions' den, and tells you all he knows,
He sticks his head into the lion's mouth, and leaves it there awhile,
And when he takes it out again, he greets you with a smile.

He died peacefully in his bed in 1865, so, if any Englishman did make the bet mentioned in *N & Q*, he lost.

TURNCOAT

N. The following is from the *Scots Magazine* for October 1747:

This opprobrious term of *turncoat* took its rise from one of the first dukes of Savoy, whose dominions lying open to the incursions of the two contending houses of Spain and France, he was obliged to temporise and fall in with the power that was most likely to distress him, according to the success of their arms against one another. So, being frequently obliged to change sides, he humorously got a coat made that was blue on one side and white on the other and might be indifferently worn either side out. While on the Spanish interest he wore the blue side out, and the white side was the badge for the French. From hence he was called Emmanuel surnamed the Turncoat, by way of distinguishing him from other princes of the same name of that house.

~ G.N., 2 Aug 1856

TURNSPIT DOGS

N. In *The Book of Days* recently compiled by Mr Chambers there is an interesting article on Turnspits. The writer mentions having a few months ago seen at an auction a box and wheel, of which no one could tell the use, till an old blacksmith solved the puzzle by stating that it was the wheel which used to be trodden by a turnspit dog. He adds that, besides the blacksmith, he has met with only one other person who can remember seeing a turnspit dog on his wheel. If I had come his way I could have given additional evidence. I well remember seeing a turnspit at work at the Sugar-Loaf Inn in Bristol at the beginning of the present century. The house was near the market, and was well frequented, and had a large kitchen where huge joints of beef were to be seen roasting every day. I remember seeing the poor turnspit in a box high up on the right-hand side of the wide fireplace, and watching the rapidity of his motion on the dreary treadwheel, where for hours he was doomed every day to confinement and hard labour. ~ F.C.H., 23 Aug 1862

R. As your correspondent F.C.H. appears to be of opinion that the use of turnspit dogs ceased in the early part of the present century, I take leave to mention an instance occurring almost fifty years later. The Rev. Thomas Parks, curate of Lismore, Ireland, died in 1854, at the age of eighty-six, in the house where he was born. He retained one of these animals in his service through life, and I saw a dog at work in the wheel in his kitchen within a few years before his death. ~ H. Cotton, Thurles, 13 Sep 1862

R2. Thirty years ago the kitchen of nearly every respectable house in Haverfordwest possessed a dog-wheel and a turnspit dog. There was no other way of roasting meat, saving the kitchen-maid turning a spit placed on andirons, as roasting jacks had not then penetrated into this faraway region. In those days we were thirty-six hours distant from London; now eight hours will bring us within view of the metropolis.

I remember two turnspit dogs in the possession of a friend, a clergyman resident in the city of St David's. They had to work in the wheel on alternate days, and, as meat was not roasted every day, some days would elapse without the services of a turnspit being required. Yet each dog knew well when it fell to his turn to occupy the wheel, and, if the cook did not lock him up before she began to prepare her meat for roasting, he infallibly made his escape. In that case the other dog had to take his place, and he would lie down in the wheel and howl dismally in expression of his sense of the injustice with which he was treated. If the cook locked up the proper dog the other one took no notice of the culinary preparations, except by significant wags of his tail and lickings of his lips, indicative of his extreme satisfaction at the prospect of dinner. ~ John Pavin Phillips, Haverfordwest, 27 Sep 1862

R3. At least two turnspit wheels still exist in Gloucestershire. One is at Wick Court, about seven miles from Bristol, and the

other is at St Briavel's Castle, on the left bank of the Wye. The wheels have a high side to keep the dog in and stand against the wall at a height from the floor which allows a person to lift a dog into them easily. I put my dog into the wheel at St Briavel's, but whether it was that the wheel would not turn easily or at all, or that my dog felt that he was not of a turnspit family, he refused to move, and laid himself down in the wheel, so that I had to take him down without the gratification of seeing the wheel in motion. ~ D.P., Stuarts Lodge, Malvern Wells, 27 Sep 1862

R4. I well remember seeing at St Briavel's a wooden turnspit wheel which was in use. I did not see the turner thereof, but was informed by his master that the old dog was in the habit of quietly slipping out of the house at the approach of strangers, fearing lest he should be called upon to do extra duty for their gratification – a great proof, were any needed, of canine wisdom. This was about the year 1844. ~ W. J. Bernhard Smith, Temple, 27 Sep 1862

R5. A friend of mine from the North of England once told me of a certain great house in Northumberland – Brancepeth Castle, if I do not forget – where turnspit dogs had been in constant request up to our own times, receiving, *virtute officii*,[1] the hereditary name of Wheeler. On one great occasion dinner was unaccountably delayed, and the lady of the house, having impatiently rung the bell to ascertain the cause, was informed, 'Please, ma'am, Wheeler's pupping!' ~ C.W.B., 27 Sep 1862

[1] By virtue of office.

UMBRELLAS: When were they first used in England?

Q. Thomas Coryate, in his *Crudities* (1611), gives us a curious notice of the early use of the umbrella by people in Italy:

> Many of them do carry other fine things that will cost at the least a ducat, which they commonly call in the Italian tongue *umbrellaes*, that is, things that minister shadow unto them for shelter against the scorching heat of the sun. These are made of leather, something answerable to the form of a little canopy, and hooped in the inside with diverse little wooden hoops that extend the *umbrella* in a pretty large compass. They are used especially by horsemen, who carry them in their hands when they ride, fastening the end of the handle upon one of their thighs: and they impart so long a shadow unto them, that it keepeth the heat of the sun from the upper parts of their bodies.

Lieutenant-Colonel (afterwards General) Wolfe, writing from Paris in 1752, says: 'The people here use umbrellas in hot weather to defend them from the sun, and something of the same kind to secure them from snow and rain. I wonder a practice so useful is not introduced in England, where there are such frequent showers, and especially in the country, where they can be expanded without any inconveniency.'

Query, what is the date of the first introduction of the umbrella into England? ~ Edward F. Rimbault, 27 Apr 1850

R. From Mr Peter Cunningham's amusing *Handbook for London*: 'The benevolent Jonas Hanway, the traveller, lived and died (1786) in a house in Red Lion Square. Hanway was the first man who ventured to walk the streets of London with an umbrella over his head. After carrying one near thirty years, he saw them come into general use.' ~ Editor, 4 May 1850

R2. It is, I think, probable that their use must have been at least partially known in London long before that period, judging from the following extract from John Gay's *Trivia, or, Art of Walking the Streets of London*, published in 1716:

Good housewives all their winter's rage despise,
Defended by the riding-hood's disguise;
Or, underneath th'umbrella's oily shade,
Safe through the wet on clinking pattens tread.
Let Persian dames the umbrella's ribs display,
To guard their beauties from the sunny ray;
Or sweating slaves support the shady load,
When Eastern monarchs show their state abroad;
Britain in winter only knows its aid,
To guard from chilly showers the walking maid.

That it was, perhaps, an article of curiosity rather than use in the middle of the seventeenth century is evident in the fact of its being mentioned in the *Museum Tradescantianum, or, a Collection of Rarities preserved at South-Lambeth neer London* by John Tradescant, 1656. It occurs under the head of 'Utensils' and is simply mentioned as 'An Umbrella'. ~ E. B. Price, 8 June 1850

R3. In the hall of my father's house at Stamford in Lincolnshire there was, when I was a child, the wreck of a very large green silk umbrella, apparently of Chinese manufacture, brought by my father from Holland somewhere between 1770 and 1780. It was, I often heard, the first umbrella seen at Stamford. ~ G. C. Renouard, Swanscombe Rectory, 8 June 1850

R4. To your extensive exhibition of umbrellas I am happy to make an addition of considerable curiosity, it being of much earlier date than any specimen at present in the collection:

Of doves I have a dainty paire
Which when you please to take the aier,
About your head shall gently hover
Your cleere browe from the sunne to cover,
And with their nimble wings shall fan you
That neither cold nor heate shall tan you,
And, like umbrellas, with their feathers
Sheeld you in all sorts of weathers.
(Michael Drayton, *The Muses' Elizium*, 1630)

~ Bolton Corney, 28 Dec 1850

R5. In 1758 Dr Shebbeare was sentenced to the pillory for a political libel. Narrating this punishment in his *Memoirs*, Horace Walpole says the doctor 'stood in the pillory, having a footman holding an umbrella to keep off the rain'. In James Burrow's *Reports of Cases Adjudged in the Court of King's Bench* there is an account of the proceedings against Arthur Beardmore, under-sheriff of Middlesex, for contempt of court in remitting part of the sentence on Shebbeare. The affidavits produced by the attorney-general stated that 'the defendant only stood upon the platform of the pillory, unconfined and at his ease, attended by a servant in livery (which servant and livery were hired for the occasion only) *holding an umbrella over his head all the time'*. Mr Justice Dennison, in pronouncing sentence on Beardmore, did not omit to allude to the umbrella.[1] ~ C. H. Cooper, Cambridge, 15 Feb 1851

R6. In Fynes Moryson's *Itinerary* (1617) is the following passage: 'In hot regions, to avoide the beames of the sunne, in some places (as in Italy) they carry umbrels, or things like a little canopy, over their heads; but a learned physician told me that the use of them was dangerous, because they gather the heate into a pyramidall point, and thence cast it down perpendicularly upon the head, except they know how to carry them for avoiding that danger.' ~ C. de D., 26 July 1851

R7. Mr Lawford, the bookseller of Savile Passage, told me that he had been informed by a very old gentleman who frequented his shop that he had witnessed several executions at Tyburn. Amongst them he said that Dr Dodd's, in 1777, had

[1] For a blatant attack on the Hanoverian succession Shebbeare was sentenced to pay £5, suffer three years' imprisonment, provide securities of £1,000 for good behaviour, and stand in the pillory at Charing Cross for one hour. However, the under-sheriff Beardmore shared his political views and arranged for him to be conveyed to the pillory not in a prisoner's cart but in one of the city's elegant coaches, and on arrival Shebbeare was greeted by cheering crowds. The umbrella was held by an Irish chairman hired for the day. Beardmore was subsequently fined £50 and imprisoned for two months.

made a particularly strong impression on his memory on account of the celebrity of the culprit and because, when the hangman was going to put the halter round the doctor's neck, the latter removed his wig, showing his bald shaved head; and, a shower of rain coming on at the same time, someone on the platform hastily put up an umbrella, and held it over the head of the man who had but a minute to live, as if in fear that he might catch cold.[1] ~ James Knowles, 8 Sep 1860

¶ As noted in *N & Q*, women in London were already using umbrellas early in the eighteenth century. However, men who followed suit were subjected to derision, as the following announcement in *The Female Tatler* of 12 December 1709 indicates: 'The young gentleman belonging to the Custom House, who, in the fear of rain, borrowed the umbrella at Will's Coffee-house, in Cornhill, of the mistress, is hereby advertised that to be dry from head to foot on the like occasion he shall be welcome to the maid's pattens.'

Umbrellas were also adopted at an early date for church use: the churchwardens' accounts at St Nicholas's, Newcastle, record a payment of £1 5s. for one in 1717, and in 1770 at Wakefield 'Dame Lofthouse' was paid five shillings per half year 'for bringing out the umbrella'.

While the traveller Jonas Hanway is generally credited with having been the first man regularly to use an umbrella in London, the footman John 'Beau' Macdonald could return from Spain with one as late as 1778 and still consider himself to be blazing a trail:

At this time there were no umbrellas worn in London, except in noblemen's and gentlemen's houses, where there was a large one hung in the hall, to hold over a lady or gentleman if it rained, between the door and their carriage. If it rained,

[1] A former chaplain to George III and a noted preacher, William Dodd had been convicted of forging a bond in the name of his pupil, Lord Chesterfield. In spite of the best efforts of Dr Johnson and others, he was executed at Tyburn on 27 June 1777.

I wore my fine silk umbrella. Then the people would call after me, 'What, Frenchman, why do you not get a coach?' In particular the hackney coachmen and hackney chairmen would call after me; but I, knowing the men well, went straight on, and took no notice. I went on so for three months, till they took no further notice of me, only 'How do you do, Frenchman?' After this the foreigners, seeing me with my umbrella, one after another used theirs – then the English. Now[1] it is become a great trade in London.

Jonas Hanway ventures out

[1] Macdonald was writing in 1790.

UNICORNS AND THE DECLINE OF WONDER

N. In a collection of *Travels* 'done into Englyshe by Richarde Eden' and published in London in 1577, there is what appears to be a copy of a publication thus entitled: *The Navigation and Voyages of Lewes Vertomannus, Gentleman of Rome, to the Regions of Arabia, Egypt, Persia, Syria, Ethiopia, and East India, both within and without the River of Ganges, etc., in the Year of our Lord 1503. Containing many Notable and Strange Things, both Historical and Natural.* From this I have made the following extract:

ON THE UNICORNS OF THE TEMPLE OF MECCA, WHICH ARE NOT SEEN IN ANY OTHER PLACE

On the other part of the temple are parks and places enclosed, where are seen two unicorns, named by the Greeks *Monocerote*, and are there showed to the people for a miracle, and not without good reason, for their seldomness and strange nature. The one of them, which is much higher than the other, yet not much unlike to a colt of thirty months of age, in the forehead groweth only one horn, in manner right forth, of the length of three cubits. The other is much younger, of the age of one year, and like a young colt: the horn of this is of the length of four handfuls. This beast is of the colour of a horse of weasel colour, and hath the head like

314

an hart, but no long neck, a thin mane hanging only on the one side. Their legs are thin and slender, like a fawn or hind; the hoofs of the fore feet are divided in two, much like the feet of a goat; the outward part of the hinder feet is very full of hair. This beast seemeth doubtless very wild and fierce, yet tempereth that fierceness with a certain comeliness. These unicorns one gave to the Sultan of Mecca, as a most precious and rare gift. They were sent him out of Ethiopia by a king of that country, who desired by that present to gratify the sultan.

~ Henry Kensington, 19 Jan 1856

R. In a note of Mr Thomas Roscoe's to his translation of the *Memoirs of Benvenuto Cellini* (1822), he says a unicorn's head was at that date being shown in London. Is there any other notice of this, or of anything similar at any other time?

~ Lyttelton, 10 Feb 1872

R2. Whatever the head exhibited in London may have been, the horn which adorned it must have been that of the sea-unicorn or narwhal (*Monodon monoceros*), probably joined neatly to the front of the head of some kind of horse. The stuffed mer-maidens and mer-men which were carried about and exhibited by men of the pedlar type, got up as sailors, twenty or thirty years ago, were probably of the same class. But the fabulous monsters which used to be taken about the country and exhibited to the unlearned have of late years greatly diminished in number. Even the performing canaries, the educated hare, and the rest have deserted us. I remember the feelings of awe with which I was taken when a child to see 'the tortoiseshell woman', 'the petrified man', 'the sand-dogs of the desert', etc. Fat women, giants, and dwarfs still visit us, but the wandering glass-blower who used to make ships and globular magnifying glasses, and who spun glass before our eyes, comes no more. However, I note that there are to be seen in Belfast at this moment 'Two sea leopards, male and female, alive, captured by the captain of a ship in the German Ocean, and brought by him into Liverpool.'

~ W.H.P., 23 Mar 1872

R3. In Sir William Dugdale's *Monasticon Anglicanum* there is a list of all the gold and silver plate delivered to Henry VIII from the stores and treasures of monastic houses. Among the plate from Glastonbury, delivered on 15 May 1539, a curious relic is thus entered: 'Item, delivered more unto his majestie the same day of the same stuff a greate pece of a unicorne-horne, as it is supposed.' ~ W.A.S.R., 23 Mar 1872

R4. In *A Catalogue of the Rarities to be seen at Don Saltero's Coffee-house in Chelsea*, No. 284 is 'A sea-unicorn's horn, seven foot and a half long.' ~ W. G. Stone, 25 May 1872

¶ Ludovico de Varthema of Bologna (*c.*1470-*c.*1515), also known as Barthema and Vartomannus, was the first European and Christian to visit Mecca and live to write the tale. His *Itinerario* (1510) is considered in many respects an accurate record – Richard Burton, for one, praised Varthema's 'correctness of observation' – while its account of unicorns has been described as 'the most important of all descriptions given by the few who claim to have seen the animal'.

The Glastonbury horn delivered to Henry VIII in 1539 was one of several held by great religious foundations before the Dissolution of the Monasteries – St Paul's Cathedral and Westminster Abbey each had at least one.

For Henry and other rulers unicorn horn had an appeal beyond mere prestige in that it was thought capable of detecting the presence of poison: 'Being put upon a table furnished with many junkets and banqueting dishes,' noted John Swan in his *Speculum Mundi* (1635), 'it will quickly descrie whether there be any poison or venime among them, for, if there be, the horne is presently covered with a kind of sweat or dew.'[1] Prices were accordingly high: as Odell Shepard notes in *The Lore of the*

---

[1] The extent of princely fear at this time is indicated by the range of other objects employed for the same purpose, from parrots, rhinoceros horns and walrus tusks to snake's tongue and raven's claw hung over a burning candle (if poison was brought to the table, the claw was supposed to clutch tight and extinguish the flame).

Unicorn, 'The cost of "true unicorn's horn" (*verum cornu monocerotis*) in its best period was a little over ten times its weight in gold when sold in small pieces or in powder, but the whole horns sometimes brought twice as much as this.'

Not surprisingly, therefore, 'fake' horn was abundant, as David de Pomis warned in 1587:

> There is very little of the true horn to be found, most of that which is sold as such being either stag's horn or elephant's tusk. The common test, which consists in placing the object in water to see whether bubbles will rise, is not at all to be trusted, and therefore, wishing to benefit the world and to expose the wicked persons who sell worthless things at great prices, I take this occasion to describe a true test by which one may know the genuine horn from the false. The test is this: place the horn in a vessel of any sort of material you like, and with it three or four live and large scorpions, keeping the vessel covered. If you find four hours later that the scorpions are dead, or almost lifeless, the unicorn's horn is a good one, and there is not money enough in the world to pay for it. Otherwise, it is false.

The idea that *all* unicorn horns might be fraudulent gained credit only very slowly. As early as 1527 the Scottish historian Hector Boethius had revealed that walrus tusks were straightened before being sold in Europe as unicorn horns, while the French traveller André Thévet, writing in 1575, claimed actually to have seen Levantine artisans straightening tusks on an island in the Red Sea preparatory to shipping them on as part of a lucrative trade. However, doubt only spread widely after 1638, when Ole Wurm, a distinguished Danish professor, pronounced in Copenhagen that most of the celebrated 'horns' of Europe were not horns at all but the teeth of narwhals. Values fell only modestly at first, but over the following decades a rising spirit of rational enquiry combined with a glut of horns[1] to produce a

---

[1] The King of Denmark owned so many that he had an elaborate new throne made out of his spares.

dramatic collapse. By 1734 Johann Zedler's great encyclopedia, the *Universal-Lexicon*, would report that horns that had previously fetched thousands of dollars could now be bought for twenty-five.

While unicorns may have lost out to rationalism in the eighteenth century, hopeful unicorn-hunters were still to be found well into the nineteenth. Indeed, the appearance of a unicorn's head in London in 1822, mentioned in *N & Q*, may have been linked to a flurry of sightings at about that time. In October 1820 the *Quarterly Review* carried a curious letter from a Major Latter, commander of the Rungpore Battalion in the hill country east of Nepal, reporting that he had been reliably informed there were unicorns in Tibet: 'I have written to the Sachia Lama, requesting him to procure me a perfect skin of the animal, with the head, horn, and hoofs.' From the *Calcutta Government Gazette* of August 1821 it seems he had some success: 'Major Latter has obtained the horn of a young unicorn from the Sachia Lama, which is now before us. It is twenty inches in length; at the root it is four inches and a half in circumference, and tapers to a point; it is black, rather flat at the sides, and has fifteen rings, but they are only prominent on one side. It is nearly straight. Major Latter expects to obtain the head of the animal, the hoofs, and the skin, very shortly...'

Meanwhile, according to the *Asiatic Journal* of July 1821, an African unicorn had been discovered by the servants of one John Campbell: ' "The animal", says Mr Campbell, "was killed by my Hottentots in the Mashow country... Never having seen or heard of an animal with *one* horn of so great a length, [they] cut off its head and brought it bleeding to me upon the back of an ox. The horn, which is nearly black, is exactly three feet long..." ' Indeed, as late as December 1860 the sober *Athenaeum* would express belief in a South African unicorn occupying 'an intermediate rank between the massive rhinoceros and the lighter form of the horse'.

As for the coffee-house rarity, Don Saltero's was established in Lawrence Street, Chelsea, in about 1695 by James Salter, a barber and former travelling servant to Sir Hans Sloane. In 1717 he moved to a new shop by the river, on the site of present day Cheyne Walk (No. 18), where, in addition to providing his customers with coffee, he would cut their hair, extract their teeth, bleed them, play the violin, and provide diversion in the form of an extensive collection of curious objects, many of them cast-offs donated by Sloane. On Salter's death, in about 1728, his daughter took over the business, and the earliest existing edition of the rarities *Catalogue* dates from 1729. It proved a long-running success: by 1795 it had reached its 48th edition. The collection itself was sold off four years later and fetched only £50 – a disappointing sum given that in its heyday, in addition to the sea-unicorn's horn, it had boasted a salamander, a small whale, a pair of nun's stockings, a basilisk, William the Conqueror's flaming sword, the King of Morocco's tobacco pipe, a frog fifteen inches long, the head of an albatross, a flying dragon, a little sultaness, the Pope's infallible candle, and a starved cat found between the walls of Westminster Abbey during repairs.

WATCHMEN: A warning to from Mr Touchit

N. The following warning was addressed to the watchmen of London on the occasion of a great fire which destroyed nearly a hundred houses in the neighbourhood of Exchange Alley, Birchin Lane, and the back of George Yard, among which were Garraway's, the Jerusalem Coffee-house, the George and Vulture, Tom's, etc. It appeared in the *Westminster Journal* of 2 April 1748 and is very characteristic of the then state of the police of the metropolis.

Mr Touchit's Warning
to the Watchmen of London

Whereas it has been represented to me, Thomas Touchit, Watchman Extraordinary of the City of Westminster, that the Watchmen of London were very remiss during the dreadful Fire on Friday morning, March 25, in not giving timely Notice of that Calamity over their several Beats, whereby the Friends of many of the unhappy Sufferers, who would have flown to their Assistance, were ignorant of their Distress till it was too late to do them Service; and also that most of the said Watchmen, on other Occasions, are very negligent, whence it happens that many Robberies, Burglaries, and other Offences, which their Care might prevent, are committed; and that even some of them are in Fee with common Harlots and Streetwalkers, whom they suffer, at unseasonable Hours, unmolested to prey on the Virtue, Health and Property of His Majesty's Liege Subjects: Be it known to the said Watchmen, and their Masters, that, having taken the Premises into Consideration, I intend whenever I set out from Spring Gardens with my invisible Cap, my irradiating Lanthorn, and my Oken Staff of correction, to take the City of London, under Leave of the Right Hon. the Lord Mayor, into my Rounds, and to detect, expose, and punish all Defaulters in the several Stands and Beats: Whereof this fair Warning is given, that none may be surprised in Neglect of Duty, I being determined to shew no Favour to such Offenders.

~ Euston Square, 12 Jan 1850

WATERHOUSE, REV. JOSHUA: The murder of a country parson

Q. Will some of your readers tell me whether the following inscription, of which I have a note, really exists at Stukeley, Huntingdonshire, in the words given?

Sacred to the Memory of the

REV. JOSHUA WATERHOUSE B.D.,

nearly 40 years Fellow of Catherine Hall, Cambridge,
Chaplain to his Majesty, Rector of this Parish, and of
Coton, near Cambridge, who was inhumanly murdered in
this parsonage house about ten o'clock on the morning of
July 3rd, 1827, aged 81: —

Beneath this Tomb his Mangled body's laid,
Cut, Stabb'd and Murdered by Joshua Slade;
His ghastly Wounds a horrid sight to see,
And hurled at once into Eternity.
What faults you've seen in him take care to shun
And look at home, enough there's to be done;
Death does not always warning give,
Therefore be carefull how you live.

~ R. W. Hackwood, 8 Mar 1856

R. There is no doubt as to the inscription. The unfortunate clergyman had some poor relations in Derbyshire, who, after his murder, came to the county of Huntingdon to attend to his funeral and administer to his estate. They erected the tombstone.

The case of Mr Waterhouse excited much interest at the time. I was then residing in the neighbourhood and forwarded notices of the deceased to my late friend Mr Mudford of the London *Courier*. Waterhouse was a parson of the Trulliber class.[1] He was the only one I ever knew drive his own pigs and sheep to market. He hated the clerical costume, usually wearing

---

[1] 'Mr Trulliber was a parson on Sundays, but all the other six days might more properly be called a farmer...' (Henry Fielding, *Joseph Andrews*, 1742)

a long blue coat. To evade the window tax he had blocked up nearly all the windows in the parsonage, and a young rogue in the village used to get into the darkened rooms, when the parson was out in the fields, and steal whatever he could carry away. One day he was detected and dragged from his lurking-place by Mr Waterhouse. The latter would promise no mercy, and the thief in desperation drew a sword (which he had stolen from an alehouse and kept concealed inside his trousers), and, pushing the old man down into a brewing tub in the passage, ran him through the throat. At his trial a billhook, the supposed instrument of death, was produced; it was stained with blood and exhibited what were considered grey hairs! The audience shuddered, but Baron Alderson was by no means satisfied with the circumstantial evidence and postponed the execution for a month. In the interval the young murderer confessed all, and told where the sword would be found.

Mr Waterhouse was a bachelor and had, up to his seventieth year, been paying addresses to a number of ladies. There was in the house at least a sackful of love letters, some – which I regret I did not copy – from the celebrated Mary Wollstonecraft, afterwards Mrs Godwin. ~ R. Carruthers, Inverness, 29 Mar 1856

¶ Born in 1746, Waterhouse went up to Cambridge in 1771, became a Fellow, served as university proctor in 1783, and was granted the living of Coton five years later.

As a young man he cut a dashing figure, dressing smartly and visiting Bath and Bristol and other fashionable resorts. It may have been at Bath that he met the young Mary Wollstonecraft, who was there from 1778 to 1780.

In later years, however, Waterhouse cut a very different figure. At Little Stukeley, to which he moved in 1813, he became notorious as a grain-hoarding miser who, when his clothes had been soiled in the hunting field, would clean them simply by going to his fishpond and brushing water onto himself. Nonetheless, it seems from a contemporary account of his murder that he retained a romantic hopefulness:

A few years since, Mr Waterhouse, believing himself to be on the brink of matrimony, had two or three of his apartments elegantly furnished. Men were employed from Cambridge to complete the undertaking, and about £300 was expended in making preparations for the expected bride. But from some undiscovered cause the match was broken off; the moreen curtains and splendid mirrors were suffered to remain in the cotton coverings which enveloped them, and the Turkey carpets, instead of being pressed by the foot of beauty, were covered with sprung grain.

As noted in *N & Q*, the murder itself caused a great stir – according to the Huntingdon *Gazette*, over 2,000 strangers visited the scene of the crime. Large crowds gathered again for the trial and execution of the murderer Joshua Slade, whose confession included a detailed account of events at the parsonage on the fatal day:

I meant to have robbed the house at night of anything I could. I was asleep from five to ten amongst the wool. Mr Waterhouse, happening to come upstairs, heard me breathe; I dare say I was snoring; upon which he came up to the chamber and called 'Holloa! Who are you? What do you do here?' I then got up, drew the sword, and laid hold of him. Mr Waterhouse tried to go in at the chamber where his blunderbuss was, but I would not let him. I led him down-stairs [and] said, 'Now, Mr Waterhouse, if you'll forgive me, I will forgive you; and if not, this is your death warrant,' holding up the sword. Mr Waterhouse said, 'No, I will suffer anything first...' He went to run by me to the kitchen door to call somebody, upon which, just as he was turning into the kitchen, I struck him a back-handed blow, [causing] the great cut across the jaw [which he suffered], and he reeled back, caught himself against the tub, and fell backwards into it. He guarded his head with his hands when in the tub. I struck him several blows with the sword. He laid hold of the sword twice, upon which I drew it out of his hands and cut his fingers. I also stabbed him in the throat, which was the last blow. Mr Waterhouse then said 'I am done,' and died immediately.

There was no blood whatever upon me except on my finger, which I spat on and wiped it on the grass, and also one spot on my waistcoat, which I scratched out with my nail immediately; it never was seen. I have heard that blood of a murdered person will not wipe out, but I am sure this did. I did not hear the dog bark all the time; he would not bark at me. He barked once when I first got over the wall, but as soon as he heard my step he knew me, and was quiet...

Among visitors to Stukeley in the following years was the actor Edmund Kean. He copied the curious tombstone inscription onto the flyleaf of his road-book, but was not impressed, adding four lines of his own:

> Worse, worse than Slade, thou murderer of verse,
> Deserving more than he the cuplrit's hearse;
> Slade killed the living, perhaps by hunger led;
> You, by your doggerel, have damned the dead.

WIFE-SELLING: An English custom?

Q. What is the origin of the popular idea that a man may legally dispose of his wife by haltering her and exposing her for sale in a public market? Some time ago the custom appears to have been very prevalent, and only a few months back there was a paragraph in *The Times* describing an occurrence of the kind at Nottingham. ~ V. T. Sternberg, 30 Apr 1853

R. About eighteen years ago a case of selling a wife actually and *bona fide* happened in the provincial town in which I reside. A man publicly sold his wife at the market cross for £15. The buyer carried her away with him some seven miles off, and she lived with him till his death. The seller and the buyer are both now dead, but the woman is alive, and is married to a *third* (or second) husband. The legality of the transaction has, I believe, some chance of being tried, as she now claims some property belonging to her first husband (the seller), her right to which is questioned in consequence of her supposed alienation by sale; and I am informed that a lawyer has been applied to in the case. ~ Sc., 9 July 1853

R2. There can be no question that this offence is an indictable misdemeanour. I made, at the time, a memorandum of the following case: 'West Riding Yorkshire Sessions, 28 June 1837. Joshua Jackson, convicted of selling his wife, imprisoned for one month with hard labour.' ~ S.R., Chiswick, 27 Aug 1853

R3. The French believe we sell our wives at Smithfield, and we call them blockheads for their ignorance of our manners. However, the following cuttings are worthy of the attention of all students of English civilisation:

A young man in Bewcastle, Cumberland, who was not on good terms with his wife, resolved a few days ago to dispose of her by auction. Not being able to find a purchaser in the place where they resided, she persuaded him to proceed to Newcastle for that purpose. Accordingly they set out, and this modern Delilah laid her plan so well that, immediately on his arrival, a press-gang conveyed him on board a frigate preparing to get under weigh for a long cruise.

(Evans and Ruffy's *Farmer's Journal*, 5 May 1810)

This barbarous occurrence actually took place in Merthyr Tydfil a few days ago between a workman of the Cyfarthfa Iron Works and another. The price for which the workman sold his wife was £3 – £2 10s. in cash and 10s. worth of beer, the latter to be drunk by the principal parties in the transaction. The husband seemed very well satisfied that he had not only got rid of his wife but also gained something in the bargain. As for the woman, she exhibited few symptoms of either shame or sorrow, and drank her share of the beer.

(*Stamford Mercury*, 27 March 1863)

~ K.P.D.E., 11 Dec 1858 & 20 June 1863

R4. There have been several notices of wife-selling in your columns, but I do not remember seeing any account of the peculiar circumstances under which the custom became a settled legal point in the minds of the labouring population.

When the war was over in 1815 and a great number of soldiers were disbanded, many of them found, on reaching what had been their homes, that their wives had married again, and that a new family had sprung up to which the unfortunate soldier or sailor had no claim. I do not suppose that the thing originated then, but the fact of taking a wife to the market, and selling her by auction, was considered as effectual a way of dissolving the *vinculum*[1] as if it had been done in the House of Lords itself. The second husband became the purchaser for a nominal sum, twopence or sixpence, the first was free to marry again, and all parties were content. In the manufacturing districts in 1815 and 1816 hardly a market day passed without such sales, month after month. The authorities shut their eyes at the time, and the people were confirmed in their sense of the perfect legality of the proceeding, as they had already been satisfied of its justice. ~ Jannoc, 5 Dec 1863

¶ Perhaps the earliest reference to a wife-selling in England comes in 1553 in the diary of Henry Machyn, the guilty party being Thomas Sowdley, a clergyman known as Parson Chicken: 'The 24th day of November did ride in a cart Chicken, parson of St Nicholas Coleabbey, about London, for he sold his wife to a butcher.'

Thomas Hardy famously featured a wife-sale in *The Mayor of Casterbridge* (1886). This part of the plot was met with disbelief and outcry at the time of publication, but Hardy had done his research: before writing he had gone through newspapers from the 1820s, when the fictional sale is set, and made careful notes of three different cases, one at Brighton, one at Stamford, and one at Buckland, near Frome.

[1] Bond.

WITCHCRAFT: An alternative test for

N. Among the many tests applied for the discovery of witchcraft was the following singular instance, but little known to the public. It was resorted to as recently as 1759, and may be found in the *Gentleman's Magazine* of February that year.

> One Susannah Hannokes, an elderly woman of Wingrove near Aylesbury, was accused by a neighbour for bewitching her spinning-wheel, so that she could not make it go round, and offered to make oath of it before a magistrate; on which the husband, in order to justify his wife, insisted upon her being tried by the church Bible, and that the accuser should be present. Accordingly she was conducted to the parish church, where she was stript of all her cloaths to her shift and under-coat, and weighed against the Bible; when, to the no small mortification of her accuser, she out-weighed it, and was honourably acquitted of the charge.

~ A.D.N., Abingdon, 16 Nov 1850

¶ The test rested on the assumption that a witch, being a spirit, would have no or very little weight.

WOOLLEN: Burial in

Q. On looking over the parish registers of Mautby, Norfolk, a few days since, I found thirteen entries of certificates of the enforced observance of burial in woollen, of which the following is a specimen: 'November the 8th, 1678. Was brought unto me an affidavit for ye burial of William the sonne of John Turner in woollen according to ye late Act of Parliament for that purpose. — Andrew Call, Rector.' In addition I find a comparatively recent trace of the practice in an affidavit from Harwich, Essex, which is in the collection of my friend R. Rising, Esq.:

> Sarah the wife of Robert Lyon, of the parish of Dovercourt in the borough aforesaid, husbandman, and Deborah the wife of Stephen Driver, of the same parish, husbandman (being two credible persons), do make oath that Deborah, the daughter of the said Stephen and Deborah, aged eighteen weeks, who was on the 7th day of April instant interred in the parish churchyard of Dovercourt, in the borough aforesaid, was not put in, wrapped, or wound up, or buried in any shirt, shift, sheet, or shroud, made or mingled with flax, hemp, silk, hair, gold, or silver, or other than what is made of sheeps' wool only; or in any coffin lined or faced with any cloth stuff, or any other thing whatsoever, made or mingled with flax, hemp, silk, hair, gold or silver, or any other material but sheeps' wool only.
>
> Taken and sworn the 15th day of April 1769 before me, one of his majesty's justices of the peace,
>
> G. Davies.

The reason is clear – to increase the consumption of wool – but I much wish to know the date of the aforesaid Act of Parliament and to how late a period it extended. ~ E. S. Taylor, 1 May 1852

R. Your correspondent is referred to Acts of 1678 and 1680. The former is entitled 'An Acte for the lessening the importation of linnen from beyond the seas, and the encouragement of the woollen and paper manufactures of the kingdome'. It prescribes

329

that the curate of every parish shall keep a register, to be provided at the charge of the parish, wherein to enter all burials and affidavits of persons being buried in woollen. The affidavit was to be taken by any justice of the peace, mayor, or such like chief officer in the parish where the body was interred. No affidavit was necessary for any person dying of the plague. The Act imposes a fine of £5 for every infringement, one half to go to the informer, and the other half to the poor of the parish.

The first entry in the book provided for such purposes in this parish bears the date August 1678, and there is no entry later than 1681, when we find the following: 'Received a fine of James Crompton ffor buringe his son and not bringinge in an affidavit according to the Acte for buryng in woollin, 02.10.00.'
~ John Booker, Prestwich, Manchester, 5 June 1852

R2. The Acts in question were repealed by another of 1814.
~ J. B. Colman, Eye, 5 June 1852

R3. The topic recalls to one's mind Alexander Pope's *Epistle to Viscount Cobham* (1734), in which he gives the following deathbed exclamation to 'Narcissa', the actress Mrs Oldfield:

> 'Odious! in *woollen*! 'twould a saint provoke!'
> (Were the last words that poor Narcissa spoke)
> 'No, let a charming chintz, and Brussels lace
> Wrap my cold limbs, and shade my lifeless face:
> One would not, sure, be frightful when one's dead –
> And – Betty – give this cheek a little red.'

~ H.W., 17 July 1852

R4. Mrs Oldfield, who died in October 1730, escaped the 'woollen'. According to the *Gentleman's Magazine* for March 1731 she was 'buried in Westminster Abbey, in a Brussels lace head dress, a Holland shift, with tucker and double ruffles of the same lace, and a pair of new kid gloves'. ~ C., 31 July 1852

¶ There had also been an earlier Act 'for burying in woollen only' passed in 1666, but it proved so ineffective that it was replaced by the more stringent legislation of 1678.

It is said that Pope based Narcissa's lines on fact, Anne Oldfield having given her maid, Elizabeth Saunders, precise instructions as to how she was to be dressed in death.

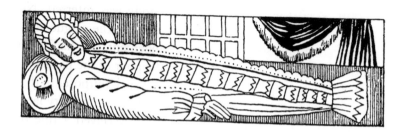

WORDS, LAST, OF THE GREAT AND FAMOUS

N. A collection of the last words of great and famous men would, I venture to suggest, be interesting and not unfit for the pages of *N & Q*. I beg to annex a few such dying speeches, each characteristic of the several men.

• Cardinal Beaufort: 'What, is there no bribing death?'

• Sir Thomas More, to the officer who escorted him onto a precariously shaky scaffold: 'I pray you, Master Lieutenant, see me safe up, and for my coming down let me shift for myself.'

• Sir Walter Ralegh, when it was complained that his head on the block was not facing east: 'So the heart be straight, it matters little how the head lieth.'

• Lord Chesterfield, bidding his valet attend to his godson, who had just arrived: 'Give Dayrolles a chair.'

• Count Mirabeau, French Revolutionary politician: 'Let me die to the sounds of delicious music.'

• Nelson: 'I thank God I have done my duty.'

• Byron: 'I must sleep now.'

• Goethe: 'Open the second shutter, so that more light can come in.'

Some of your correspondents, I have no doubt, could greatly enlarge this collection. ~ H.E.W., York, 9 Aug 1856

R. I offer the following:
- Anne Boleyn, clasping her neck: 'It is small, very small.'
- Elizabeth I: 'All my possessions for a moment of time.'
- Charles II: 'Don't let poor Nelly starve.'
- John Locke, to Lady Masham, who was reading the Psalms: 'Cease now.'
- General Wolfe, seeing the French forces retreat: 'What? Do they run already? Then I die happy.'

~ Mackenzie Walcott, 6 Sep 1856

¶ Other notable last words, actual and apocryphal, include:
- Voltaire, on being encouraged at the last to renounce the Devil: 'This is no time to make new enemies.'
- William Pitt the Younger: 'I think I could eat one of Bellamy's veal pies.'
- Heinrich Heine: 'God will forgive me. It is His profession.'
- Ramón Maria Narváez, Spanish general and political leader, asked by a priest if he forgave his enemies: 'I do not have to. I have had them all shot.'
- General John Sedgwick, scanning the horizon at the Battle of Spotsylvania in the American Civil War: 'They couldn't hit an elephant at this —.'
- Disraeli, declining the offer of a visit from Queen Victoria: 'She will only ask me to take a message to Albert.'
- Henrik Ibsen, when a nurse said he seemed a little better: 'On the contrary...'
- O. Henry, quoting a popular song: 'Turn up the lights; I don't want to go home in the dark.'

Sources

1. Text

The original fortnightly issues of *Notes and Queries* were gathered into volume form every six months, and these volumes were then numbered into series in groups of twelve, the first series running from November 1849 to the end of 1855, the second from 1856 to 1861, and so on. The material in this book is drawn mainly from series 1 and 2, with occasional forays into series 3 and 4.

The following notes consist of:

- series, volume and page references for the *N & Q* material; for example 1.02.377 indicates page 377 in the second volume of the first series.
- author, title, and date of works cited in *N & Q*, where such information is lacking in the main text. A few titles have proved elusive, however, so the listing is not complete. In some cases author dates and other basic information have been included to indicate when a work was written.
- author, title, and date of works which have been of use in compiling the additional notes.

Page references have been provided for periodical publications but not for other titles, in which treatment is often more discursive.

Quotations from the diaries of John Evelyn and Samuel Pepys appear in several entries and are not listed individually below. Texts follow the standard editions available to *N & Q* contributors (*Diary of John Evelyn*, ed. William Bray, 4 vols, 1859, and *Diary and Correspondence of Samuel Pepys*, ed. Lord Braybrooke, 3rd edition, 5 vols, 1848-9), with minor emendations by reference to their modern successors (*The Diary of John Evelyn*, ed. E. S. de Beer, 6 vols, 1955, and *The Diary of Samuel Pepys*, ed. Robert Latham & William Matthews, 11 vols, 1970-83).

Standard abbreviations are used in the text and below to indicate two reference Leviathans which have proved invaluable in the preparation of this book: *ODNB* (*Oxford Dictionary of National Biography*, online edition) and *OED* (*The Oxford English Dictionary*, 2nd edition, 1989).

Introduction. *Examiner*: quoted in the unnumbered endpages of *Notes and Queries... General Index to Series the First*, 1856. 'A work devoted...': 1.01.129. Patrick Leary, 'A Victorian Virtual Community', *Victorian Review*, vol. 25 pt 2, Winter 2000, pp62-79. Arthur Sherbo, 'William John Thoms', *ODNB*.

Actress. 2.03.206 / 2.03.238 / 2.03.471. John Payne Collier, *The History of English Dramatic Poetry*, 3 vols, 1831, vol. 2, has the 'Thomas Brande' letter. Arthur Freeman & Janet Ing Freeman, *John Payne Collier: Scholarship and Forgery in the Nineteenth Century*, 2 vols, 2004, vol. 1, outlines the case for doubting it. John Russell Brown (ed.), *The Oxford Illustrated History of Theatre*, 1995, for court masques. Colley Cibber, *Apology for the Life of Mr Colley Cibber*, 1740. Elizabeth Howe, *The First English Actresses*, 1992, for the case for Anne Marshall's priority.

Anglesey. 3.02.249 x 2. The monumental inscription appeared in *N & Q* in the original French. G. C. H. V. Paget, Marquess of Anglesey, *One-Leg: The Life and Letters of Henry William Paget*, 1961, and 'Henry William Paget', *ODNB*. Nick Foulkes, *Dancing into Battle: A Social History of the Battle of Waterloo*, 2006.

Animals. 2.02.069 / 2.07.278 / 2.07.343 / 3.05.218 x 2. Gaspard Bailly, *Traité des Monitoires, avec un plaidoyer contre les Insects*, 1668. Hieronymus Rorarius (1485-1556), *Quod animalia bruta ratione utantur melius homine*, 1654. Jacques Berriat-Saint-Prix, 'Rapport et Recherches sur le Procès et Jugemens relatives aux Animaux', in *Mémoires de la Société Royale des Antiquaires de France*, vol. 8, 1827, pp403-450. The E. P. Evans work cited in the text is the source of much of the material in the additional note, including details of Chassenée's defence of the rats. Darren Oldridge, *Strange Histories: The Trial of the Pig, the Walking Dead, and other matters of fact from the Medieval and Renaissance Worlds*, 2005. Robert Chambers, *The Book of Days*, 2 vols, 1862-4, vol. 1.

Audrey. 2.11.226 / 2.11.300. Robert Southey & S. T. Coleridge, *Omniana, or, Horae Otiosiores*, 2 vols, 1812, vol. 1. Bede, *Ecclesiastical History of the English People*, completed AD 731. Alan Thacker, 'Æthelthryth', *ODNB*. *The Winter's Tale*, Act 4, scene 4. *The Man of Mode*, Act 2, scene 2.

Basilisk. 2.11.506 / 2.12.057. Pliny the Elder, *Historia Naturalis*, written *c.* AD 77.

Bell, Book and Candle. 2.03.370 / 2.03.439 / 2.03.497. Dugdale, 3 vols, 1675-6, vol. 1. Raphael Holinshed's *Chronicles*, by himself and other hands, was first published in 1577; extracts are from *Holinshed's Chronicles of England, Scotland, and Ireland*, 6 vols, 1807-8, vol. 2. Staveley extract is from the 2nd edition, 1773. Becon, 1563. Christopher Marlowe, *The Tragical History of Dr Faustus*, first known performance 1594. *The Oxford Dictionary of the Christian Church*, 3rd edition revised, ed. F. L. Cross & E. A. Livingstone, 2005.

Bentham. 2.04.051 x 2. The Southwood Smith quotation is from a letter dated 14 June 1857 to the physician and librarian William Munk. The letter was given in full in *N & Q* in 1866 (3.10.188), when it was described as being 'among our papers'; it seems likely therefore that, before publishing D.L.'s query, *N & Q*'s editor had gathered the facts for his answer via Munk, a fellow bookman. C. F. A. Marmoy, 'The Auto-Icon of Jeremy Bentham at University College, London', *Medical History*, vol. 2, no. 2, April 1958, pp77-86. Other information from the website of University College London, which now prefers to be comma-less.

Bill of Fare. 1.05.412.

Birth, Marriage and Death. 03.03.283. Alan Cook, 'Edmond Halley', *ODNB*.

Boiling to Death. 1.02.519 / 1.05.032 / 1.05.033 / 1.05.112 / 1.05.184. John Stow, *The Annales, or, Generall chronicle of England... continued and augmented... by Edmond Howes*, 1615. Sir William Blackstone, *Commentaries on the Laws of England*, 4 vols, 1765-9, vol. 4. John Gough Nichols (ed.), *Chronicle of the Grey Friars of London*, 1852. Mr Nichols's interpretation was disputed by Mr Colman (1.05.185), but this has been omitted as little light was shed and the point remained moot. *Calendar of Letters, Despatches and State Papers*, Spanish Series, vol. 4 pt 2, 1882, has the Chapuys despatch. Henry K. J. Kesselring, 'A Draft of the 1531 "Acte for Poysoning"', *English Historical Review*, vol. 116, no. 468, September 2001, pp894-899. Maria Dowling, *Fisher of Men: A Life of John Fisher*, 1999. F. van Ortroy (ed.), 'Vie du bienheureux martyr Jean Fisher', *Analecta Bollandiana*, vol. 10, 1891, pp121-365, and vol. 12, 1893, pp97-287; the shot across the Thames is in vol. 10, pp346-347. Richard Rex, 'John Fisher', *ODNB*.

Boleyn. 1.01.468. Jennifer Westwood & Jacqueline Simpson, *The Lore of the Land*, 2005, makes the hell-wain connection. Walter Rye (ed.), *The Norfolk Antiquarian Miscellany*, 1st Series, 3 vols, 1877-87, vol. 1.

Book Titles. 1.12.403 / 2.01.174 / 1.06.299 / 2.01.176 / 3.04.400 / 2.01.337.

Bunkum. 2.06.092 x 2. Judge Halliburton: no source cited.

Burial 1. 1.08.005 / 1.08.059 / 1.08.233 / 1.08.455 x 2 / 1.09.088 / 1.09.407. Wordsworth, 1815. Thomas Whitaker, *The History and Antiquities of the Deanery of Craven in the County of York*, 1805. Thomas Ingoldsby (R. H. Barham), 'The Cynotaph', in *The Ingoldsby Legends*, 1840. Thomas Roscoe, *The German Novelists: Tales selected from the ancient and modern authors in that language*, 1826. John Murray (publishers), *A Handbook for*

Travellers on the Continent: being a guide through Holland, Belgium, &c., 1836. Marchette Chute, *Ben Jonson of Westminster*, 1954. Westminster Abbey website. Charles Rose, *Recollections of Old Dorking*, 1878.

Burial 2. 1.05.320 / 1.05.404 / 1.05.549 / 1.06.136. Thompson Cooper, rev. Philip Carter, 'Martin van Butchell', *ODNB*. *Gentleman's Magazine*, vol. 82 pt 1, April 1812, p326, has the 'full of spirits' remark.

Burial 3. 2.02.103 / 2.03.305 / 2.05.453 / 2.06.470 / 3.02.156 / 3.04.239 / 3.12.399. William Bates gave Douce's request in second-hand form from T. F. Dibdin, *Reminiscences of a Literary Life*, 2 vols, 1836, vol. 2; this has been replaced with Douce's own words as given in the *Gentleman's Magazine*, New Series, vol. 2 pt 2, August 1834, p216. Bacon quotation adjusted by reference to variant version contributed earlier by Mackenzie Walcott (1.10.233) and to *The Works of Francis Bacon*, ed. James Spedding et al., 7 vols, 1857-9, vol. 5. *Gentleman's Magazine*, vol. 71, April 1801, p378. Robert Chambers, *The Book of Days*, 2 vols, 1862-4, vol. 2, has William Blackett's will. Melanie King, *The Dying Game: A Curious History of Death*, 2008. Jan Bondeson, *Buried Alive: The Terrifying History of Our Most Primal Fear*, 2001.

Burning to Death. 1.02.006 / 1.02.050 / 1.02.090 / 1.02.261. *Gentleman's Magazine*, vol. 59 pt 1, March 1789, p272.

Byron's Brain. 2.12.028 / 2.12.116. Thomas Moore, *Letters and Journals of Lord Byron, with Notices of His Life*, 3rd edition, 3 vols, 1833, vol. 3. Pietro (Count) Gamba, *A Narrative of Lord Byron's Last Journey to Greece*, 1825, has Dr Bruno's report. Burrell, 2004. Hermann Welcker, 'On the Skull of Dante', *Anthropological Review*, vol. 5, no. 16, January 1867, pp56-71. Edward Anthony Spitzka, 'A Study of the Brain of the Late Major J. W. Powell', *American Anthropologist*, vol. 5, 1903, pp595-596. Stephen Jay Gould, *The Mismeasure of Man*, 1981.

Calumniators. 2.01.312. I have not been able to trace de Polignac's *History*. R.R. cited volume 3.

Charleston Maids. 1.07.594.

Cheshire Cats. 1.02.377 / 1.02.412 / 1.05.402. Lewis Carroll (Charles Lutwidge Dodgson), *The Annotated Alice*, ed. Martin Gardner, revised edition, 2000.

Church Bells 1. 1.09.324 / 2.05.391 / 3.06.404 / 3.06.405.

Church Bells 2. 1.06.508 & 1.12.074 (W.W. referred to the *Galignani* report in his initial letter and added the quotation in the later contribution) / 1.06.609 / 1.06.610. William Durandus, *Rationale divinorum officiorum*, written 1286-91. Dyer, 1850. *The Sermons of... Hugh Latimer*, 2 vols, 1824, vol. 2. John Brand, *Popular Antiquities of Great Britain*, ed. W. Carew

Hazlitt, 3 vols, 1870, vol. 2., has the Sandwich entry. Sir William Dugdale, *The History of St Paul's Cathedral*, 1658; ed. Henry Ellis, 1818. Details of the relics are in Henry T. Riley (ed.), *The French Chronicle of London, AD 1259 to AD 1343*, trans. from the original Anglo-Norman of the 'Croniques de London' and published with *Chronicles of the Mayors and Sheriffs of London*, 1863. W. Sparrow Simpson, *Gleanings from Old St Paul's*, 1889; Simpson cites Digby MS, Rolls 2, Bodleian Library, for the hallowing of 1498. *The true Report of the burnyng of the Steple and Churche of Poules*, imprynted at London, at the West ende of Paules Church at the Sygne of the Hedghogge, by Wylliam Seres. Anno 1561. The x of June. The anonymous Catholic response to Pilkington's sermon appeared as *An Addicion, with an Appologie to the Causes of brinnynge of Paules Church*, 1561. Pilkington's subsequent confutation appeared as *A Confutacion of an Addicion*, 1563. James Marcombe, 'James Pilkington', *ODNB*. James Calfhill, *An Aunswere to the 'Treatise of the Crosse'* (by John Martial), 1565. Thomas Kirchmeyer (also known as Neogeorgus), *The Popish Kingdome*, trans. Barnabe Googe, 1570.

Clarence. 2.02.221 / 2.02.297 / 2.02.335 / 2.03.034. R. Fabyan, *New Chronicles of England and France*, ed. H. Ellis, 1811. John Strype (1643-1737), *Annals of the Reformation*, 4 vols, 1824, vol. 1 pt 2. John Webster Spargo, 'Clarence in the Malmsey-Butt', *Modern Language Notes*, vol. 51, no. 3, March 1936, pp166-173. Spargo has the English chronicle quotation, citing *Chronicles of London*, ed. C. L. Kingsford, 1905, and gives details of Dr Goldschmidt's findings. Domenico Mancini, *The Usurpation of Richard III*, trans. and ed. C. A. J. Armstrong, 2nd edition, 1969. *Journal de Jean de Roye*, ed. B. de Mandrot, 2 vols, 1894-6, vol. 2. C. J. S. Thompson, *Mysteries of History*, 1928, has the poisoning suggestion. M. A. Hicks, *False, Fleeting, Perjur'd Clarence*, 1980, and 'George, Duke of Clarence', *ODNB*.

Coffee-houses. 1.01.026 / 1.01.154 / 1.01.314. The *N & Q* Editor gave the site of Rosee's coffee-house as George Yard, Lombard Street – a stone's throw from St Michael's Alley, the accepted location. *Aubrey's Brief Lives*, ed. Oliver Lawson Dick, 1958. Walter Rumsey, *Organon Salutis: An instrument to cleanse the stomach, as also divers new experiments of tobacco and coffee*, 1657; 3rd edition with additions, 1664. Howell's letter has been adjusted by reference to *The Familiar Letters of James Howell*, ed. Joseph Jacobs, 2 vols, 1892, vol. 2. George Sandys, *A Relation of a Journey Begun An. Dom. 1610*, 1615. *The Life and Times of Anthony Wood*, ed. Andrew Clark, 5 vols, 1891-1900, vol. 1. Markman Ellis, *The Coffee House: A Cultural History*, 2004. Brian Cowan, 'Pasqua Rosee', *ODNB*. Robert Chambers, *The Book of Days*, 2 vols, 1862-4, vol. 1, has

Pasqua Rosee, 'The Vertue of the Coffee Drink', and 'News from the Coffee-House'. Isaac D'Israeli, *Curiosities of Literature*, 9th edition revised, 6 vols, 1834, vol. 4, has 'A cup of Coffee, or Coffee in its colours', 1663, and 'The Women's Petition against Coffee', 1674.

Combustion. 1.07.286 / 1.07.440 / 1.07.458 / 1.07.632. Justus von Liebig, *Familiar Letters on Chemistry*, 3rd edition, revised and much enlarged, 1851. Two dates in the *N & Q* table have been adjusted: case 2 was mistakenly dated 1763, the year not of the death itself but of the appearance of an account of it in the *Annual Register* (see below); case 12 was dated 1830 but either this or the 1820 date given for case 11 must be wrong as the two victims are said to have burnt together in the same bed. Gordon S. Haight, 'Dickens and Lewes on Spontaneous Combustion', *Nineteenth-Century Fiction*, vol. 10, no. 1, June 1955, pp53-63. Peter Denman, 'Krook's Death and Dickens's Authorities', *The Dickensian*, vol. 82, no. 410 pt 3, Autumn 1986, pp131-141. The Bianchini extract is taken from the version reprinted in the *Annual Register*, 1763, p91, which, as Denman shows, may well be the account which Dickens used. Denman also shows that, in the dispute with Lewes, Dickens considerably overstated the extent of his own knowledge and researches. *The Letters of Charles Dickens*, 12 vols, 1965-2002, ed. Graham Storey et al., vol. 7. Jenny Randles & Peter Hough, *Spontaneous Human Combustion*, 1992.

Coventry. 1.06.318 x 2 / 1.06.589.

Cromwell. 1.03.207 / 1.03.286 / 1.05.400. Anthony Wood, *The Life and Times of Anthony à Wood*, abridged from Andrew Clark's edition by Llewelyn Powys, 1932. Edward Hyde, Earl of Clarendon, *The History of the Rebellion and Civil Wars in England*, 3 vols, 1702-4; extract is from the 1720 edition, vol. 3 pt 2. James Heath, *Flagellum, or, The Life and Death, Birth and Burial of Oliver Cromwell, the Late Usurper*, 1663; 4th edition, 1669. Samuel Butler, *Hudibras: The Third Part*, 1678; ed. Zachary Grey, 1744. Richard Westfall, *Never at Rest: A Biography of Isaac Newton*, 1980.

Curates. 1.12.160.

Custard. 1.05.321 / 1.10.174. W. L. Bowles, *The Life of Thomas Ken*, 1830. W.N. simply referred the reader to Bowles: the quotations have been added. Bowles provides no information regarding Warton: it seems likely that Joseph Warton (1722-1800) is intended, but his father Thomas (*c*.1688-1745) is another possibility. *Ingulph's Chronicle of the Abbey of Croyland with the Continuations of Peter of Blois and anonymous writers*, trans. Henry T. Riley, 1854. Thomas Fosbroke, *British Monachism, or, Manners and Customs of the Monks and Nuns of England*, 1802.

Dante. 1.01.154 / 1.01.339.

Daughters. 2.12.083. T. J. Dibdin, *The Reminiscences of Thomas Dibdin*, 2 vols, 1827, vol. 2.

Dead Men's Heads. 1.02.479 / 1.03.010 / 2.05.011. Alfred Tennyson, 'A Dream of Fair Women', in *Poems*, dated 1833 but published December 1832. Mackintosh, 1830. Thomas Stapleton, *Tres Thomae*, 1588. E. E. Reynolds, *Margaret Roper*, 1960. John Guy, *A Daughter's Love: Thomas and Margaret More*, 2008. *Gentleman's Magazine*, New Series, vol. 7 pt 1, pp494-497. Raleigh Trevelyan, *Sir Walter Raleigh*, 2003. Margaret Bowker, 'Margaret Roper', Seymour Baker House, 'Sir Thomas More', Mark Nicholls & Penry Williams, 'Sir Walter Ralegh' and 'Carew Ralegh', *ODNB*.

Death Warnings. 1.09.055 / 1.09.114. John Bernard Burke, *A Genealogical and Heraldic Dictionary of the Peerage and Baronetage of the British Empire*, 13th edition, 1851.

Deathbed Superstitions. 1.01.315 / 1.01.316 / 1.01.350 / 1.01.467. *Athenaeum*, no. 990, 1846, p1068.

Devil. 2.05.295 x 2. Ellis Wynne, *Gweledigaetheu y bardd cwsc*, 1703; ed. Daniel Silvan Evans, 1853. John Aubrey, *The Natural History and Antiquities of Surrey*, 5 vols, 1718-9, vol. 1. William Oldys (1696-1761), antiquary: no work cited. Ben Weinreb & Christopher Hibbert (eds.), *The London Encyclopedia*, 1983. Michael Dobson & Stanley Wells (eds.), *The Oxford Companion to Shakespeare*, 2001. Andrew Gurr, *Playgoing in Shakespeare's London*, 1999. E. K. Chambers, *The Elizabethan Stage*, 4 vols, 1923, vol. 3. *Gentleman's Magazine*, New Series, vol. 34 pt 2, p234.

Dog-whipping 1. 1.09.349 / 1.09.499 / 1.09.500 / 1.10.188 x 3 / 2.01.223 / 2.02.187. Stephen Friar, *A Companion to the English Parish Church*, 1996.

Dog-whipping 2. 1.08.409 / 1.09.064.

Dragons. 1.02.517 / 1.03.040 / 3.07.158 / 3.07.159. John Murray (publishers), *Handbook for Travellers in Northern Italy*, 1842. Jean de Thévenot, *Relation d'un Voyage fait au Levant*, 1665. Frederick W. Hasluck, 'Dieudonné de Gozon and the Dragon of Rhodes', *Annual of the British School at Athens*, vol. 20, 1914, pp70-79, which has the translated quotation from Giacomo Bosio, *Historia della S. Religione di S. Giovanni*, 1594.

Ear-pulling. 1.12.406 / 1.12.499. *A History of Germany... on the plan of Mrs Markham's Histories* was written by Robert Bateman Paul and published in 1847. A revised edition appeared in 1853, lacking any reference to Paul and with an introductory note by the editor, T.H.D. Taking his cue from this, P. J. F. Gantillon referred to the author as T.H.D. *Memoirs of Benvenuto Cellini... written by himself*, trans. Thomas Roscoe, 2 vols, 1822, vol. 1; quotation adapted.

Elephants. 2.02.388 / 2.02.436 / 2.04.208 / 2.04.258. Robert Dundas Thomson, *Cyclopedia of Chemistry*, 1854.

Epitaphs. 1.10.513 / 1.11.428 x 2 / 1.12.423 / 1.12.424 / 2.02.397 / 2.03.124 / 2.06.535. Abraham Newland, *The Life of Abraham Newland*, 1808. William Camden, *Remaines concerning Britaine,* the fifth impression, with many rare antiquities never before imprinted, by the industry and care of John Philipot, 1674.

Events. 1.10.202 / 1.10.294 / 2.02.043 / 2.02.152 / 2.02.232. David Hume, 'Of Parties in General,' in *Essays, Moral and Political,* 2 vols, 1741-2, vol. 1. Blaise Pascal, *Pensées,* 1670. Graves, 1773. *The Works of Alexander Pope,* ed. Joseph Warton et al., 9 vols, 1797, vol. 3. Isaac D'Israeli, *Curiosities of Literature,* 9th edition revised, 6 vols, 1834, vol. 1. Cotton Mather, *Magnalia Christi Americana,* 1702. Gilbert Burnet, *History of My Own Time,* 2 vols, 1724-34; ed. M. J. Routh with notes by Speaker Onslow and others, 6 vols, 1833, vol. 2. Edward Gibbon, *The History of the Decline and Fall of the Roman Empire,* 8 vols, 1776-88; extracts are from the 1848 edition, 8 vols, vol. 5 (Prasini) and vol. 6 (Count Julian). Antonia Fraser, *Cromwell: Our Chief of Men,* 1973. Stanley, 1855. I have not been able to trace the references to Dr Paris (possibly John Ayrton Paris, 1785-1856), Campbell (possibly the poet Thomas Campbell, 1777-1844), and M. Richer.

Familiar Phrases. 2.01.044 / 2.03.485 / 2.05.411 / 2.09.402 / 3.10.414. Stanislaus Hosius, *A Most Excellent Treatise of the Begynnyng of Heresyes in Oure Tyme... translated out of Laten in to Englyshe by R. Shacklock... and intituled by hym: The Hatchet of Heresies,* 1565.

'First Catch...' 2.11.264. G.D.Y. 'corrected' *catch* to *cast* but this has itself been corrected to *case.* *Oxford Dictionary of English Proverbs,* 3rd edition, ed. W. G. Smith & F. P. Wilson, 1970. *Brewer's Dictionary of Phrase and Fable,* 17th edition, ed. John Ayto, 2005. Henry of Bratton, or de Bracton, is thought to have been writing *De legibus* in the 1250s, but parts may not be by him and may date to a slightly earlier or later period. It was not published until 1569.

Football. 3.03.449 x 2. Percy Young, *A History of British Football,* 1968. Dr Maria Hayward's discovery of Henry VIII's order for football boots was widely reported in February 2004.

Fox-hunting. 1.01.093 / 1.01.338. Walpole alludes to the Edgehill fox-hunter several times in his *Letters,* for example in writing to the Earl of Hertford on 5 May 1765. Sir William Dugdale, *The Antiquities of Warwickshire,* 1656; new edition augmented by W. Thomas, 1730.

Frogs. 2.04.145 / 2.04.279 x 2 / 2.05.246 / 2.05.357.

Game Feathers. 1.05.341 / 1.05.413.

Glove-removal. 1.01.366 / 1.02.165 / 1.05.157.

Goat. 1.11.135 / 1.11.347. James Fenimore Cooper, *Lionel Lincoln*, 1825. A. D. L. Cary & Stouppe McCance, *Regimental Records of the Royal Welch Fusiliers*, 2 vols, 1921, vol. 1. News reports from 2006: *Telegraph*, 18 May; BBC, 24 June; Associated Press, 25 June.

Gooseberry. 2.10.307 / 2.10.308 / 2.10.376.

Hare. 1.04.208 / 2.09.492. Wright, 1857.

Hedgehogs. 1.12.383 / 1.12.477.

Hermits. 1.05.123 / 1.05.207 / 1.06.472 / 1.06.593. Florence did not cite a source for the Painshill and Lancashire stories but they had appeared verbatim in *The Cabinet of Curiosities, or, Wonders of the World Displayed*, 1824. The Lancashire gentleman was named as a Mr Powyss, but as considerable doubt was cast on this identification in *N & Q* his name has been omitted. Max Nicholson, 'Charles Hamilton', F. J. Turner, 'Thomas Weld', W. C. Sydney & S. J. Skedd, 'Sir Richard Hill', *ODNB*. John Newman & Nikolaus Pevsner, *Shropshire*, 2006. *The Oxford Companion to the Garden*, ed. Patrick Taylor, 2006. Staffordshire County Council website: article on 'Hidden Estates' project.

Hour-glasses. 1.07.589 / 1.08.082 / 1.08.083 / 1.08.209 / 1.08.279 / 1.09.253. Clive Fewins, *The Church Explorer's Handbook*, 2005. I am grateful to the Rev. John Carvosso for the Tawstock information.

Human Skin. 2.02.068 / 2.02.250 / 2.02.252 x 2 / 3.09.309 / 3.09.422 x 2 / 4.05.311 / 4.10.448 / 4.11.373.

Humble Pie. 1.01.054 / 1.01.92.

Hydrophobia. 1.05.010 / 1.06.206 / 1.06.207 x 3 / 1.06.298 / 1.06.438 / 2.11.478.

Jib. 1.10.482.

Justice. 1.12.317 / 2.01.038. J.S.M.M. said that Stratford was not only the first victim of the new Norwich gallows but also the last. This has been omitted as, while perhaps correct, it appears at odds with the fact that executions continued at the jail until 1867. *Lambeth and the Vatican, or, Anecdotes of the Church of Rome, of the Reformed Church, and of Sects and Sectaries*, 3 vols, 1825, vol. 3. Leopold von Ranke, *Die römischen Päpste*, 3 vols, 1834-6; trans. Sarah Austin as *The Ecclesiastical and Political History of the Popes of Rome*, 3 vols, 1840, vol. 1. J. Stearne, *A Confirmation and Discovery of Witchcraft*, 1648. James Sharpe, 'Matthew Hopkins', *ODNB*.

Kant's Wig. 2.06.186 / 2.10.109. The Victor Hugo quotation was given from the 1837 edition in the original French. J. H. W. Stuckenberg, *The Life of Immanuel Kant*, 1882.

Ketch. 1.12.293. The story contributed by H. Martin had appeared verbatim in William Bayley, *The Bagman's Bioscope*, 1824. Tim Wales, 'Jack Ketch', *ODNB*. The Evelyn diary entry is from 15 July 1685.

Leeches. 2.09.500 / 2.10.096 / 2.10.139. William Hayley, *The Life and Posthumous Writings of W. Cowper*, 3 vols, 1806, vol. 3. George Merryweather, *Essay explanatory of the Tempest Prognosticator in the building of the Great Exhibition for the Works of Industry of All Nations*, 1851.

Livers. 1.05.127 / 1.05.212 / 1.05.334.

London Street Characters. 1.05.270 / 1.05.376. Charles Lamb, 'A Complaint of the Decay of Beggars in the Metropolis', in *Essays of Elia*, 1st Series, 1823.

Lovell. 2.01.230 / 2.07.017. Banks, 3 vols, 1807-9, vol. 2.

Marat. 2.05.032 / 2.08.052 / 2.08.256 / 2.10.214 / 3.02.317. W.B.C. referred to 'the *Star* (Glasgow newspaper)' but this has been amended by reference to Sidney Phipson, *Jean Paul Marat: His Career in England and France before the Revolution*, 1924. Samuel Seyer was the author of *Memoirs Historical and Topographical of Bristol and its Neighbourhood*, 2 vols, 1821-3. Joseph Farington (1747-1821), *The Diary of Joseph Farington*, ed. Kenneth Garlick & Angus Macintyre, 17 vols, 1978-98, vol. 1. *Annual Register*, vol. 20, p178. J. M. Thompson, 'The Robbery from the Ashmolean Museum, 1776' and 'Le Maitre, alias Mara', *English Historical Review*, vol. 46, no. 181, January 1931, pp96-117, and vol. 49, no. 193, January 1934, pp55-73. *N & Q*, 12.11.053, has the de Ternant letter.

Marriage 1. 2.03.150 / 2.03.198. Stirling, 1852. Peter Heylin (1599-1662): no work cited.

Marriage 2. 3.03.091 x 2 / 3.06.195. Bernard Burke, *A Genealogical and Heraldic Dictionary of the Landed Gentry of Great Britain*, 1863. *Sporting Magazine*, vol. 40, no. 236, May 1812, p67, and vol. 40, no. 239, August 1812, p200.

Marriage 3. 1.12.257 / 1.12.348 / 2.08.364 / 4.04.417 / 4.04.418 / 4.04.525. The *Chronique* of Georges Chastellain (*c.*1415-1475) covers the period from 1419 to 1474. The surviving fragments were first published in 1827 and in fuller form between 1863 and 1867. *Journal d'un Bourgeois de Paris* covers the period from 1405 to 1449 and, despite its name, is thought to have been written by a cleric. It was published in part in 1653 and in full in 1729. Quotations from both works appeared in *N & Q* in the original French. *Diary of John Manningham, of the Middle Temple*, ed. John Bruce, 1868.

Marriot. 2.02.006 / 2.02.031 / 2.03.455. Dunton, 1705. Smyth, 1849. Cotton, 1689. Commonplace book of William Oldys: British Library, Add. MS 4245, fol. 97r. Eleanor O'Keeffe, 'William Marriott', *ODNB*.

Melancholy. 1.02.505 / 1.03.230. Sir Walter Scott (compiler), *Minstrelsy of the Scottish Border*, 3 vols, 1802-3, vol. 3. The *Henry IV part 1* scene reference is to the Oxford Shakespeare: in many editions the quotation falls in Act 2, scene 4. The Icelandic *Saga of Egil Skallagrimson* is thought to have been written by Snorri Sturluson (1179-1241) and to date from *c*.1230.

MPs' Salaries. 3.01.149. Prynne, 4 vols, 1659-64, vol. 4. Sir William Blackstone, *Commentaries on the Laws of England*, 4 vols, 1765-9, vol. 1. Cuthbert Johnson, *The Life of Sir Edward Coke*, 2 vols, 1837, vol. 1, has the Dunwich agreement. R. C. Latham, 'Payment of Parliamentary Wages – The Last Phase', *English Historical Review*, vol. 66, no. 258, January 1951, pp27-50.

Mice. 1.01.397 / 1.01.430 / 1.02.004 / 1.02.197 / 1.02.435 / 1.04.052.

Mince Pies. 2.10.470. Sir Roger Twysden (1597-1672), antiquary: no work cited.

Monks. 1.06.053 / 1.06.110 / 1.06.205 / 1.06.328 x 2 / 3.08.524. 'All unruffled was his face...': adapted by Frances Trollope from Canto 2, verse 19 of Sir Walter Scott's *The Lay of the Last Minstrel*, 1805. John Murray (publishers), *Handbook for Travellers in France*, 1843.

Moustaches. 2.03.507 / 2.08.266.

Nelson 1. 2.01.170 / 3.06.060. *The Dispatches and Letters of Vice Admiral Lord Viscount Nelson*, with notes by Sir Nicholas Harris Nicolas, 7 vols, 1845-6, vol. 3.

Nelson 2. 4.01.223 / 4.01.277 / 4.02.357. *The Dispatches and Letters of Vice Admiral Lord Viscount Nelson*, with notes by Sir Nicholas Harris Nicolas, 7 vols, 1845-6, vol. 7. Sir Samuel Burdon Ellis, *Memoirs and Services*, ed. Lady Ellis, 1866.

Newton's Apple. 2.05.312 / 2.06.170. The 1738 Voltaire quotation was given in *N & Q* in the original French. Gauss biography: no work cited. David Brewster, *Memoirs of the Life, Writings and Discoveries of Sir Isaac Newton*, 2 vols, 1855, vol. 1. Robert Greene, *The Principles of the Philosophy of the Expansive and Contractive Forces, or, an Inquiry into the Principles of the Modern Philosophy*, 1727. Voltaire, *An Essay upon the Civil Wars of France... And also upon the Epick Poetry of the European Nations*, 1727. *Memoirs of Sir Isaac Newton's Life by William Stukeley*, ed. A. Hastings White, 1936. Douglas McKie & G. R. de Beer, 'Newton's Apple' and 'Newton's Apple: An Addendum', *Notes and Records of the Royal Society of London*, vol. 9, 1951-2, pp46-54 and pp333-335. Richard Westfall, *Never at Rest: A Biography of Isaac Newton*, 1980.

North Sides. 1.02.055 / 1.02.092 / 1.02.126 / 1.02.189 / 1.02.254 / 1.03.333. 'That close behind...': adapted by Alfred Gatty from S. T. Coleridge,

'The Rime of the Ancient Mariner', 1798. Coverdale quotation is from 'An Exhortation to the Carrying of Christ's Cross' in *The Remains of Myles Coverdale*, 1846.

Omens. Hares, Magpies, Swallows et cetera: 1.03.003. Mice and Robin Redbreast: 1.02.164. Cornish Village: 1.11.397 & 1.12.037.

Owls. 2.10.212 x 2 / 2.10.254 / 2.10.255.

Parisian Punishments. 1.02.480 / 1.02.522 / 1.03.091 / 1.05.043. Louis-Sébastien Mercier, *Tableau de Paris*, 12 vols, 1782-9, vol. 9.

Pigs. 1.05.245 / 1.05.304. *Gentleman's Magazine*, vol. 83 pt 1, p513.

Pocket-Handkerchief. 2.06.481 / 2.07.018 / 2.07.096 / 2.07.097 / 2.07.226.

Polperro. 1.10.178 & 1.10.300 & 1.10.318 & 1.10.358 & 1.10.418 & 1.10.440 & 1.10.479. Thomas Bond, *Topographical and Historical Sketches of Looe*, 1823.

Pope the Poet. 1.10.418 / 1.10.458 / 1.10.478.

Quarrelsome, Careless and Hairy. 2.03.262. *Chambers Biographical Dictionary*, 8th edition, ed. Camilla Rockwood, 2007. Robert Easton, *The Good, the Bad and the Unready*, 2008. Jean Froissart (*c.*1333-*c.*1404), *Chroniques*, trans. Lord Berners as *Chronicles*, 2 vols, 1523-5; extract is from W. P. Ker's edition, 6 vols, 1901-3, vol. 5, and has been adapted.

Rain. 2.10.207. I have not been able to trace the newspaper cutting or information regarding the effectiveness of Mons. Otto's invention.

Rats 1. 2.12.502 / 3.01.078 / 3.01.296.

Rats 2. 2.03.307. *Secret Agent's Handbook of Special Devices: World War II*, 2000. SOE report quoted in *Guardian*, 27 October 1999.

Remedies. Ague 1: 1.02.130 / 2.03.519 / 2.10.173. Ague 2: 1.04.053 / 1.04.111 / 1.04.251. Baldness and Tired Feet: 4.09.484. Fits: 2.06.522. Gout: 4.08.023. Lethargy in the Head: 2.02.333. Plague et cetera: 2.02.261 / 2.02.333. Rheumatism: 1.02.037. Whooping Cough: 1.03.258. *Memoirs of that Learned Antiquary Elias Ashmole, Esq., drawn up by himself by way of diary*, 1717. *Calendar of State Papers*, Domestic Series, of the Reign of James I, 1858.

Rhinoceros. 3.09.139 / 3.09.200 x 2. Biographies by Roger North (1651-1734) of his kinsmen Francis North (Baron Guilford), Sir Dudley North, and the Rev. Dr John North were published in 1742 and 1744 and subsequently collected under the title *Lives of the Norths*. T. H. Clarke, *The Rhinoceros from Durer to Stubbs*, 1986. L. C. Rookmaaker et al., *The Rhinoceros in Captivity: A List of 2439 Rhinoceroses Kept from Roman Times to 1994*, 1998.

Richelieu. 1.11.222. The letter's authorship has been questioned. In a later series of *N & Q* (5.01.214) it was attributed to Mazarin.

Riding Whip. 1.12.184.

Royal Positions. Whipping Boy: 1.05.468. Cock-crower: 2.03.069. Ratcatcher: 3.03.395. Joculator: 2.02.111 / 2.03.157. Keepers: 2.07.456. Yeomen: 3.10.232 x 2. 'The cock's shrill clarion': Thomas Gray, 'Elegy written in a Country Churchyard', 1751. *Gentleman's Magazine*, vol. 55 pt 1, p341. Ellis, 1805. *The Regulations and Establishment of the Household of Henry Algernon Percy, the Fifth Earl of Northumberland... begun anno domini MDXII*, edited with notes by Thomas Percy, Bishop of Dromore, 1827. 'Copy of the booke of the Household of Queen Elizabeth as it was ordered in the 43 yeare of her Raigne': British Library, Harley MS 293, article 76.

Running Footmen. 2.01.009 / 2.01.080 / 2.01.178 / 2.01.279 / 2.01.439. *Recollections of the Life of John O'Keeffe, written by himself*, 1826. Beckford, 1805.

Rural Nutrition. 1.03.132 / 1.03.207 / 1.03.221 x 2 / 1.03.336. Borrow, 1841.

Russia. 1.10.127 / 1.10.209 x 2 / 1.10.512 & 1.12.109 (J. Virtue Wynen provided the Milton details first and added the Pepys extract in the later contribution). *Quarterly Review*, vol. 17, no. 34, pp474-475. Milton's *Brief History of Moscovia* was published posthumously in 1682. *Calendar of State Papers*, Foreign Series, 1584-85, 1916. M. Unkovskaya, 'Sir Jerome Bowes', *ODNB*.

Salting. 1.04.006 / 1.04.043. *Historia Caroli Magni* (History of Charles the Great) is a twelfth-century Latin forgery ascribed to Charlemagne's contemporary, Turpin, Archbishop of Rheims; trans. Thomas Rodd as *History of Charles the Great and Orlando*, 2 vols, 1812, vol. 1. Anna Eliza Stothard, afterwards Mrs Bray, *Traditions, Legends, Superstitions, and Sketches of Devonshire... in a series of Letters to Robert Southey, Esq.*, 3 vols, 1838, vol. 1. *Gentleman's Magazine*, vol. 55 pt 2, p760.

Schoolmaster's Career. 2.01.053. Dibdin, enlarged edition, 1842.

Sedan Chair. 2.01.345. *The Autobiography and Correspondence of Mary Granville, Mrs Delany...*, ed. Lady Llanover, 1st series, 3 vols, 1861, vol. 1: the letter is dated 16 April. 'Perhaps the longest journey...': John Timbs, *The Romance of London*, 3 vols, 1865, vol. 2.

Sermon. 1.11.232. *Sermons by the Late Rev. W. B. K. Kirwan, with a Sketch of his Life*, 1815.

Sic Transit. 1.06.100 / 2.12.215. Philo of Alexandria, also known as Philo Judaeus (*c.*20 BC-*c.*40 AD), 'A Treatise on the Meeting for the Sake of Seeking Instruction'. Guillaume de Saluste Du Bartas (1544-1590): no work cited. Filippo Picinelli (1604-*c.*1667): no work cited; likely source is his best known work, *Mondo Simbolico*, 1653. I have not been able to identify the work ascribed to W. Mason. Agostino Paravicini, trans. David S. Peterson, *The Pope's Body*, 2000, has the Damiani reference. *Chronicon Adae de Usk, AD 1377-1421*, ed. E. M. Thompson, 1876.

Sleepers. 2.02.266 / 2.02.516.

Spur Money. 1.01.373 / 1.01.374 / 1.01.462 / 1.01.494 / 2.12.229. Ray, 1846. Thoms, 1838.

Stagecoach Travel. 2.02.126 / 2.02.313. 'The pelting...': adapted by C.T. from *King Lear*, Act 3, scene 4. 'Cabined, cribbed...': *Macbeth*, Act 3, scene 4.

Suicide. 1.07.180 / 1.07.316 / 1.07.511. Michel de Montaigne, *Essais*, first published between 1580 and 1595; extracts are from *The Complete Works of Michael de Montaigne*, trans. Charles Cotton, rev. William Hazlitt, 1842. 'On the Virtuous Deeds of Women', in *Plutarch's Moralia*, with an English translation by Frank Cole Babbitt et al., 16 vols, 1927-2004, vol. 3.

Sundial Motto. 2.09.279. Timbs, revised edition, 1867.

Surnames 1. 1.10.059 & 1.12.040 / 1.12.114 x 2 / 1.12.391 / 2.01.103.

Surnames 2. 1.05.425 / 3.04.163 / 3.04.333 / 3.07.506 / 3.08.236 / 4.12.082 / 4.12.164 x 2. 'Waste its sweetness...': Thomas Gray, 'Elegy written in a Country Churchyard', 1751. Percy, 1823 (Fredk. Rule placed the Valavoir story in quotation marks but did not name a source; the story appears verbatim in Percy).

Swans. 1.02.510 / 1.03.075.

Swearing. 1.06.367 x 2 / 1.06.471.

Swot. 1.01.352 / 1.01.369.

Taxes. Beards: 3.11.416. Chimneys: 2.05.172 x 2. Clocks: 1.11.145. Hair-powder: 1.11.027. Windows: 1.03.447.

Thames. 2.11.086 / 2.11.139 / 2.11.219 x 2. *Holinshed's Chronicles of England, Scotland, and Ireland*, 6 vols, 1807-8, vol. 4. William Andrews, *Famous Frosts and Frost Fairs*, 1887, has the quotation from *Dawks's News-Letter*.

Toad-Eaters. 1.05.419 x 2 / 3.01.128 / 3.01.276. Ogilvie, 1850. The Haines letters are in Thomas Brown, *Letters from the Dead to the Living*, 1702. John Dryden, 'Georgics', in *The Works of Virgil*, 1697.

Trafalgar. 2.02.444.

Travellers. 2.11.132 x 2 / 2.11.156. Thackeray, serialised 1847-8. H. Frost, *A Brief Biographical Sketch of I. A. Van Amburgh*, 1860.

Turncoat. 2.02.086. *Scots Magazine*, vol. 9, pp477-478.

Turnspit. 3.02.149 / 3.02.219 / 3.02.255 x 3 / 3.02.256. Robert Chambers, *The Book of Days*, 2 vols, 1862-4, vol. 1.

Umbrellas. 1.01.414 / 1.01.436 / 1.02.025 x 2 / 1.02.523 / 1.03.126 / 1.04.75 / 2.10.198. Wolfe's letter is given in Robert Wright, *The Life of Major-General James Wolfe, founded on original documents*, 1864. Cunningham, 2nd edition, 1850. Horace Walpole (1717-1797), *Memoirs of the Last Ten Years of the Reign of George II*, ed. Lord Holland, 1822. James Burrow's *Reports* appeared in various editions from 1766 to 1790. M. John Cardwell, 'John Shebbeare', *ODNB*. William Andrews, *Bygone England*, 1892, has the Newcastle and Wakefield references. John Macdonald, *Travels in various parts of Europe, Asia, and Africa*, 1790.

Unicorns. 2.01.056 / 4.09.119 / 4.09.245 / 4.09.246 / 4.09.437. Dugdale, 3 vols, 1655-73; extract is from the English translation, ed. John Caley et al., 6 vols, 1817-30, vol. 1. Odell Shepard, *The Lore of the Unicorn*, 1930; Shepard is the source of the quotation regarding the importance of Varthema's account and of much of the information in the additional note. David de Pomis, *Dittionario Novo Hebraico, Molto Copioso, Dechirato in Tre Lingue*, 1587. Hector Boethius, *Historia Gentis Scotorum*, 1527. André Thévet, *Cosmographie universelle*, 1575. *Quarterly Review*, vol. 24, no. 47, pp120-121. *Calcutta Government Gazette* is quoted in Augustine Calmet, *Calmet's Dictionary of the Holy Bible*, 9th edition, 5 vols, 1847, vol. 4. *Asiatic Journal*, vol. 12, July to December 1821, p36. *Athenaeum*, no. 1730 (22 December), July to December 1860, p875. W. W. Wroth, *rev.* P. E. Kell, 'James Salter', *ODNB*.

Watchmen. 1.01.167.

Waterhouse. 2.01.193 / 2.01.262. Anon., *Narrative of the murder of the late Rev. J. Waterhouse, with a full report of the trial, confession, and execution of the murderer*, 1827. Elizabeth Nitchie, 'An Early Suitor of Mary Wollstonecraft', *PMLA*, vol. 58, no. 1, March 1943, pp163-169. Kean's lines were quoted in the *Manchester Guardian*, 18 October 1870.

Wife-selling. 1.07.429 / 1.08.043 / 1.08.209 / 2.06.490 & 3.03.486 (K.P.D.E.'s initial remarks are from the former and the Bewcastle and Merthyr Tydfil accounts are from the latter) / 3.04.450. *The Diary of Henry Machyn*, ed. John Gough Nichols, 1848. Christine Winfield, 'Factual Sources of Two Episodes in *The Mayor of Casterbridge*', *Nineteenth-century Fiction*, vol. 25, no. 2, September 1970, pp224-231.

Witchcraft. 1.02.404. *Gentleman's Magazine*, vol. 29, p93.

Woollen. 1.05.414 / 1.05.542 / 1.05.543 / 1.06.058 / 1.06.111. *Gentleman's Magazine*, vol. 1, p114.

Words, Last. 2.02.105 / 2.02.192. Various details have been added to H.E.W.'s contribution. *Oxford Dictionary of Quotations*, 6th edition, ed. Elizabeth Knowles, 2004.

2. Illustrations

The handful of illustrations not listed below are taken from undated prints and engravings, nineteenth-century and earlier, belonging to the editor.

Andrews, William, *Bygone England*, 1892 (Running Footmen; Umbrellas: Jonas Hanway); *The Church Treasury*, 1898 ('The End'); *Famous Frosts and Frost Fairs*, 1887 (endpaper: The Thames in 1684; Thames: detail from the same).

Animal Illustrations, Dover Publications, 1987 (Fox-hunting; Pigs: pig; Rural Nutrition: hedgehog).

Ashton, John, *Curious Creatures in Zoology*, 1890 (Basilisk); *The Dawn of the Nineteenth Century*, 2 vols, 1886, vol. 1 (Stagecoach); *The Devil in Britain and America*, 1896 (Devil); *Social Life in the Reign of Queen Anne*, 2 vols, 1882, vol. 1 (Sedan Chair; Woollen), vol. 2 (Watchmen: the watch).

Bell, Thomas, *A History of British Quadrupeds*, 1837 (Goat; Mice; Rats).

Bewick, Thomas, *Bewick Gleanings...* ed. Julia Boyd, 1886 (Travellers: lion); *Quadrupeds*, 1807 (Turnspit: small dog).

Biré, Edmond, *The Diary of a Citizen of Paris during the Terror*, 3 vols, 1896, vol. 1 (Marat).

Blessington, Marguerite (Countess of), *Conversations of Lord Byron with the Countess of Blessington*, 1834 (Byron: image in the text).

Book of Public Arms: A Cyclopaedia, ed. Arthur Charles Fox-Davies & M. E. B. Crookes, 1894 (Animals: dog; Nelson).

Boreman, Thomas, *A Description of Three Hundred Animals*, 1730; revised edition, 1786 (jacket: toad).

Brehm, A. E., *Merveilles de la Nature*, 9 vols, 1869-85, vol. 9 (Rural Nutrition: snail).

Byron, George Gordon (Lord), *The Works...* ed. R. E. Prothero, 6 vols, 1898-1901, vol. 6 (jacket: Byron).

Calmet, Augustine, *Calmet's Dictionary of the Holy Bible*, 9th edition, 5 vols, 1847, vol. 5 (Rhinoceros).

Carroll, Lewis (Charles Lutwidge Dodgson), *Alice's Adventures in Wonderland*, 1865 (Cheshire Cat). Illustration by Sir John Tenniel.

Chambers, Robert, *The Book of Days*, 2 vols, 1862-4, vol. 1 (Animals: sow; Coffee-houses; Turnspit: wheel in action; Watchmen: man with bell; Witchcraft), vol. 2 (Epitaphs: 'The Puzzle'; Hour-glasses: first image).

Correspondence of Sir Isaac Newton and Professor Cotes... ed. J. Edleston, 1850 (Newton's Apple).

Dickens, Charles, *Bleak House*, 1853 (Combustion). Illustration by 'Phiz' (Hablot Knight Browne).

English Encyclopedia, The, 10 vols, 1802, vol. 3 (jacket: hedgehog; endpaper: elephant; Elephants; Hedgehogs), vol. 4 (Cromwell; Glove-removal: cannon; Justice: petard), vol. 5 ('First Catch...').

Fairholt, F. W., *Costume in England: A History of Dress*, 2nd edition, 1860 (jacket: spurs; Actress; Curates; Glove-removal: glove; Quarrelsome: crowned heads; Spur Money: both images; Taxes: beards).

Fleury, Ch. Rouault de, *La Messe: Etudes Archéologiques*, Paris, 8 vols, 1883-9, vol. 6 (jacket: belfry and three figures below; Bell, Book and Candle; Church Bells 2: bell-ringer and trumpeter; Epitaphs: crosses).

Fosbroke, Thomas, *Encyclopedia of Antiquities*, 2 vols, 1843, vol. 2 (Football).

Gelzer, M., & König, Gustav, *The Life of Martin Luther the German Reformer* in fifty pictures from designs by Gustav König, 1853 (Events).

Gentleman's Magazine, The, vol. 67 pt 2, 1797 (Church Bells 2: Caldecot Church, Rutland); vol. 74 pt 2, 1804 (Quarrelsome: Charles the Bad; Sleepers: Steyning Church, Sussex); vol. 83 pt 1, 1813 (Pigs: Norton by Twycross Church).

Graphic Ornaments, The Pepin Press, 2007 (Book Titles; Kant's Wig: auctioneer; Richelieu: letter head and foot and quills; Royal Positions: fool; Swans).

Hearne, Thomas, *The History and Antiquities of Glastonbury*, 1722 (Monks).

Hildebrant, A. M., *Heraldisches Musterbuch*, 1872 (Burial 1: three skulls; Justice: figure of; Dog-whipping 1 & 2: three separate dogs; Omens; Owls; Royal Positions: cockerel).

Illustrated Catalogue of the Heraldic Exhibition, Burlington House, 1894, 1896 (Unicorn: unicorn).

Ingoldsby, Thomas (R. H. Barham), *The Ingoldsby Legends*, with illustrations by George Cruikshank, John Leech, and John Tenniel, 1864 (Boleyn; Burial 2: Tray; Clarence: barrel; Custard; Pocket-Handkerchief). Sir Thomas Boleyn is of course not the headless man depicted and the last three images have been adjusted for use here.

Instrumenta Ecclesiastica, 2nd Series, edited by The Ecclesiological (late Cambridge Camden) Society, 1856 (Burial 3).

Knapp, Andrew, & Baldwin, William, *The New Newgate Calendar*, 6 vols, 1826, vol. 1 (Burning).

Mivart, St George, *The Common Frog*, 1874 (Toad: *Bufo vulgaris*).

Rees, Abraham, *The Cyclopaedia, or, Universal Dictionary of Arts, Sciences and Literature*, 45 vols, 1819-20, plates vol. 5 (Animals: bug; Ear-boxing; Frogs; Riding Whip: sturgeon; Unicorn: narwhal).

Rous, John, *This rol was laburd and finished by Master John Rows of Warrewyk*, ed. William Courthope, 1859 (Clarence: portraits).

Russell, Constance (Lady), *Swallowfield and its Owners*, 1901 (Thames: printed card).

Simpson, W. Sparrow, *Gleanings from Old St Paul's*, 1889 (Church Bells 2: St Paul's).

Stuckenberg, J. H. W., *The Life of Immanuel Kant*, 1882 (Kant's Wig: Kant).

Tales and Jest of Mr Hugh Peters... to which is prefixed a short account of his life, 1660; reprinted 1807 (Hour-glasses: Hugh Peters).

3,800 Early Advertising Cuts, Deberny Type Foundry, ed. Carol Belanger Grafton, 1991 (Dragon: first image; Riding Whip: whip).

Wall, J. Charles, *An Old English Parish*, 1907 (Dog-whipping 1: dog-whipper and dog tongs).

Wright, Thomas, *Caricature History of the Georges*, 1898 (Remedies).